BATTLEFIELD 2

™

BATTLEFIELD 2

PRIMA OFFICIAL GAME GUIDE

David Knight
Michael Knight

Prima Games
A Division of Random House, Inc.

3000 Lava Ridge Court
Roseville, CA 95661
(800) 733-3000
www.primagames.com

Product Manager: Jill Hinckley
Editor: Alaina Yee
Design & Layout: Graphic Applications Group, Inc.

Acknowledgments
Prima would like to thank Darren Montgomery, Andrew Stein, John Vifian, Benjamin Smith, and Jose Gonzales From EA; and Sean Decker, Erik Sjövold, Jamil Dawsari, Jonas Åberg, Linus Josephson, and James Salt from DICE for all their help in the creation of this guide.

ISBN: 0-7615-4885-8
Library of Congress Catalog Card Number: 2004117799
Printed in the United States of America

05 06 07 08 LL 10 9 8 7 6 5 4 3 2 1

CONTENTS

BATTLEFIELD

INTRODUCTION

Three years ago, Electronic Arts and DICE released a demo of an upcoming game. This map from the game was playable only online against other human players and was set in the middle of the Pacific Ocean during World War II on Wake Island. It was a team-based shooter that seamlessly combined the use of air, ground, and naval vehicles with an ease and balance never seen before in an online game. The response was overwhelming, resulting in a huge dedicated fan base, prompting the organization of clans, teams, and tournaments—and all before *Battlefield 1942* was even released. With the release of two expansions to the original—*The Road to Rome* and *Secret Weapons of WWII*—new maps, vehicles, and weapons were added. *Battlefield Vietnam* introduced helicopters, and took gamers into the Southeast Asian conflict approximately 25 years after the original setting.

Now the series has reached the present time. With the release of *Battlefield 2*, players can experience modern combat. The old jeeps that were only good for getting you around the map quickly have been replaced by fast attack vehicles which compliment their speed with the firepower of a couple of machine guns. Infantry now have guided missiles for firing at enemy armor, while aircraft and helicopters carry a variety of deadly ordnance, including heat-seeking missiles, TV-guided missiles, laser guided missiles, and dumb bombs. However, one of the most impressive additions to the *Battlefield* series is the ranking and command systems. While playing online, players' points and results are recorded to provide a history of the missions played, number of kills, and many other stats. The command system allows players to join squads or assume leadership as either a squad leader or commander. This further enhances the ability to play as a team and encourages cooperation among players.

Whether you are a veteran from the Wake Island demo or a new recruit to *Battlefield 2*, this guide will help you understand the game's basics as well as the new features. In "Basic Training," you will find the basics on how to play the game. Look at how to use some of the new features of the game. The next three sections cover the infantry, surface vehicles, and airpower, respectively. That is where you will find all the info on troop kits, personal weapons, tanks, jets, and helicopters in the game. For a detailed look at the command structure as well as tactics for playing as a squad leader or commander, check out "Chain of Command." Finally, the next 12 sections cover the game's maps. In addition to tactics for each side, there are also individual maps showing the locations of all control points and lists of vehicle spawns for 16-, 32-, and 64-player games. The last two sections include charts and tables with information to help you better understand the intricacies of the game.

BATTLEFIELD 2

BASIC TRAINING

Welcome to *Battlefield 2*! The wait is over and now it's time to jump into combat. Think of this section as a refresher course. Although many of the basic controls and concepts are untouched, there are plenty of new additions to the game you'll want be aware of before rushing into action. So whether you're a veteran or a rookie, set your gear aside for a few minutes and read up.

MOVEMENT FUNDAMENTALS

Moving your soldier around the battlefield is simple, especially if you've played the earlier installments or any other FPS. The standard combination of keyboard and mouse controls allows for quick and precise movement. Your left hand controls all movement, using [W] to move forward, [S] to move backward, and [A] and [D] to strafe left and right, respectively. Jump by pressing [Spacebar], useful for hopping over short barriers like sandbags and low walls. The mouse is used to change directional facing, as well as to aim and fire weapons. By using the mouse and strafe keys, it's possible to move laterally in one direction, while aiming in a different direction. This form of strafing is useful in close combat situations, helping you evade incoming fire.

> **NOTE** It's possible to move while peering through your weapon's iron sight or scope, but your speed reduces to a slow walk.

In addition to standing, your soldier can also crouch ([Ctrl]) or drop prone ([Z]). While crouched, your soldier can duck behind low objects for cover. It's possible to move while crouched, too, but your speed reduces. Dropping prone is the best way to stay out of sight as well as evade incoming gunfire when there's no cover available. Crawling on your belly is the slowest but stealthiest way to move around. Snipers and other reconnaissance-oriented troops should stay as low as possible to avoid detection. The crouched and prone stances also improve the accuracy of firearms. We'll discuss the importance of these stances more in the "Weapons Training" section.

> **CAUTION** Be careful where you take cover. High-caliber rounds can penetrate light objects like flimsy sheets of metal or wooden structures. For the best protection, take cover behind heavy solid objects constructed from concrete or stone.

Sprinting

New to *Battlefield 2* is the sprinting function. Your soldier can now run at high speed by either holding down [⇧Shift] while moving forward or by double-tapping [W]. Sprinting makes your soldier tougher to hit, especially if an enemy sniper has you in his sights. While sprinting, your soldier can't fire his weapons—but he can reload, as long as the reloading process is initiated before sprinting. Each soldier has a sprint meter below his health meter. The meter drops every time the soldier sprints (or jumps) and won't build up until the soldier stops to rest. Troop kits equipped with body armor (anti-tank, assault, and support) have shorter sprint durations due to their gear's weight. Sprinting also increases the distance your soldier can jump, so get a running start before leaping across large gaps.

> **TIP** When descending a ladder, hold down [⇧Shift] to quickly slide down the rails.

Swimming

If you are in deep water, swim using the forward and backward movement keys—you can't strafe. While swimming, you cannot access your kit's weapons. However, you can sprint, allowing you to swim to shore faster. Avoid swimming, as it leaves you out in the open with no way to defend yourself. If you must cross a river or other body of water, look for shallow spots or hitch a ride on a boat or APC. Although you can no longer drown from exhaustion, the larger maps make for long swim times.

Parachuting

Whether jumping out of a damaged aircraft or hopping off a tall building, you can avoid cratering into the ground by deploying your parachute. While in free fall, repeatedly tap [9] until the parachute opens. Steer the parachute by using the strafe keys ([A] and [D]) to turn left and right. Press [S] to flare the parachute, reducing forward momentum. It's possible to use your troop's kits' weapons while drifting downward, but your accuracy won't be great. At high altitudes, drop grenades on enemy infantry below—make sure they explode long before you reach the ground. You can use parachutes multiple times, so don't worry if it takes a few jumps to descend a deep canyon or multi-tiered structure. But the longer you're in the air, the more attention you're likely to attract. For this reason, free fall as long as possible and open the parachute just before you reach the ground. This is a great way to sneak into enemy-held control points.

NAVIGATION

While the maps in *Battlefield 2* vary in size, they all require rudimentary navigational skills to find your way around. There are a couple of ways to do this. The first is the mini-map in the upper-right hand corner of the screen. At the center of the map is a white vector. You are always in the mini-map's center, and the vector shows which way you are facing, with north at the mini-map's top. The mini map is for seeing your surroundings, the location of control points, and any nearby friendly troops. Your troops appear as blue while enemy units are red, no matter whether you are playing as USMC, Chinese, or Middle East Coalition (MEC). You can cycle through three zoom levels for the mini map by pressing [N]. For an expanded view of the map, press [M]. This shows you the battlefield and the position of your friendly units. [N] cycles through zoom levels for this larger map, as well. Use this larger map to get an overall view of the battle's status. Because the fog of war is in effect on the maps, you will not see the location of enemies unless they are detected by a UAV or radar scan; or a teammate spots and reports on an them. Unoccupied vehicles, support structures, artillery, and defensive machine guns and turrets appear as gray icons. In addition to the two maps, you can also toggle flag icons to appear on your HUD to show you the direction and distance to the game's control points. Press [Alt] to toggle these icons on and off as needed.

WEAPONS TRAINING

For the most part, the weapons in *Battlefield 2* work the same way they did in the previous games, but there are some slight variations worth taking note of. Let's look at each weapon type.

Knife

The knife kills in one hit, but you can only use it at extreme close-range. Unless challenged to a knife duel, there aren't too many opportunities to use the knife. However, if your opponent is attempting to reload a firearm, rush in close for a quick stab. You can also use it when sneaking up behind enemies for a quick stealthy kill. The concept of a knife fight may sound silly in a game loaded with so many projectile weapons, but it's something for which you should prepare. To defend against a knife attack, strafe left and right while continually facing your opponent. Look for opportunities to strike, lunging forward to stab, and immediately step back to avoid the counter-thrust. Depending on the skill of the combatants, knife fights can last anywhere from a couple of seconds to more than a minute. By the way, it's bad etiquette to pull out your firearm and shoot your opponent after a knife fight has been initiated—then again, honor isn't one of the stats tracked by *Battlefield 2*.

> **NOTE** The medic's shock paddles can be used in close combat like the knife. Two medics fighting with shock paddles is one of the many bizarre things you're likely to encounter on public servers.

Firearms

Although there are more than 20 firearm types available to infantry, they all function similarly. Aiming your weapon is as simple as moving the mouse. Place the cross hairs over your target, and click the left mouse button to fire. For more precise aim, and a boost in accuracy, click the right mouse button to switch to the weapon's iron sight view—if the firearm is equipped with a scope, this will bring up the scope's view. This magnified view has you looking down the weapon's sights. The rear and front sighting apertures are automatically aligned, so place the front sight post's tip over your target and fire. When engaging infantry, aim for their upper torso to maximize the chances of scoring a hit. If you hit an enemy, the cross hairs icon will "bloom." Use this hit information to place your following rounds in approximately the same area. Although scoring a head-shot is fatal, an opponent's head is smaller than his torso and difficult to hit unless using a sniper rifle.

Use the iron sight view when engaging targets at intermediate to long range. Switch to semi-automatic to help keep your target centered.

NOTE Snipers do not have a cross hairs icon on their HUD when their sniper rifle is selected, and cannot accurately aim their weapon until they peer through the scope view by right-clicking. This is inconvenient and dangerous when engaging enemies at close range, as the magnification of the scope is disorienting and peripheral vision is nonexistent. Therefore, the sniper should move with his pistol drawn, using his sniper rifle only when he finds a good hiding spot.

Most of the game's weapons have two firing modes. The most common are automatic and semi-automatic. You can toggle the firing modes by pressing (3), the same key used to select a kit's primary weapon. Automatic fire is useful in close-range engagements when accuracy takes a backseat to rate of fire. Switch to semi-automatic when engaging distant targets or when you need to conserve ammo. The M16A2, used by the Marine assault and medic kits, offers a three-round burst mode instead of automatic. This provides a nice balance of firepower and accuracy; it's capable of placing three rounds in a tight cluster.

Accuracy

Movement and stance affect firearm accuracy. While moving, watch the cross hairs increase in size, indicating a reduction in accuracy. When you halt movement, the cross hairs shrink, representing a more stable firing position. For this reason, fire from stationary positions. Accuracy increases more by crouching or

dropping prone. Crouched firing is the most practical of the two stances, particularly when on the move. Take a knee before squeezing off a few rounds. To maximize your weapon's accuracy, drop prone and use your weapon's iron sights or scope. This combination is the most stable and accurate firing position. Support troops will benefit most from firing in a prone position, as it helps stabilize their cumbersome light machine guns.

NOTE The body armor included with the anti-tank, assault, and support kits reduces damage dealt to a soldier's torso by approximately 33 percent.

Reloading

After you expend ammunition from a magazine, you must reload before you can resume firing. If the Auto Reload function is checked in the Options menu, reloading will occur automatically every time a magazine runs dry. Reload the weapon by pressing

(R). Keep a full magazine at all times, as you never know when you'll need every last round. But you also need to conserve ammunition, unless a support soldier or supply crate is nearby to keep you stocked. Reload your weapon after the magazine reaches the half-capacity mark. Monitor how much ammo is left in a magazine by glancing at the ammo meter in the screen's bottom-right hand corner.

TIP When firing bolt-action sniper rifles like the M24 and M95, continue holding down the left mouse button after firing to keep peering through the scope. Otherwise the bolt will retract and a new round will load, often causing you to lose sight of your target.

Hand Grenades

There are a couple of ways to throw a hand grenade in *Battlefield 2*. The most common option is to click the left mouse button. This causes you to throw the grenade at full strength. But by clicking the right mouse button and holding it down, you can specify how hard you throw a grenade. After you begin holding down the right mouse button, a small meter appears in the screen's bottom-right hand corner. The longer you hold down the right mouse button, the harder you will throw the grenade. After the meter tops out, you will hold the grenade until you release the right mouse button—don't worry, it won't explode in your hand. Specifying the strength of a throw is useful when you want to drop a grenade off a high elevation, or roll it down an incline. Each grenade has a four second fuse, so it will bounce and roll around until it detonates.

Specialized Weapons

In addition to their primary weapon, most troop kits are equipped with a unique weapon. We'll discuss these weapons and specific tactics at greater length in the next section, but here's a brief overview on how to operate each one.

Wire-Guided Missiles

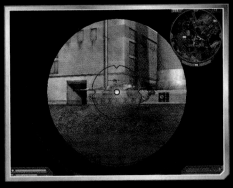

Accuracy is no longer a problem for anti-tank troops, thanks to this new weapon. The missile launcher functions like a sniper rifle, but with more explosive results. Right-click to bring up the weapon's magnified scope view. After you spot a target, click and hold down the left mouse button to launch the missile. While holding down the left mouse button, you can steer the missile toward the target by moving the mouse in any direction— wherever you aim, the missile will go. The stationary TOW/HJ-8 anti-tank missile turrets fire the same way, but are more powerful than their shoulder-fired counterparts.

Grenade Launchers

Mounted beneath the barrels of the assault kit's assault rifles, use these launchers to lob grenades at great distances. Press [4] to select the launcher, then aim by elevating the rifle's barrel. However, it's difficult to judge the proper barrel elevation you need to hit a distant target, because the grenade travels in an arc-like trajectory. Raise the barrel for distant targets and level it out for closer targets. The grenade launcher is most accurate when used as a direct-fire weapon, particularly against vehicles. While hand grenades bounce around, launched grenades explode on impact, making them effective against light armored vehicles or stationary weapons.

AT Mines

Still carried by engineers, the mines in *Battlefield 2* work the same way as they did in the previous games. Drop them on the ground to prevent enemy vehicles from moving through a particular chokepoint. These are anti-vehicle mines, and will not explode if infantry walk across them. But a mine is powerful enough to destroy any vehicle, whether it's friendly or not.

Claymores

The function of claymores has changed since their introduction in *Battlefield Vietnam*. Although they're still directional anti-personnel mines, they can no longer be detonated by remote. They're proximity-activated, detonating whenever someone walks in front of them. Carried by snipers, these nasty mines are great for setting up booby traps near control points. However, be careful when placing them, as your teammates can set them off, too. Place one by pressing the left mouse button, and move away, staying behind it till you're a safe distance away.

> **CAUTION** When entering a friendly mine field (with AT mines or claymores), a red skull and crossbones icon appears on the right side of the screen.

C4

The C4 charges are associated with the special forces kit. Press the left mouse button to either toss them on the ground or stick them to surfaces. After you place the charges, press the right mouse button to equip the detonator. Move to a safe distance and press the left mouse button to simultaneously set off all of the charges. C4 is useful for blowing up bridges and destroying commander stations. They're also effective in defensive situations. Planting them around a control point's flagpole.

BATTLEFIELD SUPPORT

The icons on top of the vehicles indicate their support capability. Vehicles must be in close proximity to support each other.

Unlike *Battlefield 1942* and *Battlefield Vietnam*, there are no land vehicle repair stations, but there are helipads and airfields for repairing aircraft and helicopters. Your troops must rely on the medic, support soldier, and engineer for most of their logistical needs. The medic carries medic bags which he can use to heal injured soldiers. His shock paddles can also revive downed teammates. In addition to a light machine gun, the support soldier carries ammo bags, capable of re-supplying teammates with ammunition of every type. It's up to the engineer to repair vehicles and other damaged objects, using his versatile wrench.

By riding in vehicles, these troops can also extend their services to friendly infantry and vehicles on the battlefield. For example, a medic riding in a Humvee can heal any nearby troops. An engineer and a support soldier in a helicopter can hover over a tank to rearm and repair it. A pair of tanks, driven by engineers, can repair each other. You can use numerous support combinations to give your team an edge, so experiment with these troop kits and vehicle combos.

NOTE Supply crates dropped by the commander dispense ammunition and health; they also repair vehicles. This is discussed in "Chain of Command."

GAMEPLAY CONCEPTS

If you're a veteran of the *Battlefield* series, you can easily jump in and play, as little has changed. But if it's been a while, or if you're new, here's a rundown of how the game works.

Spawn Screen

This is where you select your troop kit and your spawn point. Spawn points are represented by white dots on the map and are usually located next to control points, but they can also be on ships and other areas—your squad leader can also act as a spawn point. Access the spawn screen at any time during the game by pressing Enter.

Tickets

Tickets represent the number of reinforcements your team has at any given time. These fluctuating numbers are prominently displayed in the screen's upper-right hand corner—above the mini-map. Every time a teammate dies, one ticket subtracts from your team's total count. The side with tickets at the game's end wins; the side with no tickets loses. A medic can prevent ticket loss by reviving wounded teammates with his shock paddles.

Control Points

These are locations of strategic importance that either side can capture. View the location of a battlefield's control points on the mini-map in the screen's upper right-hand corner, or by expanding the map view by pressing M. On the map, the control points are marked by small flag icons indicating their locations and current states. When your team holds a control point, your nationality's flag appears here and vice versa if your opponent controls it. Control points can also be neutral, represented by a gray flag icon on the map. In addition to being a spawn point, most control points also produce vehicles and stationary weapons when captured. The types and number of assets a control point produces vary based on the map size and occupier's nationality.

Control Point Capture

You must occupy a control point's radius to capture it. Think of this as a large invisible dome emanating from the flagpole. The capture progress meter appears below the mini-map any time you're within a control point's radius; it disappears when you move out. Use this to scout the boundaries of the radius, as well as monitor the status of the conversion process. The raising and lowering of flags on the flagpole is another visual cue to gauge progress. No opponents can be present within the control point's radius at the time of capture, so you must eliminate or route all resistance. Multiple teammates gathered within the radius can reduce the amount of time necessary to capture the control point.

Game Types

The popular conquest battles are back in *Battlefield 2*, and little has changed. There are three battle types, each with their own rules and victory conditions.

Double Assault

All of the 16-player maps are double assault battles, consisting of no more than four control points. On these maps, each side begins with one control point. A ticket drain can be initiated on the opposing team by controlling more than half of the map's control points. For example, if there are four control points, a team must control three to bleed their enemy's ticket count. Achieve a quick victory by capturing the control points, denying the opposing team a spawn point.

Assault

During assault battles, there is an attacker and a defender. The attacker begins with at least one base that cannot be captured. Defenders hold most of the map's control points. The attackers' job is to capture the map's control points, preventing the defenders from spawning new troops. The attackers begin the battle with more tickets, but a ticket drain is in effect till they capture and hold at least one of the defenders' control points. The defenders' tickets cannot be drained unless they lose all of the control points.

Head-On

In head-on battles, both sides are on an even footing, each beginning with a base on opposite sides of the map. The control points are neutral to begin with, resulting in races to capture the most. Like double assault, bleeding the opposing side's tickets is possible by holding more than half of the map's control points—bases not included. Because the bases cannot be captured, each side will have at least one spawn point.

SCORING

Unlike the previous games, in *Battlefield 2* you get credit for everything you do. While you're still likely to make the majority your points through kills, you can now boost your score by healing/reviving, repairing, and supplying. There are also points awarded for kill assists and driver assists, when your actions contribute to a kill. But you can also lose points by accidentally killing teammates. So watch your fire, or your score will suffer. For more details on scoring, let's look at the scoreboard.

Scoreboard

Access the scoreboard at any time during gameplay by pressing and holding [Tab]. There are three sections of the scoreboard, the first being the Players tab. Here are two side-by-side lists detailing the scores of every player in the game—players with the highest

scores are at the top. There are five statistics the scoreboard tracks, indicated by the columns to the right of each player's name. These columns are topped by a different icon:

Trophy Icon: This is your overall score, taking into account all actions.

Kits Icon: This is your teamwork score. Any points earned by providing team support are listed here. Points deducted for team kills show up here, too.

Skull Icon: Your kills are tracked in this column.

Cross Icon: How many times you've died. No points are deducted for dying, but tickets are.

Computers Icon: Your ping. A low number (100 or less) indicates a good connection and is less likely to result in lagged gameplay. If this number is high (200 or more), find a different server.

Scoring Breakdown

Overall Score: The overall score is a 1 for 1 representation of scores accumulated in all categories listed here:

Skill-Based Score:
- Kill = 2 points

Team-Based Score:
- Capture Control Points = 2 points (2 points to make it neutral and 2 points to capture it for your side)
- Capture Assist CP = 1 point (1 point to make it neutral and 1 point to capture it for your side)
- Defend Control Point = 1 point (kill opponent within your flag radius)
- Kill Assist = 1 point (do 50 percent damage to opponent whom teammate subsequently kills)
- Heal = 1 point
- Revive = 2 points
- Resupply = 1 point
- Repair = 1 point
- Driver Score = 1 point (every time passenger uses special ability or kills opponent)

Scoring Breakdown (continued)

Commander Score:
- Winning Commander = 2x average team score
- Losing Commander = average team score

Score Punishments:
- Team Kill = -4 points
- Team Damage = -2 points
- Team Vehicle Damage = -1 point

The scoreboard has two more tabs you can access by right-clicking to activate the cursor—you still need to hold down [Tab] to keep the scoreboard open. Under the scoreboard's Squads tab, you can view the scoring status of each squad on your team. In addition to individual scores, the total points accrued by a squad are also tabulated, making it easy to see which squads are effective and which one's aren't.

The Manage tab is where you can mute a teammate's VOIP chatter as well as initiate votes to either kick a player off the server or suggest a new map. If a player is racking up team kills or being a pain, kick him off. Click the Kick Vote button next to his name in the list. This initiates a vote, allowing all players to decide the fate of the problem player. A majority of players must agree to kick a player, otherwise he'll be allowed to stay. When prompted with a vote, press [Page Up] to vote yes, or [Page Down] to vote no. Voting for new maps works the same way. At the top of the Manage tab, click on the Map Vote pull-down menu. Select from a list of maps available on the server.

YOUR PROFILE

When you start *Battlefield 2*, you're prompted to create a multiplayer profile. Come up with a nickname, then enter your e-mail address, a password, and country. Your profile is used to keep track of your gameplay stats. These stats determine your rank and your eligibility for any awards or kit unlocks.

To look at your stats, click the BFHQ button on the main menu. The first section is the Kit Info screen. Here you can get the basics, such as your rank, score, and time logged playing. For more detailed information, click on the Stats tab. The Stats screen lists everything you've done in every online game you've played. Included are statistics on your most played kits, vehicles, weapons, maps, and nationalities—it even logs how long you've played each, down to the second! Your teamwork and combat stats are listed here, too. Next is the Leaderboards screen, where you track your statistics against everyone else in the online community. You can

sort data based on scores, kits, vehicles, and individual kit equipment. The Awards screen is where you view your acquired medals, badges, and ribbons. Information on the individual awards is in the charts at the back of the guide.

Moving up the Ranks

The rank system in *Battlefield 2* is based on the total number of points you earn. In addition to score, achieving some of the higher ranks require certain badges. Seven of the ranks allow you to unlock one of the weapons found in the troop kits. For example, when you achieve Lance Corporal, you can choose one of the seven troop kit weapons to unlock. Additional weapon unlocks are available at higher ranks. The following table shows what you'll need to achieve each rank:

Ranks		
Rank	Triggers Unlock?	Criteria
Private	No	None
Private First Class	No	Score
Lance Corporal	Yes	Score
Corporal	Yes	Score
Sergeant	Yes	Score
Staff Sergeant	Yes	Score
Gunnery Sergeant	Yes	Score
Master Sergeant	Yes	Score
First Sergeant	N/A	Score
Master Gunnery Sergeant	Yes	Score
Sergeant Major	N/A	Score
Sergeant Major of the Corps	N/A	*

* = The highest ranking person at Master Gunnery Sergeant or Sergeant Major level gets this special rank. Recalculated each month.

EXTENDED PLAY

Battlefield 1942 generated an enthusiastic gaming community, even before its release. Over the years, the community has grown larger, fueled by mods and organized team play. It only takes a few minutes of poking around the internet to find numerous fan sites dedicated to everything *Battlefield*. With the new Battle Recorder and a fresh set of mods under development, the community is poised for another major growth spurt.

Battle Recorder

If you've been playing these games for any period of time, you have a *Battlefield* story. You know, like the time you saved your team from defeat by ditching your plane and capturing an undefended control point. Instead of just bragging to your friends about your incredible skills, you can now back it up with footage, thanks to the new Battle Recorder function. With this server side option, individual rounds record to a file and save to a URL where participants can download them. After completing a gaming session, click on the Community tab in the main menu. Under the Battle Recorder tab is a list of URLs allowing you to download files of the game rounds you've played. Files downloaded here are saved to the \My

Documents\Battlefield 2\Profiles\Default\Demos directory. Once downloaded, you can play back these files and share them with other players. But download them before the server overwrites them. A server stores 30 recordings at a time.

To play a recorded file, select it from the Battle Recorder Library list on the screen's right side. During playback, use the number keys to control the speed. If you prefer to follow individual players, press [Spacebar] to toggle through the participants, using the mouse to move the camera around and the mouse wheel (or [W] and [A]) to zoom in and out. Enter free cam mode by right-clicking the mouse. This allows you to fly through the battle using the standard movement keys. In addition to backing up your prowess on the battlefield, the Battle Recorder is also a great tool for reviewing team strategies, and helping determine what worked and what didn't.

Mods

Mods, or modifications, describes user-created content. Using the *Battlefield* engine and basic gameplay fundamentals, users design their own maps, vehicles, and weapons, making for new gaming experiences. Given the game's world-wide following, the number of mods under development for *Battlefield 2* grows daily. The variety of mods is impressive, ranging from historical to sci-fi. The best thing about mods is that they're free! As long as you have *Battlefield 2* (and the appropriate updates) you can download mods and play them. To activate a mod, choose the Community tab at the main menu, then click on the Custom Games button. This opens a new screen, allowing you to choose from a list of installed mods. Select the mod you want to play from the list on the screen's left side, then click the Activate button in the bottom-right corner to load the mod.

The *Battlefield 2* Mod Tool Development Kit is available for download from EA's web site. This kit consolidates a number of tools, making mod creation easier than ever. EA also hosts a number of mod tutorials on their web site, offering step-by-step instruction. Here are the main tools available in the kit:

- **Level Editor:** This lets you move objects around a map and import new objects to create a new map. Also set your control points, spawn points, and object spawners.
- **Terrain Editor:** Allows you to change a map's physical features by adjusting the terrain, adding and deleting vegetation (undergrowth and overgrowth), and changing the texture.
- **Object Editor:** Using meshes imported from a 3D modeling program, tweak objects such as vehicles, weapons, kits, and more.
- **Material Editor:** This lets you determine how objects interact with one another. Set an object's inherent material properties (e.g., elasticity, resistance, damage loss) as well as its properties when interacting with a specific object.
- **Animation Editor:** Change the behavior of existing animations, including animation states, how much of the animation plays, looping, triggers, and more.

Online Resources

Official Battlefield 2 Web Site

http://www.eagames.com/official/battlefield/battlefield2/us/home.jsp

This is your first stop for patches and other official add-ons.

Planet Battlefield

http://www.planetbattlefield.com/bf2/

This is one of the most comprehensive and frequently updated *Battlefield* sites on the web. Check it for news and mod updates, as well as details on clans and upcoming tournaments. The forums are also an excellent source of information. Bookmark this one!

Total BF2

http://www.totalbf2.com/

Here's another great source for news, with daily updates and links to other community web sites around the world.

INFANTRY

In *Battlefield 2*, nothing is predictable. The tactical situation changes from minute to minute, requiring your team to respond to a variety of threats and opportunities. Success mostly hinges on picking the right tools for the job and applying them in a way to best benefit the team's progress.

The seven available troop kits each have their own strengths and weaknesses. A competent player should be familiar with the nuances of each and know how to apply them to the ever-changing situation on the battlefield. In this chapter we'll rummage through each troop kit and offer some tips on how to use them. We'll also take a look at the stationary weapons, vital to any defensive effort.

ANTI-TANK

| Sprint: Short |
| Armor: Heavy |
| Equipment: |
| • Knife |
| • Pistol |
| • Sub-Machine Gun |
| • Guided Anti-Tank Missile |

The anti-tank missile packs the biggest single punch of any hand-held weapon. You can even guide your missile after firing by repositioning your viewfinder's crosshairs while the missile is in air. This comes in handy not only for tracking a moving target but also for firing around corners. Your sub-machine gun fires in two modes. In single-shot mode you have the accuracy to take out targets at a distance, while automatic mode gives you better chances at close range.

Chinese Anti-Tank

Chinese Anti-Tank Kit

Key	Weapon/Item	Magazine Capacity	Ammo Count
1	Knife	—	—
2	QSZ-92	15	120
3	Type 85	30	150
4	Eryx	1	6

Damage: 19
Accuracy: Low/Medium
Fire Modes: Full-Auto

Primary Weapon: Type 85

The Type 85 can be fired on full automatic fire and is ideal for close-quarter battles. It makes a perfect sidearm for the anti-armor soldier.

US Anti-Tank

US Anti-Tank Kit

Key	Weapon/Item	Magazine Capacity	Ammo Count
1	Knife	—	—
2	92FS	15	120
3	MP5	30	150
4	SRAW	1	6

Damage: 19
Accuracy: Low/Medium
Fire Modes: Full-Auto/Semi-Auto

Primary Weapon: MP5

The MP5 is a scaled-down version of the G3 assault rifle. It uses 9mm bullets and is very effective at close range.

MEC Anti-Tank

MEC Anti-Tank Kit

Key	Weapon/Item	Magazine Capacity	Ammo Count
1	Knife	—	—
2	MR-444	15	120
3	PP-19	45	135
4	Eryx	1	6

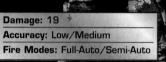

Damage: 19
Accuracy: Low/Medium
Fire Modes: Full-Auto/Semi-Auto

Primary Weapon: PP-19

The PP-19 is based on the AKS-74, but uses 9mm ammunition and a very unconventional magazine solution.

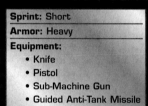

Specialized Equipment

SRAW

Affiliation: USMC	
Type: Wire Guided	
Damage: Armor-Piercing	
Accuracy: High	

The Mk40 Short Range Assault Weapon (SRAW) is the US military response to armored vehicles on the battlefield. Explosive reactive armor is not a problem for this ultra-modern weapon system.

Eryx

Affiliation: China and MEC	
Type: Wire Guided	
Damage: Armor-Piercing	
Accuracy: High	

The Eryx is a shoulder-fired Short Range Anti-Armor weapon which can be used to defeat modern tanks.

Kit Unlock: DAO-12

Damage: 12x8	
Accuracy: Low	
Fire Modes: Semi-Auto	

The DAO-12 has a big revolver-style cylinder holding 12 shots—a large number compared to other automatic shotguns. This shotgun is extremely effective in close-range encounters.

Anti-Tank Tactics

Equipped with a deadly-accurate AT missile, the anti-tank kit is the answer when facing enemy vehicles. Anti-tank troops are effective in offensive roles, and should always be part of any attacking squad. Their body armor gives them the ability to withstand serious damage, making them useful in frontline combat. But anti-tank troops are even more valuable when defending. Use them to guard control points, preferably from an elevated but concealed position. Like a sniper, the anti-tank soldier can pick off targets at long range, guiding their AT missile across the battlefield with near pinpoint accuracy. Use the guidance system to steer the missile at the weaker side and rear armor of tanks and APCs. However, the AT missile leaves behind a smoke trail when fired, making it possible to trace its path back to the shooter. For this reason, move after firing each missile to avoid falling victim to enemy snipers. With only six AT missiles total, these troops will run low on ammo quickly, so make sure a support soldier with an ammo bag is nearby. The commander's supply crate is another good way to keep the anti-tank soldier stocked up on ammo, especially when defending a control point or any other static location on the battlefield.

Anti-Tank: Tester Tips
by Jose Gonzales

- The Chinese & MEC Eryx/US SRAW are the nastiest weapons in the game. The user-guided round can do the following:

  1. Easily kill enemy soldiers with the splash damage alone.
  2. Quickly destroy light armor, helicopters, or manned stations (IGLA/Stinger or TOW/HJ-8).
  3. If aimed at the most vulnerable areas of a vehicle, it can destroy heavy armor (tanks, APCs, or AA vehicles).

- The SRAW and Eryx take awhile to reload and are relatively poor weapons in close combat fighting. This is where you use your sub-machine gun (US MP5/MEC PP-19/China Type 85). The SMGs don't do much damage, nor carry many rounds in a clip, but are good enough to put away enemies that see you trying to reload your AT weapon.

- The US MP5/MEC PP-19/China Type 85 don't have that many rounds in the clip. Make the shots count, and aim for the enemy's head or upper body.

- The US MP5/MEC PP-19 have semi-auto fire mode (NOT the Chinese Type 85), so use them in conjunction with the gun's iron sights for more accurate/controlled fire.

- If all else fails, rely on your trusty sidearm. It makes a fierce combination with the AT class's body armor.

ASSAULT

The workhorse of any attack team, the assault soldier combines heavy firepower with high mobility. You'll be a force on any battlefield with your assault rifle/grenade launcher combo—switch it to automatic mode for rapid firing or single-shot mode for accuracy. Using the gun's grenade launcher targeting apparatus can be tricky, so practice before entering combat. If you find yourself taking fire from all sides, use your smoke grenades to make a stealthy retreat.

Sprint: Short	
Armor: Heavy	
Equipment:	
• Knife	
• Pistol	
• Assault Rifle	
• Grenade Launcher	
• Smoke Grenade	

US Assault

US Assault Kit

Key	Weapon/Item	Magazine Capacity	Ammo Count
1	Knife	—	—
2	92FS	15	120
3	M16A2	30	210
4	M203	1	5
5	Smoke Grenade	—	1

Primary Weapon: M16A2/M203

The M16A2 was developed as an improvement over the standard M16A1. It has proven itself superior in many ways. The M203 is a 40mm

Damage: 30	
Accuracy: High	
Fire Modes: Burst/Semi-Auto	

under-barrel grenade launcher mounted on the M16A2. It fires single-shot explosive grenades capable of doing significant damage to both infantry and soft targets, but isn't as effective against armored vehicles. Because of its lightweight construction, the M203 has a limited impact on the accuracy of the M16A2.

Chinese Assault

Chinese Assault Kit

Key	Weapon/Item	Magazine Capacity	Ammo Count
1	Knife	—	—
2	QSZ-92	15	120
3	AK-47	30	210
4	GP-25	1	5
5	Smoke Grenade	—	1

Primary Weapon: AK-47/GP-25

The AK-47 is an extremely robust weapon that has sacrificed some accuracy for reliability. It fires powerful 7.62mm ammunition from

Damage: 38	
Accuracy: Medium	
Fire Modes: Full-Auto/Semi-Auto	

a 30-round magazine. The predecessor of the GP-30, the GP-25 is a muzzle-loaded under-barrel grenade launcher. Intended for lobbing grenades long distances, it is effective against infantry and soft targets but does minimal damage to armored vehicles.

MEC Assault

MEC Assault Kit

Key	Weapon/Item	Magazine Capacity	Ammo Count
1	Knife	—	—
2	MR-444	15	120
3	AK-101	30	210
4	GP-30	1	5
5	Smoke Grenade	—	1

Primary Weapon: AK-101/GP-30

The gas-operated AK-101 is a modern version of the classic AK-47. It uses 5.56mm NATO ammunition which can be fired at

Damage: 37	
Accuracy: Medium/High	
Fire Modes: Full-Auto/Semi-Auto	

the rate of 600 bullets per minute, and is far more accurate than its predecessor. The GP-30 is an under-barrel launcher firing high-explosive 40mm rounds. It can be used as indirect fire to eliminate enemies who are hidden behind walls or cover. The grenade launcher is also effective against infantry and soft targets but does minimal damage to armored vehicles.

Specialized Equipment

Smoke Grenade

The J4-M35 Smoke Grenade has helped many soldiers out of dire situations. Simply throw the grenade, wait for the smoke to spread, and charge firing positions when the enemy can't see you.

Kit Unlock: G3

Damage: 40	
Accuracy: High	
Fire Modes: Full-Auto/Semi-Auto	

The G3 is the big brother to many modern weapons such as the MP5 and the G36C. It's heavy and somewhat clumsy but reliable, very accurate, and extremely powerful.

Assault Tactics

When you're not quite sure what kind of resistance you might face, a well-rounded assault kit is always a good choice. The assault rifles associated with this kit offer a fine balance of accuracy and firepower useful for downing enemy infantry at any range. Each assault rifle is also equipped with a grenade launcher, mounted below the weapon. By elevating the rifle's barrel, grenades can be lobbed at impressive distances. While intended primarily as an anti-infantry weapon, the grenade launcher can also inflict heavy damage against vehicles and stationary weapons. Unlike hand grenades, launched grenades explode on impact, dealing more direct damage to the target. The assault soldier also carries one smoke grenade. These hand-tossed canisters dispense a thick cloud of gray smoke which lasts for a few precious seconds. Smoke screens are vital when crossing known fields of fire. Use them in urban settings to avoid being cut down by enemy snipers and machine gunners when crossing streets or other open areas.

Assault: Tester Tips
by Jose Gonzales

- The assault class is great for general anti-infantry mayhem, thanks to his weapon loadout and body armor.

- The US M16A2 in burst mode is great for a three-round burst into the enemy up close. When zoomed in conjunction with semi-auto fire mode, it's also decent to use for sniping.

- The MEC AK-101 and China AK-47 in full-auto mode are awesome in close quarters, but are even more deadly against long-range targets when zoomed in conjunction with semi-auto fire mode.

- The smoke grenade is the perfect tool to conceal your squad mates as they attempt to get past lethal choke points (down streets overlooked by rooftops, at cross street sections, and through alleyways) covered by enemy snipers and support soldiers with heavy MGs.

- Smoke is also a good distraction device. Throw a smoke grenade down to bring the enemy out to investigate. When he exposes his position, get the jump on him.

- The US M209/MEC GP-30/Chinese GP-25 grenade launchers are great to not only take out infantry, but also infantry manning stations (stationary MGs, IGLA/Stinger stations, or TOW/HJ-8 stations). The armor of the station itself may deflect bullets if fired upon, but the splash from the grenade rounds will surely kill the occupant.

ENGINEER

Teams rely on engineers to keep their vehicles up and running, so keep that wrench ready. Engineers can even ride in certain vehicles and turn them into mobile repair vehicles, automatically repairing any nearby friendly vehicles. As good as they are at fixing vehicles, they're just as good at destroying them—it takes just one well-placed anti-vehicle mine to destroy an enemy tank. Place these mines on well-traveled roads, but just over a rise or around a bend, so the driver never sees what hit him. They can also repair bridges vital to your side's effort.

| Sprint: Long |
| Armor: None |
| Equipment: |
| • Knife |
| • Pistol |
| • Shotgun |
| • Hand Grenades |
| • AT Mines |
| • Wrench |

US Engineer

US Engineer Kit

Key	Weapon/Item	Magazine Capacity	Ammo Count
1	Knife	—	—
2	92FS	15	120
3	M11-87	7	31
4	Hand Grenade	—	4
5	AT Mine	—	5
6	Wrench	—	—

Primary Weapon: M11-87

This pump-action, magazine-fed shotgun takes six shells plus one in the chamber. It uses 12 gauge Magnum ammunition and comes with a rubber-padded butt stock to reduce recoil.

| Damage: 25x8 |
| Accuracy: Low |
| Fire Modes: Pump-Action |

Chinese Engineer

Chinese Engineer Kit

Key	Weapon/Item	Magazine Capacity	Ammo Count
1	Knife	—	—
2	QSZ-92	15	120
3	NOR982	7	31
4	Hand Grenade	—	4
5	AT Mine	—	5
6	Wrench	—	—

| Damage: 25x8 |
| Accuracy: Low |
| Fire Modes: Pump-Action |

Primary Weapon: NOR982

This shotgun has a standard 12-gauge pump-action which has become very popular due to its low fabrication cost. Its internal magazine has a capacity of six rounds, plus one additional round in the chamber.

MEC Engineer

MEC Engineer Kit

Key	Weapon/Item	Magazine Capacity	Ammo Count
1	Knife	—	—
2	MR-444	15	120
3	S12K	7	56
4	Hand Grenade	—	4
5	AT Mine	—	5
6	Wrench	—	—

Damage: 12x8
Accuracy: Low
Fire Modes: Semi-Auto

Primary Weapon: S12K

Imagine an AK-47 limited to semi-automatic fire, with a rebuilt chamber to house shotgun shells, and you have this automatic shotgun. Extremely powerful at short range, it loses accuracy at longer ranges.

Specialized Equipment

AT Mine

The landmine is an anti-vehicle explosive which is detonated whenever a vehicle passes over it. The landmine does not distinguish between friend or foe.

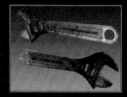

Wrench

The HOFF-3 wrench was adopted by modern day armies in the late 90s. It's one of the most comprehensive tools designed as it can be used to repair everything from damaged vehicles to destroyed bridges.

Kit Unlock: MK3A1

Damage: 15x8
Accuracy: Low
Fire Modes: Full-Auto/Semi-Auto

The Jackhammer is a heavy shotgun loaded with a 10-round revolver-type cylinder. Due to its long reload time, it's important to be careful when firing on the full-auto setting, or you'll find yourself out of ammunition at an inconvenient moment.

Engineer Tactics

The wrench is back, and this time the engineer gets some credit for using it. Like before, the engineer is the master of repairs and mines. If it can be damaged, the engineer can fix it. Use the wrench to restore vehicles and other damaged items to full strength. The engineer can also turn any vehicle into a mobile repair station by simply riding in it. When an engineer is inside a vehicle, a small repair radius is emitted outward from the vehicle, slowly repairing any nearby objects. Repairs conducted in this manner are slower than if performed directly with the wrench, but staying in a vehicle provides the engineer with much more protection than standing out on the battlefield. The engineer's mines are only effective against vehicles—they won't explode if you step on one. These are useful in defensive situations, when it's necessary to close off roads, bridges, or other narrow choke points to vehicle traffic. One mine is enough to turn any vehicle into a flaming hulk of charred metal, and mines don't distinguish between friend or foe—so think twice before dropping them. No more than five mines can be dropped at one time. Each engineer is also armed with a shotgun, a weapon that is nearly useless at intermediate and long ranges, but outright devastating at close range. When fired, the shotgun spits out eight spherical pellets which leave from the barrel in a cone-shaped spread. As such, accuracy diminishes drastically over distance. Unless conducting close quarter combat, engineers are better off using their pistol. It causes less damage but is much more likely to hit distant targets.

> **TIP** Need to drop some mines fast? Try dropping them out of a moving vehicle like a heavy jeep or even a transport helicopter. However, you must be sitting in a passenger spot that allows you to access your kit. You can even drop mines while parachuting, as a last ditch effort at survival when you find yourself drifting toward an enemy tank.

Engineer: Tester Tips
by Jose Gonzales

- The engineer is the class of choice for battlefield commanders. Commanders can hang out around stations vital to their team use (UAV trailer, radar station, and artillery), supply commander assistance to squads (UAV sweeps, radar scan, artillery fire, supply drops, and recon-naissance), and defend/repair the stations upon attack/sabotage.

- The US M11-87 and China Norinco 982 pump-action shotguns are lethal close-quarters weapons. These weapons can easily lay waste to poor soldiers without body armor (special forces, snipers, engineers, or medics).

- The MEC Saiga 12K is awesome in not only its power, but in its rate of fire as well, as it is semi-auto. Your soldier can spray away with the shotgun fire without having to compensate for the time it takes to pump the shotgun.

- Anticipate your landmine needs, as the mines have a specified arm time. Place them ahead of time at entrances that enemy armor will come through.

- Booby trap vehicles with landmines. To do this, jump and toss the landmine on top of the stationed enemy vehicle roof or on top of unmanned vehicles. Once the enemy moves the vehicle forward or backward, the mine triggers and kills the occupants.

Engineer: Tester Tips (continued)
by Jose Gonzales

- The engineer isn't equipped with body armor. Make sure your squad mates are covering you, or you'll die quickly.

- The engineer can indirectly repair his teammate's vehicles by being a passenger in a nearby vehicle. For example, a teammate in a M1A2 tank can benefit from a repair, if you as an engineer drive up behind/beside him in a Humvee (staying in close proximity).

- Your team's placed landmines are displayed with a skull and crossbones on it within your 3D map (which is enabled by default).

- The wrench is an all-purpose, helpful tool, as it can do the following:

  1. Repair destroyed bridges.

  2. Repair stations vital to the commander (UAV Trailer, Radar Station, and artillery).

  3. Directly repair your team's vehicles. This proves most useful when repairing the vehicle you are sitting in, when occupying an exposed passenger position (found in the RIB, US Seahawk, US Bradley Linebacker, US Humvee, MEC Mi-17, MEC Tunguska, MEC Vodnik, Chinese Z-8, Chinese Nanjing, and Chinese Type 95 AA).

  4. Indirectly repair nearby vehicles, if an engineer is sitting in a nearby vehicle.

  5. Remove enemy landmines from the ground.

  6. Remove enemy claymores, if carefully approached from the rear.

  7. Repair damaged supply crates from the commander.

  8. Repair destructible items that you want to preserve as defensive tools. Engineers can repair destructible fence sections to prevent the enemy from entering. Repair explosive fuel wagons/barrels to use/shoot later when an enemy runs near one. Or, repair damaged destructible wooden crates to use as cover.

MEDIC

The medic's main role is healing and reviving teammates with medic bags and shock paddles. A serious injury can send a soldier into revive mode for a short period of time, during which you can save his life—if you get there in time. Also keep in mind that the shock paddles can deliver a big enough charge to kill an enemy soldier. Medics can also hop in certain vehicles and turn them into "ambulances" to automatically heal other passengers and nearby teammates.

Sprint:	Long
Armor:	None
Equipment:	

- Knife
- Pistol
- Assault Rifle
- Hand Grenades
- Medic Bag
- Shock Paddles

US Medic

US Medic Kit

Key	Weapon/Item	Magazine Capacity	Ammo Count
1	Knife	—	—
2	92FS	15	120
3	M16A2	30	150
4	Hand Grenade	—	4
5	Medic Bag	—	3*
6	Shock Paddles	—	—

* = Replenishable

Primary Weapon: M16A2

The M16A2 was developed as an improvement over the standard M16A1. It has proven itself superior in many ways.

Damage:	30
Accuracy:	High
Fire Modes:	Burst/Semi-Auto

Chinese Medic

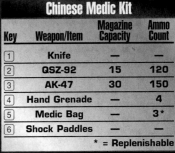

Chinese Medic Kit

Key	Weapon/Item	Magazine Capacity	Ammo Count
1	Knife	—	—
2	QSZ-92	15	120
3	AK-47	30	150
4	Hand Grenade	—	4
5	Medic Bag	—	3*
6	Shock Paddles	—	—

* = Replenishable

Primary Weapon: AK-47

The AK-47 is an extremely robust weapon that has sacrificed some accuracy for reliability. It fires powerful 7.62mm ammunition from a 30-round magazine.

Damage:	38
Accuracy:	Medium
Fire Modes:	Full-Auto/Semi-Auto

MEC Medic

MEC Medic Kit

Key	Weapon/Item	Magazine Capacity	Ammo Count
1	Knife	—	—
2	MR-444	15	120
3	AK-101	30	150
4	Hand Grenade	—	4
5	Medic Bag	—	3*
6	Shock Paddles	—	—

* = Replenishable

Primary Weapon: AK-101

The gas-operated AK-101 is a modern version of the classic AK-47. It uses 5.56mm NATO ammunition which can be fired at the rate of 600 bullets per minute, and is far more accurate than its predecessor.

Damage: 37
Accuracy: Medium/High
Fire Modes: Full-Auto/Semi-Auto

Specialized Equipment

Medic Bag and Shock Paddles

The medic bag is used to heal friendly soldiers. Hold the bag when you are near friendly soldiers to gradually heal them. Alternately, you can throw one on the ground and any teammate who runs over it will be fully healed. The defibrillator is standard

equipment in all modern armies, and are used to save mortally wounded soldiers. There are rumors that medics have used them as weapons in close-action combat.

Kit Unlock: L85A1

Damage: 32
Accuracy: High
Fire Modes: Full-Auto/Semi-Auto

The L-85 is part of the SA80 weapons family. It's a completely new design, and when introduced to the British Army, proved so accurate that they had to redesign their Army Marksmanship tests.

Medic Tactics

Now that first-aid cabinets and crates are no longer available, the medic kit is more valuable than ever. Administer first aid by selecting the medic bag and simply standing next to a wounded teammate. Medic bags can also be dropped on the ground—a total of five can be dropped by one medic at any given time, and only three at a time in quick succession. One medic bag fully heals any wounded teammate. The medic has an unlimited supply of medic bags, but they must be regenerated one at a time. Similar to the engineer, the medic can heal while riding in a vehicle. As a passenger, the medic generates a healing zone around the vehicle, slowly healing any nearby teammates.

The shock paddles are used to revive seriously wounded teammates. When a player's health reaches zero, they enter revive mode for a few seconds. If the medic can make it to a downed teammate during this short period and use the shock paddles on them, the teammate will be revived. Cheating death not only keeps a teammate in the fight, but it spares the team the cost of a ticket—something that could make a huge difference in the long term. Before rushing to a downed teammate, analyze the situation first and make sure it's safe. Otherwise, there's a good chance you could face the same fate as your teammate, and the loss of one ticket could quickly become two. Medics receive points for both healing and reviving teammates. Offensively, the medic is similar to the assault kit, using the same assault rifle, but without the grenade launcher. The medic also lacks body armor, making the kit a bit more vulnerable to damage. Still, at least one medic should accompany every squad, prioritizing the survival of the squad leader above all else.

Medic: Tester Tips
by Jose Gonzales

- The medic is able to heal soldiers by throwing medic bags on the ground for his teammates to walk over, or also by simply holding up the medic bag when in the proximity of soldiers.

- It's a good idea to actively heal your teammates when defending a flag. The best way to do this is to randomly drop medic bags around the CP for your teammates to pick up if needed.

- Not only are the shock paddles handy in reviving teammates, but they can also be used as a nasty melee weapon. Enemy soldiers die in one hit upon shock paddle contact.

- The M16A2 in burst mode is great for a three-round burst into the enemy up close. It's also decent enough to snipe with, when zoomed in conjunction with semi-auto fire mode.

- The MEC AK-101 and China AK-47 in full-auto mode are awesome in close quarters but are even more deadly against long-range targets when zoomed in conjunction with semi-auto fire mode.

- The medic is not equipped with body armor. Make sure your squad mates are covering you, or you will die quickly.

TIP You can exchange your current kit for a dead player's by approaching their kit and pressing [G]. This can come in handy if you're low on ammo or simply want to try out the opposing team's weapons. Even if you're satisfied with your kit, you can still use other kits to your advantage. For instance, if you're a wounded assault soldier, pick up a medic's kit, throw out some medic bags to heal yourself and teammates, then pick up your assault kit again. The same tactic works when restocking on ammo using the support kit's ammo bags.

SNIPER

s a sniper you can move quickly when ou need to, but the key to your eadliness is staying still. Wearing amouflage allows you to remain oncealed in a good hiding spot so you an pluck off your enemies from a istance without being spotted. Or, sneak hrough tall grass and plant claymore nines for unsuspecting enemy troops. he claymore explodes when somebody walks in front of it, so lant it and get out of there fast.

Sprint: Long
Armor: None
Equipment:
• Knife
• Pistol (silenced)
• Sniper Rifle
• Hand Grenades
• Claymore Mines

Chinese Sniper

Chinese Sniper Kit

Key	Weapon/Item	Magazine Capacity	Ammo Count
1	Knife	—	—
2	QSZ-92 (silencer)	15	120
3	Type 88	10	50
4	Hand Grenade	—	4
5	Claymore	—	2

Damage: 45
Accuracy: High
Fire Modes: Semi-Auto

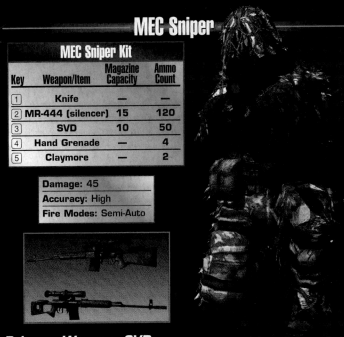

Primary Weapon: Type 88

The Type 88 is a member of the same family of guns as the Type 95 rifles, and fires a similar type of 5.8mm ammunition. It is semi-automatic and loaded from a 10-round box magazine.

US Sniper

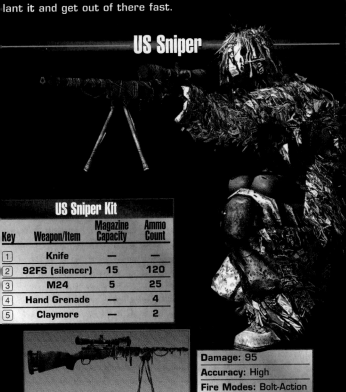

US Sniper Kit

Key	Weapon/Item	Magazine Capacity	Ammo Count
1	Knife	—	—
2	92FS (silencer)	15	120
3	M24	5	25
4	Hand Grenade	—	4
5	Claymore	—	2

Damage: 95
Accuracy: High
Fire Modes: Bolt-Action

Primary Weapon: M24

he M24 sniper rifle replaced the older M21 in the late 1980s. The Jnited States returned to bolt-action sniper rifles with this light-veight weapon. It has an effective range of nearly 1,000 meters.

MEC Sniper

MEC Sniper Kit

Key	Weapon/Item	Magazine Capacity	Ammo Count
1	Knife	—	—
2	MR-444 (silencer)	15	120
3	SVD	10	50
4	Hand Grenade	—	4
5	Claymore	—	2

Damage: 45
Accuracy: High
Fire Modes: Semi-Auto

Primary Weapon: SVD

The SVD is a lightweight rifle used for mid-range sharp shooting. It's slightly less accurate than its American counterpart, but shoots significantly faster.

Specialized Equipment

Claymore

The claymore is an anti-personnel mine which explodes in a cone-shaped pattern. A claymore explodes whenever someone moves in front of it. Be careful, as the claymore does not distinguish between friend and foe.

Kit Unlock: M95

Damage:	95
Accuracy:	High
Fire Modes:	Bolt-Action

The M95 Barret is the most massive sniper weapon to date. It fires 12.7mm (.50) ammunition and is one of the few handheld weapons that can penetrate armored glass such as the type used in helicopter cockpits.

TIP When using the M24 or M95, take some time to line up your shot and make it count. After each shot, the bolt must be retracted and reinserted to load a new round, often causing you to lose sight of the target when your eye is pulled back from the scope. The semi-automatic Type 88 and SVD inflict less damage but allow the shooter to fire multiple rounds while keeping their target centered in the scope.

Sniper Tactics

Although popular, the sniper is one of the most difficult kits to master, as stealth and patience are just as important as marksmanship. The rifles provided by this kit are the most powerful and accurate firearms in the game. Still, unless you score head shots every time, it'll probably take two or three hits to down an opponent. When engaging enemies at long range through the scope, the most difficult aspect of scoring a hit is determining how much to lead a moving target. It all depends on the direction and speed of movement. For instance, you'll need to lead a sprinting target a bit more than one that is just walking. For the most part, it's all guess work. But with practice, you'll be able to accurately predict where your bullet and target will converge down range, increasing the likelihood of scoring a hit.

Before taking your first shot, find a well concealed place to hide. Each sniper is equipped with a ghillie suit, a bulky camouflaged outfit adorned in grass and foliage designed to break-up the wearer's silhouette. This suit makes the sniper extremely difficult to see when deployed in tall grass or within bushes or shrubs. To maximize concealment, try to stick to natural settings as much as possible. In urban environments, seek the cover of building interiors and only take to rooftops if objects are available to hide

behind. When sniping, background is just as important as the foreground, as it helps conceal the sniper's visible profile—a sniper outlined against the blue sky makes an easy target for everyone. The sniper's ability to remain concealed for long periods of time makes this kit useful for reconnaissance, helping keep the commander informed of enemy movement. Snipers are also equipped with a couple of claymores. Use them to booby trap control points or to simply cover your flanks while sniping.

Sniper: Tester Tips
by Jose Gonzales

- The sniper is great to have out in the hills overlooking CPs, in thickets of grass, under small trees/shrubs (with help of the ghillie suit), or on a rooftop/crane somewhere.
- Using the US M24 or Chinese Type 88, aim at targets using the center of the crosshairs.
- For the MEC SVD, fit your target inside the top-most triangle-shaped reticule in zoom mode.
- Make the sniper responsible for relaying proper recon to the squad. Snipers can report their findings via VOIP, or can also place markers of the enemy on the mini-map via the commo rose *Spotted* function.
- As the sniper class, you will be for the most part looking through the scope of your rifle. Knowing this, be prepared for someone trying to sneak up on you when providing recon or covering fire. Place claymore mines around the perimeter of your desired sniping position, or at the exit point of the building roof/crane ladder(s) to prevent the enemy from getting the jump on you.
- The sniper isn't equipped with body armor. Make sure your squad mates are covering you, or you will die quickly.
- Claymores are also great to cover entrances that enemy infantry may use to assault a flag. Place them at angles/locations where the enemy will trigger them unknowingly (in their blind spots, like to the side of a fence entrance as they run through).
- Finally, claymores make for great booby traps. Place them near some tempting tanks or planes/choppers, and you will surely get a kill off a greedy enemy player.
- Your team's placed claymores will be displayed with a skull and crossbones on it within your 3D map (which is enabled by default).

SPECIAL FORCES

Swift and deadly, special forces soldiers come armed with silenced pistols, allowing you to take out targets with ultimate stealth. But when you want to make some noise, your C4 explosives should do the trick. You can plant a C4 pack out of sight and detonate it when troops walk by, blow bridges to cut off your enemy, or attach the pack to a vehicle and wait for enemy troops to gather around it before setting off the charge.

Sprint:	Long
Armor:	None
Equipment:	

- Knife
- Pistol (silenced)
- Assault Carbine
- Hand Grenades
- C4

US Special Forces

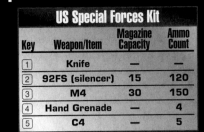

US Special Forces Kit			
Key	Weapon/Item	Magazine Capacity	Ammo Count
1	Knife	—	—
2	92FS (silencer)	15	120
3	M4	30	150
4	Hand Grenade	—	4
5	C4	—	5

Damage: 25
Accuracy: High
Fire Modes: Full-Auto/Semi-Auto

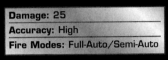

Primary Weapon: M4

The M4 is a lightweight version of the M16 and fires the same type of ammunition. It has similar handling and accuracy but does less damage, and comes equipped with a red-dot scope.

MEC Special Forces

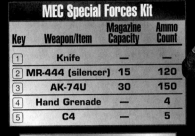

MEC Special Forces Kit			
Key	Weapon/Item	Magazine Capacity	Ammo Count
1	Knife	—	—
2	MR-444 (silencer)	15	120
3	AK-74U	30	150
4	Hand Grenade	—	4
5	C4	—	5

Damage: 29
Accuracy: Medium
Fire Modes: Full-Auto/Semi-Auto

Primary Weapon: AK-74U

The AK-74U is a shortened version of the AK-74 and is intended as a personal defense weapon for tank and helicopter crews. It lacks accuracy at longer ranges, but is easier to handle in confined spaces.

Chinese Special Forces

Chinese Special Forces Kit			
Key	Weapon/Item	Magazine Capacity	Ammo Count
1	Knife	—	—
2	QSZ-92 (silencer)	15	120
3	QBZ-97	30	150
4	Hand Grenade	—	4
5	C4	—	5

Damage: 25
Accuracy: High
Fire Modes: Full-Auto/Semi-Auto

Primary Weapon: QBZ-97

The QBZ-97 carbine is the latest addition to the PLA armory. It is a lightweight, air-cooled assault rifle built of polymer materials which fires 5.8mm rounds from a 30-round magazine.

Specialized Equipment

C4

C4 is an extremely powerful explosive charge which can be attached to vehicles and structures. A remote detonator is used to set off the explosive. It's very effective against vehicles or as a booby-trap—just make sure you are at a safe distance away before you press the detonator, as it has a large blast radius!

Kit Unlock: G36C

Damage: 25
Accuracy: High
Fire Modes: Full-Auto/Semi-Auto

The G36C is the commando version of the G36. It weighs 2.8 kilos and is only 500mm long when the butt stock is folded; in full auto mode, it can fire 750 rounds per minute.

Special Forces Tactics

Like the assault kit, the special forces kit is another well-rounded option capable of filling both offensive and defensive roles. The compact assault carbines offered by this kit are a bit more accurate than their full-sized assault rifle counterparts (found in the assault and medic kits), but not quite as powerful. This kit also lacks body armor, making it less suitable for frontal assaults. Instead, use special forces for sneak attacks and sabotage missions behind enemy lines. Using light jeeps, RIBs, or helicopters for transport, a small squad of special forces troops can successfully conduct surprise attacks on enemy held control points, especially if they're lightly defended.

Their C4 charges are also ideal for taking out the opposing team's commander stations—it takes two charges to destroy each. On defense, C4 can be used to booby trap control points or demolish bridges. Destroying bridges is a great way to slow down an enemy advance, but the damage is never permanent since engineers can repair the bridges. Three charges are needed to blow a hole in a bridge. Long bridges can often be blown in two or three separate spots, requiring three C4 charges for each demolished span. The more damage dealt to a bridge, the longer it takes an enemy engineer to repair it, buying defenders more time to counter the crossing.

Special Forces: Tester Tips
by Jose Gonzales

• The special forces soldier is the most balanced of the classes, and is probably the best choice to use for lone wolf play.

• The US M4/China QBZ-97/MEC AK-74U do great up-close damage against infantry in full-auto mode. They're also great for distance targets in zoom mode in conjunction with semi-auto fire mode.

• This class is equipped with several C4 explosives. C4 is the best solution to destroy enemy armor and also to defend choke points or flags.

• C4 can stick to materials—you can place C4 on your vehicle (like a jeep), drive into the enemy, jump out, run away, and hit the C4 detonator for a rolling car bomb.

• During the game, have special forces soldiers focus on using C4 on the opposing team's commander stations (UAV trailer, Radar station, or artillery).

• The special forces soldier is not equipped with body armor. Make sure your squad mates are covering you, or you will die quickly.

• Your team's placed C4 charges are displayed with a skull and crossbones on it within your 3D map (which is enabled by default).

SUPPORT

Crates of ammo are hard to come by in war zones. That's where the support soldier comes in. These troops provide an invaluable service by supplying ammunition bags to their team. Though carrying all that ammo weighs them down, their body armor provides some protection against

Sprint: Short
Armor: Heavy
Equipment:
• Knife
• Pistol
• Light Machine Gun
• Hand Grenades
• Ammo Bag

enemy fire while they lay down some serious lead with their machine guns. They also automatically replenish ammo for any squad mates riding with them in a vehicle.

US Support

Key	Weapon/Item	Magazine Capacity	Ammo Count
1	Knife	—	—
2	92FS	15	120
3	M249	200	1,200
4	Hand Grenade	—	4
5	Ammo Bag	—	3*

* = Replenishable

Damage: 25
Accuracy: Medium/High
Fire Modes: Full-Auto/Semi-Auto

Primary Weapon: M249

The Squad Automatic Weapon (SAW) is the basis of firepower for an infantry squad. Its high rate of fire affects accuracy. For best results, the M249 should be fired from a prone position in controlled bursts.

Chinese Support

Key	Weapon/Item	Magazine Capacity	Ammo Count
1	Knife	—	—
2	QSZ-92	15	120
3	Type 95	200	600
4	Hand Grenade	—	4
5	Ammo Bag	—	3*

* = Replenishable

Damage: 25
Accuracy: Medium/High
Fire Modes: Full-Auto

Primary Weapon: Type 95

The Type 95 is the light machine gun version of the Type 95 carbine. It uses the same ammunition, but has a slightly longer barrel and is drum-loaded.

MEC Support

MEC Support Kit

Key	Weapon/Item	Magazine Capacity	Ammo Count
1	Knife	—	—
2	MR-444	15	120
3	RPK-74	130	650
4	Hand Grenade	—	4
5	Ammo Bag	—	3 *

* = Replenishable

Damage: 35	
Accuracy: Medium	
Fire Modes: Full-Auto	

Primary Weapon: RPK-74

The RPK is a very efficient squad-level light-support weapon using small-caliber ammunition. Due to its high rate of fire, the RPK is most accurate when fired from a prone, stationary position.

Specialized Equipment

Ammo Bag

Ammo bags are used to refill friendly soldiers' ammunition stock. Hold the bag when you are near friendly soldiers to gradually refill their ammunition stock. Alternatively, you can throw one on the ground and any teammate who runs over it will be fully resupplied.

Kit Unlock: PKM

Damage: 45	
Accuracy: Medium	
Fire Modes: Full-Auto	

The 7.62mm PKM is a 16-kilo machine gun which has amazing firepower but is extremely inaccurate due to its massive recoil. Firing from a prone, stationary position gives the best results.

Support Tactics

Laying down suppressive fire has never been easier (or more fun) than with the support kit's light machine gun. What these hulking automatic weapons lack in accuracy, they make up for in volume, capable of spraying the battlefield with a sustained barrage of hot lead. For best results, always drop prone before firing these weapons. At the very least, take a knee. Attempting to fire while standing causes these weapons to buck wildly about, usually hitting everything except your target. Accuracy improves dramatically when fired from a stationary prone position. As such, this kit is great for defensive roles, especially when covering narrow choke points like streets, alleys, and bridges. Like any automatic weapon, fire in short bursts to keep the weapon on target and prevent overheating. Support troops are also responsible for supplying their teammates with ammo since there are no ammo crates scattered about. The ammo bag works just like the medic's medic bag. When selected, the ammo bag slowly replenishes the ammo stocks of nearby friendly troops. These bags can also be dropped on the ground, allowing teammates to restock themselves. Like the medic and engineer, the support soldier can also extend ammo supplies to surrounding friendlies when riding in a vehicle. This is a good way to rearm tanks and other vehicles on the battlefield. Supplying teammates with ammo gives the support soldier points.

Support: Tester Tips
by Jose Gonzales

- The support soldier can directly re-supply his teammates by throwing ammo bags on the ground for them to walk on. He can also re-supply them by simply holding the ammo bag out as soon as they're nearby.

- The support soldier can indirectly re-supply his teammates' vehicles by being a passenger in a nearby vehicle. For example, a teammate in a M1A2 tank can benefit from an ammo re-supply if a support soldier drives up behind/beside him in a Humvee (staying in close proximity).

- The support soldier's primary weapon, when fired standing up, sprays far too wildly to be of any good use. Stay prone when firing this weapon.

- The US M249/MEC RPK-74/China Type 95 can deal heavy damage to infantry or light-armor vehicles (US Humvee, US DPV, MEC FAV, MEC Vodnik, Chinese Paratrooper Vehicle, or Chinese Nanjing), but the downside is that they overheat. Watch the overheat meter during sustained fire.

- Place this soldier somewhere prone, then have him throw down cover fire for the squad as they make their way across a nasty choke point.

- Actively rearm your teammates when defending a flag. The best way to do this is to randomly drop ammo bags around the CP for your teammates to pick up if needed.

STANDARD-ISSUE INFANTRY WEAPONS

The standard-issue combat knife is very deadly when used in hand-to-hand combat. Many soldiers have survived thanks to quick thinking and fast reflexes when they found themselves suddenly out of ammunition.

Pistols

92FS

The 92FS is a 9mm semi-automatic pistol which carries 15 rounds in the magazine. The 92FS is used by military and law enforcement all over the world.

Affiliation:	USMC
Damage:	20
Accuracy:	Low
Fire-Modes:	Semi-Auto

QSZ-92

Affiliation:	China
Damage:	20
Accuracy:	Low
Fire-Modes:	Semi-Auto

The QSZ-92 is a recoil-operated semi-automatic pistol built for the PLA. It fires 5.8mm ammunition and has 15 shots in a clip.

MR-444

Affiliation:	MEC
Damage:	20
Accuracy:	Low
Fire-Modes:	Semi-Auto

The Russian made MR-444 is a polymer-framed semi-automatic pistol firing 9mm ammunition. It is sold worldwide and is well-known for its reliability.

Hand Grenade

The hand grenade, an effective fragmentation explosive, can be thrown long distance or rolled for more accurate placement. It has a four second fuse.

STATIONARY WEAPONS

Machine Guns

Stationary machine guns are found at control points, usually configured in a defensive arrangement. Like vehicles, the type of machine gun that spawns at a control point is determined by the nationality of the captor. You would find mounted versions of either the US M249, the Chinese Type 95, or the MEC RPK-74. The stability of these weapons greatly increases their accuracy, making them surprisingly effective at mowing down enemy infantry even at long range. Gunners can duck incoming fire by pressing and holding left `Ctrl`.

Anti-Tank Turrets

Both the US TOW and Chinese/MEC HJ-8 are wire-guided anti-tank missiles. Functionally, they work identically to the SRAW and Eryx systems used by anti-tank troops, but these larger missiles pack a much bigger punch, particularly against tanks. Be aware: while manning these stations you're vulnerable to gun fire and grenades, and a sitting duck for snipers.

Anti-Aircraft Turrets

The US Stinger and Chinese/MEC IGLA are anti-aircraft, heat-seeking missiles useful for downing enemy helicopters and jets. The operator must first attain a lock on the target's heat signature before the missile will track. But flares and other heat sources can confuse the missile's guidance system, causing it to miss. For best results, wait until the targeted aircraft dumps its flares before firing.

TIP Stationary weapons can be damaged and eventually destroyed. Use the engineer's wrench to restore them to full strength. But even if destroyed, they'll spawn back into place just like a vehicle.

Phalanx and Sea Sparrow Battery

Two of these devastating anti-aircraft batteries are mounted on the Marine USS *Essex* aircraft carrier. Both weapon systems are linked and can rotate 360 degrees, allowing a single operator to rapidly fire cannon rounds and missiles at approaching enemy aircraft. The awesome Phalanx auto-cannon can shred enemy aircraft with only a few hits, but can quickly overheat if not fired in short bursts. Equally impressive is the Sea Sparrow battery, capable of firing eight heat-seeking missiles in quick succession. When playing as the Marines, man at least one of these batteries at all times to protect friendly aircraft parked on the flight deck.

SURFACE VEHICLES

Like the infantry troop kits, the game vehicles are a different set of tools you must understand and master if you hope to lead your team to victory. In this section, we'll look at every ground vehicle as well as the Rigid Inflatable Boat. Before reading over the tips and strategies for each vehicle type, here is a refresher course on driving.

DRIVER TRAINING

Some players find the first-person view too confining when driving. Press F10 for a rear third-person perspective.

Driving a vehicle is as intuitive as moving your soldier. To get inside any vehicle, stand near it and press E. You'll enter the vehicle's driver position, assuming it's unoccupied. Switch to other positions by using the function keys like F2 and F3. Press F1 to return to the driver position. All surface vehicles use the same default movement keys as the solider: W to move forward, S to reverse, A to steer left, and D to steer right. If the vehicle is equipped with a turret, pan the mouse to rotate it and click the mouse buttons to fire its weapons. Moving the mouse while driving a vehicle without a turret causes the player to turn his head left and right. To make driving easier, switch to one of the third-person external views by pressing C. If you prefer the first-person perspective, press F9. Hop out of a vehicle by pressing E at any time.

You crashed your vehicle into a tree? No problem. The engineer can fix anything with his trusty wrench.

Vehicles in the game respond to their environment in the same way they would in the real world. For instance, you can move faster on roads than you can through marshlands and mud. Depending on the vehicle's durability, it can also sustain damage by running into objects—the higher the speed of impact, the more damage dealt to the vehicle. And unless you're in an amphibious APC, no land vehicle is salvageable if driven into deep water. So take care of your vehicle and keep it at full strength. Otherwise you're making it easier for your opponents to destroy it.

> **NOTE** All vehicle machine guns have unlimited ammo, but they can still overheat.

LIGHT JEEPS

DPV

Affiliation: USMC
Speed: Very Fast
Armor: None

What this lacks in armor it makes up for in agility and firepower. The Desert Patrol Vehicle (DPV) has two gunner positions— one for the light machine gun and the other for the heavy machine gun. It is not effective against armored vehicles, but it helps clear out infantry.

DPV Armament		
Key	**Crew Position**	**Weapon**
F1	Driver	—
F2	Passenger 1	Heavy Machine Gun
F3	Passenger 2	Machine Gun

Paratrooper Vehicle/FAV

Affiliation: China/MEC
Speed: Very Fast
Armor: None

The PLA and MEC operate the fast attack vehicle (FAV) for both airborne and special operations. Developed by a former aircraft manufacturing company, the FAV is known for its rugged construction and light weight as well as the impressive amount of firepower it can carry into battle.

Paratrooper Vehicle/FAV Armament

Key	Crew Position	Weapon
F1	Driver	—
F2	Passenger 1	Heavy Machine Gun
F3	Passenger 2	Machine Gun

NOTE The heavy machine gun in the Paratrooper Vehicle/FAV can rotate 360 degrees—the DPV's only faces forward. This makes the DPV vulnerable to side and rear attacks.

Light Jeep Tactics

The light jeeps are the fastest land vehicles in the game, useful for rushing neutral control points at a battle's start. But their lack of armor and exposed positions make them death traps if driven into heavy action. Most explosive munitions can destroy these small vehicles in one hit, killing everyone inside. The driver and passengers are also exposed to small arms fire. The light jeep's greatest defensive assets are its speed and off-road capability. To ensure survival, use these vehicles to traverse terrain on a map's periphery, staying away from heated battles near control points. Although the vehicle can attain high speeds on roads, many roads will be used by larger and more deadly vehicles. Instead, stay off-road and out of sight. Such stealthy tactics are effective when staging raids on distant enemy-held control points and commander stations.

Light Jeeps: Tester Tips
by Jose Gonzales

- The vehicles in this category are very fast, but can withstand little damage.

- You can use its speed to your advantage, as you can run enemy ground troops over while you make your CP approaches.

- The position 2 occupant mans the 50 cal. roof gun. It can quickly destroy enemy troops, light armor, and helicopters. The rounds from the gun are also powerful enough to damage APCs and tanks. Protect this gunner at all costs, as he is fully exposed and can't duck into the turret.

- The position 3 occupant in the light jeep mans the passenger seat machine gun. The MG quickly tears through enemy infantry and light armor, but is limited by a small turning radius and its ability to overheat.

HEAVY JEEPS

HMMWV

Affiliation: USMC
Speed: Fast
Armor: Weak

The American HMMWV (High Mobility Multipurpose Wheeled Vehicle, or "Humvee" sets the world standard for light high-performance military trucks. The Humvee was designed as a multi-purpose infantry vehicle for use in all areas of the modern battlefield. It can maneuver over trenches and steep slopes or wade through deep water.

HMMWV Armament

Key	Crew Position	Weapon
F1	Driver	—
F2	Passenger 1	Heavy Machine Gun
F3	Passenger 2	Kit Weapons
F4	Passenger 3	Kit Weapons

Nanjing (NJ) 2046

Affiliation: China
Speed: Fast
Armor: Weak

The NJ 2046 is a heavy troop transport and field command vehicle. Derived from a civilian minivan and enhanced for use in the field, it features 4-wheel drive transmission, a turbocharged diesel engine and armor plating. You can equip its cargo bed with benches for transporting infantry, or configure it with a canvas or steel roof to provide shelter during inclement weather.

NJ 2046 Armament

Key	Crew Position	Weapon
F1	Driver	—
F2	Passenger 1	Heavy Machine Gun
F3	Passenger 2	Kit Weapons
F4	Passenger 3	Kit Weapons

GAZ 39371 Vodnik

Affiliation:	MEC
Speed:	Fast
Armor:	Weak

The rugged Vodnik is the Russian answer to the American HMMWV. It has nearly two feet of ground clearance and is fitted with bulletproof windows and tires. The Vodnik's most apparent advantage is its unique design. The vehicle consists of two modules: one in front housing the driver and engine and one in the rear for personnel or cargo.

GAZ 39371 Armament

Key	Crew Position	Weapon
F1	Driver	—
F2	Passenger 1	Heavy Machine Gun
F3	Passenger 2	Kit Weapons
F4	Passenger 3	Kit Weapons

Heavy Jeep Tactics

Although slower than light jeeps, the heavy jeeps benefit from more armor and one extra passenger position. The heavy jeep's armor isn't capable of repelling tank rounds or anti-tank missiles, but it does provide its driver and passengers limited protection from small arms fire and even the large munitions fired by APC and AA vehicle auto-cannons. Use these vehicles primarily as troop transports, and once on the move, keep moving to avoid falling victim to enemy tanks and aircraft. The roof-mounted heavy machine gun is a decent defensive weapon, capable of easily mowing down infantry. Its ability to rotate 360 degrees also makes it a fine air defense weapon if tasked with defending a control point without any AA Turrets. Turn it skyward and let it rip to punch holes in enemy helicopters and jets. Just be ready to jump out if the enemy aircraft retaliates.

Heavy Jeeps: Tester Tips
by Jose Gonzales

- Compared to the jeeps in *Battlefield 1942* and *Battlefield Vietnam*, jeeps in *Battlefield 2* should never be underestimated, and serve a greater purpose than just quick infantry transport. Make sure your team fills the jeep up before heading into combat, rather than just using it as a taxi to drive to empty vehicles.

- The vehicles in this category are not as fast as the light jeeps, but compensate by being able to take a little more damage.

Heavy Jeeps: Tester Tips (continued)
by Jose Gonzales

- The position 2 occupant mans the 50 cal. roof gun. It can quickly destroy enemy troops, light armor, and helicopters. The rounds from the gun are also powerful enough to damage APCs and tanks. The roof gunner in heavy jeeps luckily has the option to duck in the turret when under fire.

- The rest of the occupants in the heavy jeep will man exposed passenger positions. They are exposed to gunfire, but are able to use their kit weapons during transport.

- The heavy jeep is great to have fully manned to capture flags. The flag turns faster when more soldiers are in the flag radius.

- Its high occupant number makes it a great vehicle to use for squads.

ARMORED PERSONNEL CARRIERS (APCS)

LAV-25

Affiliation:	USMC
Speed:	Medium
Armor:	Medium

The LAV-25 is an all-weather, all-terrain, light armored vehicle capable of quickly moving firepower and troops around the battlefield. Powered by a 275 hp diesel engine, the LAV-25 can reach speeds up to 65 mph. It is fully amphibious and can traverse rivers or lakes—or even operate offshore during a beach assault.

LAV-25 Armament

Key	Crew Position	Weapon 1	Weapon 2	Weapon 3
F1	Driver	25mm auto-cannon (450)	Anti-Tank (6) Missile	Smoke Grenades
F2	Passenger 1	Machine Gun	—	—
F3	Passenger 2	Machine Gun	—	—
F4	Passenger 3	Machine Gun	—	—
F5	Passenger 4	Machine Gun	—	—

WZ 551

Affiliation:	China
Speed:	Medium
Armor:	Medium

The WZ 551 offers the People's Liberation Army (PLA) the ability to quickly deploy infantry to almost any battlefield location. The six-wheeled armored personnel carrier is designed to cross rugged terrain, from trenches to rivers to steep grades. It's amphibious, carries a 25mm auto-cannon, and is fitted with an NBC (nuclear, biological, chemical) protection system, allowing it to operate in inhospitable environments. Because the PLA's current imperative is to transform its forces into rapid reaction units, the WZ 551 provides the ideal method of transportation.

WZ 551 Armament

Key	Crew Position	Weapon 1	Weapon 2	Weapon 3
F1	Driver	25mm auto-cannon (450)	Anti-Tank (6) Missile	Smoke Grenades
F2	Passenger 1	Machine Gun	—	—
F3	Passenger 2	Machine Gun	—	—
F4	Passenger 3	Machine Gun	—	—
F5	Passenger 4	Machine Gun	—	—

BTR-90

Affiliation:	MEC
Speed:	Medium
Armor:	Medium

The BTR-90 is the Russian Army's next-generation armored personnel carrier. Designed during the mid-1980s and presented publicly for the first time in 1994, the BTR-90 is larger and more powerful than its predecessors. In terms of armament, the BTR-90 carries a complete weapon set in addition to a 30mm main gun; these include machine guns and a launcher for anti-tank guided missiles. Like the other APCs, the BTR-90 is amphibious.

BTR-90 Armament

Key	Crew Position	Weapon 1	Weapon 2	Weapon 3
F1	Driver	30mm auto-cannon (450)	Anti-Tank (6) Missile	Smoke Grenades
F2	Passenger 1	Machine Gun	—	—
F3	Passenger 2	Machine Gun	—	—
F4	Passenger 3	Machine Gun	—	—
F5	Passenger 4	Machine Gun	—	—

APC Tactics

The APCs are the most versatile vehicles in the game, and are armed to the teeth when fully manned. Its auto-cannon rapidly fires small explosive shells, effective against infantry, armored vehicles, and aircraft. The driver can also launch wire-guided anti-tank missiles with the secondary fire key. These work like the game's other wire-guided missiles. Launch it and use the mouse to guide it into the target. Although they take a long time to reload, these missiles are an APCs best chance at surviving an encounter with an enemy tank—fire a missile, pop smoke, and hide until a new missile is loaded and ready to fire. In addition to the driver-operated auto-cannon and anti-tank missiles, machine guns line each APC's flanks, allowing passengers to fire on enemy troops attempting to blindside the vehicle. Unlike any other vehicle in the game, all APCs are amphibious. Use this capability to launch surprise attacks on coastal control points or to flank the enemy. But be aware, APCs are slower in the water, potentially making them easy targets for enemy aircraft and ground-based missiles. Be ready to dispense smoke if you come under attack.

> **CAUTION** If enemy aircraft are present, be wary of fully loading an APC. One laser-guided or TV-guided missile is all it takes to destroy these vehicles, crediting the enemy aircraft's crew with as many as five kills.

APCs: Tester Tips
by Jose Gonzales

- The APC is a perfect vehicle to have fully manned. The APC driver can take out targets out in front with the cannon/missiles while the passengers can man the gun ports and take out assaulting enemy infantry around the vehicle. This helps since the APC's sides and rear are vulnerable areas.

- Do not fire wildly with the APC's driver weapons. The primary fire cannon overheats quickly, and the vehicle only has one missile to fire at a time (the missile carries a slow missile reload time).

- The APC is best used as a mobile repair/healing/re-supply depot with the proper soldier classes occupying its seats. Other soldiers can enter the APC and heal up if a medic is in the APC, while attack choppers, for example, can hover over the APC (occupied by an engineer and support soldier) and be repaired/rearmed.

- APCs are amphibious (can travel on land and over water), so don't be afraid to go off-road to avoid enemy ambushes or potential hazards on the road.

- The APC has the ability to pop smoke. This helps the vehicle conceal itself from AT soldiers, or from enemy soldiers manning TOW/HJ-8s.

- The APC is great to have fully manned to capture flags. The flag turns faster when more soldiers are in the flag radius.

- Its high occupant number makes it a great vehicle to use for squads.

AA VEHICLES

M6 Bradley Linebacker

Affiliation: USMC
Speed: Slow
Armor: Medium

In the late 1990s, the US Army needed for a new short-range air defense system to protect advancing armored units. To provide these units with a mobile defense capable of maintaining their pace, the Army combined the combat-tested M6 Bradley with the proven Stinger anti-aircraft missile system to produce the M6 Bradley Linebacker. The Linebacker is capable of engaging and destroying helicopters and low-flying aircraft. With the help of a sophisticated tracking computer and laser range finder, the Linebacker can fire its missiles while either stationary or on the move.

M6 Bradley Armament

Key	Crew Position	Weapon 1	Weapon 2
F1	Driver	25mm auto-cannon (450)	Anti-Air Missile (12)
F2	Passenger 1	Kit Weapons	—

Type 95

Affiliation: China
Speed: Slow
Armor: Medium

Until the appearance of the Type 95 in the mid-1990s, the PLA relied on older, conventional air defense systems to combat low-flying aircraft and helicopters. Commanders pushed for a better solution, and with the Type 95 they received one. With four rapid-fire 25mm cannons and four SAM launch tubes turret-mounted on top of an armored chassis, the Type 95 is a formidable weapon and the backbone of the PLA's mobile air defense.

Type 95 Armament

Key	Crew Position	Weapon 1	Weapon 2
F1	Driver	25mm auto-cannon x 4 (600)	Anti-Air Missile (12)
F2	Passenger 1	Kit Weapons	—

Tunguska

Affiliation: MEC
Speed: Slow
Armor: Medium

The Russian military began development of the Tunguska in the early 1980s, and the final version rolled off the assembly line in 1988. A combination gun and missile system, the Tunguska can engage targets while stationary or on the move. Its surface-to-air missiles are used for long-range targets, while its twin barrel 30mm anti-aircraft guns are used for close-in defense. The Tunguska's combined radar/optical target detection and tracking system ensures accurate fire from these weapons.

Tunguska Armament

Key	Crew Position	Weapon 1	Weapon 2
F1	Driver	30mm auto-cannon x 2 (600)	Anti-Air Missile (12)
F2	Passenger 1	Kit Weapons	—

AA Vehicle Tactics

Despite their rugged-armored appearance, these vehicles aren't intended for toe-to-toe slug-fests with enemy tanks. In fact, their armor isn't different from that found on the APCs. Move them to strategically advantageous locations to shoot down enemy aircraft. Each AA vehicle is equipped with an anti-aircraft missile battery capable of firing up to four missiles in quick succession. Like all AA missiles, these missiles must attain a lock on an aircraft before they can track it. To ensure a hit, wait until the enemy aircraft dumps its decoy flares before firing. The auto-cannons are effective against aircraft, too, but they can also shred infantry and light-armored vehicles. AA vehicles are rare, so take extra steps to keep them alive and hold the control points where they spawn. Before moving out, analyze the team's air defenses and fill in any gaps with the AA vehicle, parking it where it's well-protected and out of sight from advancing enemy troops and tanks.

> **TIP** The exploding shells fired by the auto-cannons of the AA vehicles and APCs make a distinctive percussive sound, like a string of fire crackers popping. If you're on foot and you hear this sound approaching, take cover fast!

AA Vehicles: Tester Tips
by Jose Gonzales

- The primary fire weapon on the AA vehicle does great damage on light armor, infantry, and helicopters.
- When locked, the barrage of missiles fired from secondary fire mode can quickly take out enemy aircraft.
- The occupant in seat #2 is an exposed passenger position. The soldier in here can provide small arms fire, but can be killed easily as he is fully exposed and can't duck in the turret. The soldier will want to cover the sides and rear of the AA vehicle, as those sides are its most vulnerable.

TANKS

M1A2

Affiliation:	USMC
Speed:	Slow
Armor:	Strong

The backbone of the US Military's armored forces, the M1A2 Abrams exemplifies high tech firepower. Its main armament, a 120mm smooth bore cannon, can fire a variety of rounds. A sophisticated fire control system stabilizes the cannon for accurate shooting on the move, while a laser range finder, thermal imaging sight, and a digital ballistics computer give the Abrams a "first shot, first kill" advantage. Protected by an NBC (nuclear, biological, chemical) system and surrounded by steel-encased depleted uranium armor, the M1A2 can operate in nearly any conceivable battlefield environment.

M1A2 Armament

Key	Crew Position	Weapon 1	Weapon 2	Weapon 3
F1	Driver	120mm cannon (40)	Coaxial Machine Gun	Smoke Grenades
F2	Passenger 1	Heavy Machine Gun	—	—

Type 98

Affiliation:	China
Speed:	Slow
Armor:	Strong

Developed during the early 1990s, the Type 98 represents the latest in Chinese design and manufacturing. Engineers based its hull on proven Russian and European models, and incorporated high technology to maximize its performance: a laser range finder, wind sensor, ballistic computer, and axis stabilization system ensure accurate firing of its 120mm cannon while on the move, and a combination warning/defense system protects the tank from enemy-guided weapons.

Type 98 Armament

Key	Crew Position	Weapon 1	Weapon 2	Weapon 3
F1	Driver	120mm cannon (40)	Coaxial Machine Gun	Smoke Grenades
F2	Passenger 1	Heavy Machine Gun	—	—

T-90

Affiliation:	MEC
Speed:	Slow
Armor:	Strong

In the early 1990s, the Russian Army began production on a successor to the problematic T-80 tank. Dubbed the T-90, the new tank is a powerful weapon system that combines advanced armaments and equipment. It carries a 125mm main gun capable of firing various projectiles. Most of the T-90 is covered with Explosive Reactive Armor bricks. These bricks detonate upon contact with a warhead, projecting the explosive force away from the tank.

Type 98 Armament

Key	Crew Position	Weapon 1	Weapon 2	Weapon 3
F1	Driver	125mm cannon (40)	Coaxial Machine Gun	Smoke Grenades
F2	Passenger 1	Heavy Machine Gun	—	—

Tank Tactics

While tanks are still at the top of the food chain during ground combat, they're no longer as dominant as they once were. Guided missiles fired by infantry, APCs, and aircraft pose a threat to a tank's survivability. The only way a tank can counter these new threats is by deploying a smoke screen ([X]). When popping smoke to avoid an incoming missile, move in reverse while staying within the smoke cloud—it doesn't do you any good to move out of the smoke screen. As usual, a tank's side and rear armor are the weakest. For this reason, keep the front armor facing a threat. This is important when duking it out with an enemy tank. Despite advances in firepower, the rounds fired by the main gun travel in an arc-like trajectory, especially when fired at distant targets. As such, compensate for range by elevating the barrel, aiming above your target. Use the horizontal lines on the tank's HUD to determine the correct elevation setting and score a hit.

CAUTION A tank's driver position offers poor visibility. Unless a teammate is manning the machine gun up top, switch to an external view when driving the tank through city streets. This allows you to spot enemy troops attempting to sneak up on your tank—special forces troops can ruin your day with a couple of C4 charges. If enemy troops are around your tank, keep moving and retreat to a safe distance until you can turn the tank's coaxial machine gun on the attackers.

Tanks: Tester Tips
by Jose Gonzales

- Be aware that the sides and rear end on the tank are the most vulnerable areas. Have the tank's roof gunner cover those specified sides from enemy AT soldier fire.
- The tank has the ability to pop smoke. This helps the tank conceal itself from AT soldiers, or from enemy soldiers manning TOW/HJ-8s.
- The tank roof gunner is able to duck in the turret. When you are under fire from enemy infantry, you cannot be harmed when ducking.

BOATS

Rigid Inflatable Boat (RIB)

| Affiliation: All |
| Speed: Very Fast |
| Armor: None |

The RIB is a high-speed extreme-weather vessel whose hull is partially rigid and partially inflatable to allow it to traverse long distances at high speed. Developed in the late 1990s, the RIB is used for

insertion or extraction of special operations teams such as the US Navy SEALS or the Army's Delta Force. Portable, lightweight, and rugged, the RIB's hull is constructed from glass-reinforced plastic, and a new neoprene and nylon-reinforced fabric makes up its inflatable tube.

Key	Crew Position	Weapon
	RIB Armament	
F1	Driver	—
F2	Passenger 1	Machine Gun
F3	Passenger 2	Kit Weapons
F4	Passenger 3	Kit Weapons
F5	Passenger 4	Kit Weapons
F6	Passenger 5	Kit Weapons

Boat Tactics

The RIB is used by all nationalities and spawns next to control points near rivers and other large bodies of water. This not a heavy assault vehicle, as small arms fire easily destroy it. Even worse, it provides no protection for its occupants. Therefore, remain stealthy and out of harm's way when using this boat. It's a transport, not a gunboat. Instead of staging frontal assaults, circumvent the enemy's main defenses and launch surprise attacks on rear positions. The RIB can speed through shallow water without running aground, so hit the enemy where it least expects it.

TIP When on defense, use RIBs to mine river fords. An engineer sitting in one of the side passenger positions can toss mines out the side of the boat, hiding them in the shallow water where enemy vehicles have a hard time spotting them. Do not run the RIB over the mines after they're placed.

Boats: Tester Tips
by Jose Gonzales

- RIB boats are great solutions for soldiers who want to make stealth approaches across enemy lines, over to flags that the enemy may otherwise ignore defending. It may be too risky for you to fly, since you can be locked onto, and it can be too risky driving around on land, heading into fortified enemy positions.
- The RIB's seat #2 occupant mans a rotating M249 SAW machine gun (360-degree turning radius), which easily tears through infantry and light armor.
- The rest of the occupants (aside from the driver) are able to man exposed passenger positions and provide small arms fire support.
- Its high occupant number makes it a great vehicle to use for squads.

AIR POWER

Offering a mix of unparalleled speed and amazing fire power, the aircraft and helicopters in the game are the most deadly vehicles available. But they're also the most difficult vehicles to master, requiring hours of practice. In this section, we help you get the hang of the various air assets as well as provide tips on how to use each type.

FLIGHT SCHOOL

Flying the game's jets and helicopters is more difficult than maneuvering the ground vehicles. Beginner pilots are often more of a danger to themselves and their passengers than they are to the enemy. In this section, we offer quick tips to help get you into the air without crashing, whether your control preference is a keyboard or joystick. We also take a look at the various weapon systems available to both jets and helicopters, and offer some pointers on how to use each.

Flying with the Keyboard

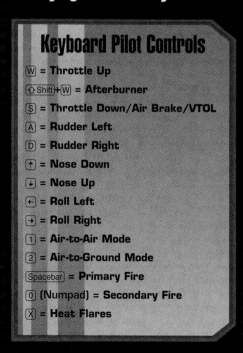

Keyboard Pilot Controls

W = **Throttle Up**

⇧Shift + W = **Afterburner**

S = **Throttle Down/Air Brake/VTOL**

A = **Rudder Left**

D = **Rudder Right**

↑ = **Nose Down**

↓ = **Nose Up**

← = **Roll Left**

→ = **Roll Right**

1 = **Air-to-Air Mode**

2 = **Air-to-Ground Mode**

Spacebar = **Primary Fire**

0 (Numpad) = **Secondary Fire**

X = **Heat Flares**

Flying a plane with the keyboard isn't as daunting or clumsy as it may sound. In fact, the default key setup makes flying easy and intuitive. Place your left hand over the basic movement keys of W, S, A, and D. These keys are used to adjust the aircraft's speed and heading. Your right hand should hover over the arrow keys, responsible for pitch and roll.

Use the afterburner on take-off. The faster you can get in the air, the less likely enemy pilots are to strafe you.

Give the aircraft throttle by holding down W. Using the afterburner when taking off gets you in the air fast, so hold down ⇧Shift+W. Alternatively, you can double-tap W to kick in the afterburner. Like sprinting, the afterburner has its limits and must recharge, so don't keep it lit for long periods. After you're racing down the runway, leap into the air by pressing ↓. Once airborne, level out by tapping ↑ while continually holding down W to maintain speed. Turn by using A and D to activate the rudders. This is the easiest way to change an aircraft's heading and is vital when lining up for bombing or strafing runs. To turn faster, roll left or right using ← or → and pull back on the stick using ↓. Banking is the quickest way to change directions, and is useful when making evasive maneuvers. To reduce speed, let go of W. A reduction in speed allows the aircraft to make tighter turns, a useful tactic when dog fighting. Pressing S deploys the aircraft's speed break, reducing speed faster. If the speed drops too low, the aircraft will stall and drop toward the ground. If this happens, get on the throttle before you crash.

TIP Pressing S when flying the F-35B, activates its VTOL function, allowing it to vertically take off or land. The fighter can use this function to slow its speed and can reduce its forward speed, coming to a steady hover.

In many respects, flying helicopters with the keyboard is easier than flying fixed-wing aircraft. But it takes practice to master the skill, not to mention a light touch on the keys. Keep your hands in the same positions used to fly the jets. Pressing W increases rotor speed, eventually lifting the chopper into the air. The longer you hold down W, the higher you'll go. After you are a few feet in the air, release W to hover and use the rudder controls (A and D) to spin the chopper left and right to change its heading. The arrow keys control pitch and roll, allowing the helicopter to move in any direction. Tap ↑ to pitch the helicopter's nose forward, causing forward motion. While moving, the helicopter will lose altitude, so compensate by tapping W—read the chopper's altitude and air speed on the HUD.

If you master hovering, you can convert control points without landing—just watch out for incoming anti-tank missiles! A fully loaded transport helicopter can convert any control point within a few seconds.

To stop moving forward, tap ↓ to reduce speed. Reduce speed until the helicopter stops. This is made easier by aligning the HUD's center reticule with the artificial horizon line. You'll know you've stopped when a circular icon appears at the center of the HUD—this is the hover position box. This icon's movements across the HUD reports your helicopter's drifting movements while in a hover. To maintain a stationary position in the air, tap the pitch and roll keys to keep the icon centered. While in a hover, you can cause the helicopter to side-slip left and right by using [◄] and [►]. This is useful for peeking around buildings and hills. The helicopter can fly backward by using [↓]. Just remember, each movement causes the rotors to lose lift, resulting in altitude loss, so compensate by tapping or holding down [W]. When you want to lose altitude, press [S] to reduce rotor speed. To land, bring the helicopter to a hover and slowly reduce rotor speed until it touches the ground. Land on even terrain, or else the helicopter may tip over and explode, killing everyone inside.

> **TIP** Choose a transport helicopter when learning to fly. Their sluggish controls are more forgiving than the hyper-sensitive attack helicopters'. If you find the controls too sensitive, reduce the sensitivity in the Options menu under Controls.

Joystick Setup

All controls in the game are customizable for each vehicle type. Use this menu to assign joystick controls for aircraft and helicopters.

The game allows players to customize their control configuration to suit their preferences for the unit types—infantry, ground vehicles, aircraft, helicopters, and boats. For most, the standard keyboard and mouse combination works. However, many players like to use a joystick when piloting aircraft and helicopters. Because the game does not automatically configure controls for a joystick, you will have to do so manually from the Options menu.

Following are quick tips on how best to get your joystick up and running.

Before you start your game, be sure your joystick is connected to your computer and ready to go. Once in the game, select the Options button, then click on the Controls button to open a menu that allows you to select from the various unit types you can control. Let's start with Aircraft. Here you can designate secondary controls for various functions. To assign a control, click on the empty box to the right of the function and on the right side in the secondary column. Input the control you want to use (i.e., push a button on the joystick).

Under the Weapons category, click on the Fire slot, then assign that to your trigger. Assign the Alt-fire to a secondary fire button. Because an aircraft pilot has a choice between missiles and bombs, assign the Cycle Weapons function to another button on the joystick, if available.

Center your throttle, select accelerate from the menu, then move your throttle forward. You do not need to assign decelerate separately. The game will detect the throttle and automatically assign decelerate to moving your throttle back from center. The same goes for all the axis controls. You only need to assign one direction—not both. For the Movement category, assign accelerate and decelerate to the throttle, if your joystick is so equipped. For Steer Right, use the rudder control on your joystick, if so equipped. For Pitch Forward, push your joystick away from you. Then for Roll Right, move your joystick to the right. Depending on the number of buttons on your joystick, you many want to assign both flares and afterburner to your joystick, as well.

The final step is to set the sensitivity. This is under Mouse Settings, but it also affects your joystick. Because the game is set up for mouse use by default, the sensitivity is around 3.00. Leaving it at that means you have to be light on the joystick or you will overcorrect all over the map—until you crash. Reduce the sensitivity to 1.00, and flying will be easier. Repeat the same steps for the Helicopter control setup.

Flying with the Joystick

Once configured, the joystick allows for more precise control, particularly when performing attacks against ground units.

Flying aircraft with the joystick is easy. If you have played flight simulation games, you will have no trouble. Keep the throttle forward of the center position. Pulling it back applies brakes and slows you, and will often cause a stall. The exception to this is with the US F-35B fighter. Negative input on the throttle activates the VTOL function—putting the plane into a hover. Make sure you have enough altitude before changing between hover and flight modes, or you will crash because you lose altitude in the process.

Helicopters are trickier to fly with the joystick. To fly one, you must understand the mechanics of helicopter flight. The throttle is your collective. It controls how much lift the rotor provides. In the center position, the helicopter maintains the same altitude while hovering or not horizontally moving. When you move horizontally, your lift is redirected to provide motion. Therefore, to maintain altitude, you have to give it more throttle. Horizontal motion is created by moving the joystick in the direction of the motion, and tilts the helicopter in that direction. To stop this motion type, tilt the helicopter in the opposite direction to slow it, then return to level to hover. To land, decrease the throttle back from center to reduce the lift. To prevent your helicopter from being damaged during a landing, make sure you have as little horizontal motion as possible.

Practice, practice, practice. Start a LAN game with only you playing. Then you can fly around without having to worry about people shooting at you. This training also works well for aircraft. It is easier to practice bombing targets such as bridges without the risk of enemy fire.

Aircraft Weapons

Auto-Cannon

Switch to air-to-ground mode when strafing. The bounding boxes around enemy vehicles make them easier to spot.

Whether dogfighting or strafing, the auto-cannon is a reliable weapon capable of inflicting serious damage. This is available in both air-to-air and ground-to-air modes, and can be fired with the primary weapon button or key. Line up your target in the HUD's center aiming reticule and fire a burst.

Heat-Seeking Missiles

Wait until an enemy aircraft is flying level and away from you before firing a missile. You're less likely to hit with missiles when the enemy aircraft is in a steep bank.

These missiles work like the land-based versions AA vehicles and turrets fire. Switch to air-to-air mode by pressing [1]. Maneuver your aircraft so the target is within the HUD. The missile will begin attaining a lock, indicated by a beeping sound. When a lock is achieved, the beeping sound will turn into a solid tone. Before firing the missile, wait for the enemy pilot to drop his flares, as these

decoys may break the missile's lock. When the flares are out of view, you must attain a new lock on the enemy aircraft before firing. On average, it takes two heat-seeking missiles to shoot down an enemy jet or helicopter.

> **TIP** When dogfighting, watch for the contrails your opponent's wing forms. This makes them easier to spot and follow while performing tight turns.

Bombs

Fighters and fighter bombers carry two bomb types. The fighter bomber's retarded bombs are more accurate due to the high-drag fins which deploy when dropped.

Both fighters and fighter bombers carry bombs. Drop them by switching to air-to-ground mode ([2]). Aim bombs using the vertical line in the center of the HUD and the dashed lines at the bottom of the HUD. Where these lines intersect is where the bomb drops. Manned enemy vehicles appear on the HUD, represented by either square or triangle icons. Use these icons to line up bombing runs at a distance, then fly over the target, using the rudders to fine-tune your aim. When the lines on the HUD intersect the target, release the bombs with the secondary fire button or key.

> **CAUTION** The bounding icons of friendly vehicles and aircraft show up on the HUD superimposed by an "X." Don't attack them!

Laser-Guided Missiles

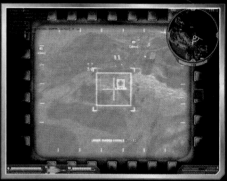

It only takes a couple of seconds to lock up a ground target, but this is difficult, due to the fighter bomber's speed and evasive movements.

Laser-guided missiles are carried by fighter bombers and are fired from the co-pilot position. By right-clicking, the co-pilot can access a TV screen which she can pan and tilt by moving the mouse. The co-pilot must use the mouse to locate enemy ground targets. After she spots a target, the co-pilot must keep it centered in the screen's cross hairs until the laser can achieve a lock. This is difficult, especially if the fighter bomber is pitching or rolling, so the pilot should remain level. After the co-pilot attains a lock, fire the missile, which automatically homes in on the ground target. These missiles are great for taking out enemy vehicles, and are also effective against the commander stations.

Helicopter Weapons

Miniguns/Heavy Machine Guns

The automatic weapons mounted on the transport helicopters are good for engaging troops and light vehicles, but they can't penetrate the armor of tanks.

These side-mounted weapons carried by transport helicopters are effective against both air and ground targets, but are difficult to aim while on the move. Their high rate of fire helps compensate for the instability, especially in the case of the miniguns mounted on the US HH-60H Seahawk. Passengers must man these weapons.

Unguided Rockets

Fire multiple rockets at tanks. It takes several hits to puncture their thick armor.

The rockets are the only weapon available to attack helicopter pilots. Aim them with the circular reticule at the center of the HUD, and launch them with the primary fire key/button. They aren't accurate, even when properly aimed, but they're useful against ground targets, especially when fired in large volleys.

Auto-Cannon

The gunner should tap C once to turn off the cockpit view. This increases visibility, allowing the gunner to spot and engage more targets, including enemy helicopters, with the auto-cannon.

Unlike the auto-cannon used by the jets, the attack helicopter is mounted in a turret operated by the gunner. The ability to pan and tilt this weapon (with the mouse) gives it targeting flexibility regardless of the helicopter's orientation. Press the primary fire key or button to fire, using it to shred enemy vehicles or aircraft. The splash damage the impacting rounds cause also makes it devastating against infantry. This is one of the most deadly weapons in the game.

TV-Guided Missiles

Find an enemy target on the TV screen before launching. The pilot must help by aiming the chopper in the target's direction and staying level.

The attack helicopter's gunner also has access to these guided missiles. By right-clicking, the gunner can access a TV screen. But unlike the laser-guided missiles, the gunner cannot move this screen view. The helicopter's current facing dictates the forward-facing view. Therefore, it's up to the pilot to turn the helicopter in the target's direction. For best results, the gunner should make visual contact with an enemy vehicle before firing a missile. Use the mouse to move the cross hairs over the target, then fire by clicking the left mouse button. You can change the missile's heading while in flight by moving the cross hairs over the intended target and clicking. But the missile's high speed makes it difficult to make more than a few minor course corrections before the missile impacts—more the reason to line up the shot before launching. Scoring a direct hit with one of these missiles turns any vehicle into a charred hunk of metal.

Rearming and Repairs

Swoop over runways to load up on more missiles and bombs.

Like troops on the ground, aircraft and helicopters take damage and run out of ammo. Fortunately, you can remedy both problems. Jets can rearm by flying low over a friendly or neutral airfield—there's no need to land. Flying over the hangar at a runway's end can repair damage, but it may take several passes before the aircraft reaches full-strength. Helicopters can rearm and repair by either landing on or hovering above a helipad. They can get the same benefits by hovering or landing near a friendly vehicle occupied by an engineer and a support soldier.

FIGHTERS

F-18 E/F Super Hornet

Affiliation: USMC
Speed: Very Fast
Armor: Weak

Originally conceived as a fighter for the US Air Force, the F-18 ended up in the hands of the US Navy, which saw it as a perfect replacement for older carrier-based aircraft. Production of the plane began in the late 1970s, and the first Hornet arrived on station in 1983; the upgraded "Super" Hornet made its appearance a decade later. The F-18 is the most versatile aircraft ever produced for the US military. It can perform a variety of missions, including strike, air superiority, and reconnaissance—sometimes even during the same sortie.

F-18 E/F Armament					
Key	Crew Position	Weapon 1	Weapon 2	Weapon 3	Countermeasure
F1	Pilot	20mm Auto-cannon (900)	Heat-seeking Missiles (6)	Bombs (2)	Heat Flares

F-35B Joint Strike Fighter

Affiliation: USMC
Speed: Very Fast
Armor: Weak

Also known as the Joint Strike Fighter (JSF), the F-35B is a multi-role aircraft designed for the US Marine Corps, the UK Royal Air Force, and Royal Navy as a replacement for the AV-8B Harrier. In addition to possessing the same VTOL capability of its predecessor, the F-35B also employs stealth technology, apparent in the airframe's angular design. To further reduce the aircraft's radar cross-section, all weapons are stored in an internal bay.

F-35B Armament					
Key	Crew Position	Weapon 1	Weapon 2	Weapon 3	Countermeasure
F1	Pilot	20mm Auto-cannon (900)	Heat-seeking Missiles (6)	Bombs (2)	Heat Flares

Jian J-10

Affiliation: China
Speed: Very Fast
Armor: Weak

While the PLA Air Force's fighter aircraft are regarded as obsolete by US, Russian, and European standards, China has taken great strides in the past decade to upgrade its fleet. The J-10 consequently embodies China's dedication to producing an indigenous modern fighter. A single-seat, single-engine, multi-role aircraft, the J-10 incorporates the latest avionics technology. The fighter can reach speeds of Mach 1.5 and faster, and is equipped to carry air-to-air guided missiles and bombs for ground attack.

J-10 Armament					
Key	Crew Position	Weapon 1	Weapon 2	Weapon 3	Countermeasure
F1	Pilot	20mm Auto-cannon (900)	Heat-seeking Missiles (6)	Bombs (2)	Heat Flares

Mig-29 Fulcrum

Affiliation: MEC
Speed: Very Fast
Armor: Weak

The Mig-29 Fulcrum is the newest and most technologically advanced fighter in Russia's inventory. Developed to counter Western fighters such as America's F-15 Eagle and F/A-18 Hornet, the Fulcrum has proven itself an equal to these planes in terms of maneuverability and firepower. Its twin turbofan engines provide it with excellent acceleration and climbing power, as well as superior low-speed turn rates in comparison with the American planes.

Mig-29 Armament					
Key	Crew Position	Weapon 1	Weapon 2	Weapon 3	Countermeasure
F1	Pilot	20mm Auto-cannon (900)	Heat-seeking Missiles (6)	Bombs (2)	Heat Flares

Fighter Tactics

Establishing and maintaining air superiority over the battlefield is the primary responsibility of the fighters. Their heat-seeking air-to-air missiles make shooting down enemy aircraft easy. Attain a lock and fire. However, firing missiles at helicopters is tricky. Due to the fighter's high speed, it's difficult to lock on to a slow chopper, especially if it deploys heat flares. Your fighter will zoom past the helicopter before you can acquire a lock. Therefore, use the auto-cannon against enemy helicopters. This requires more skill, but if your aim is true, the enemy chopper is toast. The auto-cannon is also a good option when dogfighting enemy jets, because heat flares can't fool its rounds. The fighters are more agile and maneuverable than their fighter bomber counterparts, giving them an edge in dog fights. But when it comes to close air support, the fighters are inferior. The fighter's two "slick" bombs are effective against ground targets, but less accurate than the fighter bomber's high-drag retarded bombs. The "slick" bombs drift apart during free fall, usually impacting in two distant areas, sometimes missing the target. Instead of glide bombing ground targets, begin your bombing run in a shallow dive. This increases accuracy, helping ensure that the bombs detonate in a tight cluster. For greater precision against ground targets, strafe enemy vehicles with the auto-cannon—just make sure you have enough time and space to pull up.

CAUTION Don't drop the fighter's bombs while flying level at low altitude. When they impact into ground, they detonate beneath the fighter, causing damage.

FIGHTER BOMBERS

F-15E Strike Eagle

Affiliation:	USMC
Speed:	Very Fast
Armor:	Weak

After learning some harsh lessons in the skies over Vietnam, the US Air Force resolved to develop a fighter dedicated to air superiority—something the USAF had lacked since the late 1950s. Experimental versions of the F-15 were produced and flown during the early 1970s, and full production and deployment of the plane began in 1976. The F-15's impact was immediate; pilots and crews loved it. Its superior maneuverability, speed, and advanced avionics were—and remain—unequaled. The Eagle's twin engines generate an unprecedented 50,000 lbs of thrust, and its advanced radar and missile systems can detect, track, and acquire targets up to 100 miles away.

F-15E Armament

Key	Crew Position	Weapon 1	Weapon 2	Weapon 3	Countermeasure
F1	Pilot	20mm Auto-cannon (900)	Heat-seeking Missiles (4)	Retarded Bombs (5)	Heat Flares
F2	Co-pilot	Laser-guided (20) Missiles	—	—	—

SU-30MKK

Affiliation:	China
Speed:	Very Fast
Armor:	Weak

A Soviet-designed and manufactured fighter/bomber, the SU-30 is a long range aircraft capable of air superiority and ground attack missions. China began importing the two-seat fighter in 2000, and it has since been deployed to various training centers and PLA Air Force bases. Among its many assets, the SU-30's advanced Doppler radar and an infrared optic and laser designation system can simultaneously find and track up to 10 targets. After you acquire and lock a target, the SU-30 can unleash a variety of weapons.

SU-30 Armament

Key	Crew Position	Weapon 1	Weapon 2	Weapon 3	Countermeasure
F1	Pilot	20mm Auto-cannon (900)	Heat-seeking Missiles (4)	Retarded Bombs (5)	Heat Flares
F2	Co-pilot	Laser-guided Missiles (20)	—	—	—

SU-34 Flanker

Affiliation:	MEC
Speed:	Very Fast
Armor:	Weak

The SU-34 Flanker is a two-seat, long-range fighter/bomber built to replace earlier Soviet-era attack aircraft. Appearing in 1991, the Flanker was designed as a carrier-based aircraft. However, because the Russian navy no longer operates a ship capable of carrying the plane, the Flanker was re-designated as a land-based strike fighter—a role it fills with success. Fitted with 10 weapons stations under its wings, the Flanker can carry a range of missiles. The aircraft's distinctive flattened nose houses a terrain-avoidance phased-array radar that allows the Flanker to fly safely even at low altitudes.

SU-34 Armament

Key	Crew Position	Weapon 1	Weapon 2	Weapon 3	Countermeasure
F1	Pilot	20mm Auto-cannon (900)	Heat-seeking Missiles (4)	Retarded Bombs (5)	Heat Flares
F2	Co-pilot	Laser-guided Missiles (20)	—	—	—

Fighter Bomber Tactics

The fighter bombers are versatile, capable of shooting down enemy aircraft as well as destroying ground units with their bombs and laser-guided missiles. Two players should man these two-seater aircraft, so don't take off till a teammate climbs aboard. The pilot can handle the air-to-air missiles and bombs on his own, but teamwork is required to deploy the co-pilot's laser-guided missiles. To make it easier for the co-pilot to achieve a lock on a ground target, the pilot should fly as level as possible and in the target's direction. Clear communication between the pilot and co-pilot makes the job of locating and hitting targets easier. For this reason, form a squad for the fighter bomber crew and use the VOIP function to talk to each other. The pilot's five high-drag retarded bombs are less accurate than the laser-guided missiles, but more effective when engaging high concentrations of enemy units. Unlike the fighter's "slick" bombs, these bombs deploy fins when dropped, slowing them, allowing the aircraft to speed away before they impact. This makes them ideal for low-level glide bombing attacks. Drop these bombs on congested chokepoints or other areas where enemy troops and vehicles gather. It's not uncommon to score four or five kills with each bombing run. These bombs are also perfect for taking out bridges. Line up with the bridge as if you were going to land on it, and drop a string of bombs to knock it out. If it's a long bridge, it's possible to blow three large holes in it with a bombing run.

Fighters and Fighter Bombers: Tester Tips
by Jose Gonzales

- Planes can handle two roles: air-to-air support, and air-to-ground support.

- As the pilot, switching your plane's weapon payload is as easy as using the weapon number keys or scrolling with your mouse wheel. Your on-screen cockpit HUD will change to accommodate the mode currently in use.

- Count your shots. The planes do not carry that many missiles/bombs in their payloads. They will have to do frequent re-supplying at their team's airfields.

- To avoid the enemy in dogfights, the pilot can activate the afterburner to get away (activated through the same key assigned to your soldier sprint).

- The occupant that takes up seat #2 in the fighter bomber can lock onto enemy land targets and fire a missile that kills in one hit. You want to make sure you don't take the fighter bomber up in the air without a co-pilot.

- Pilots in first-person view can turn their heads in the cockpit by holding down the left `Ctrl` and moving the mouse around. This is a great thing to know when trying to get a visual on enemy aircraft in dogfights.

- Pilots can break a heat-seek lock by throwing flares down.

- On some maps, the out of bounds "red zone" area is extended out, to allow for aircraft occupants to dogfight easier.

- Be aware that you can be shot out of the pilot seat if you decide to idle for too long. The M95 sniper rifle (unlockable kit for sniper class) round can penetrate the cockpit enclosure.

TRANSPORT HELICOPTERS

HH-60H Seahawk

Affiliation:	USMC
Speed:	Fast
Armor:	Weak

In the early 1970s, the US Army began looking for a new front-line helicopter to replace the aging UH-1 "Huey." Sikorsky was awarded the contract, and the company provided the Army with a helicopter with expanded troop capacity and cargo lift capability, and increased firepower for close air support. While its armor can tolerate most small arms fire and medium-caliber explosive projectiles, the Seahawk is also fitted with redundant flight systems in the event it does take damage.

HH-60H Armament

Key	Crew Position	Weapon	Countermeasure
F1	Pilot	—	Heat Flares
F2	Passenger 1	Minigun	—
F3	Passenger 2	Minigun	—
F4	Passenger 3	Kit Weapons	—
F5	Passenger 4	Kit Weapons	—
F6	Passenger 5	Kit Weapons	—

Z-8

Affiliation:	China
Speed:	Fast
Armor:	Weak

The medium-sized Chinese Z-8 is based on the French Super Frelon transport helicopter. China purchased 13 of these helicopters in the early 1970s, and reverse-engineered them to produce their version to use in rapid-deployment operations. Two door-mounted machine guns give the Z-8 the ability to assist infantry with close-in fire support.

Z-8 Armament

Key	Crew Position	Weapon	Countermeasure
F1	Pilot	—	Heat Flares
F2	Passenger 1	Heavy Machine Gun	—
F3	Passenger 2	Heavy Machine Gun	—
F4	Passenger 3	Kit Weapons	—
F5	Passenger 4	Kit Weapons	—
F6	Passenger 5	Kit Weapons	—

Mi-17 Hip

Affiliation: MEC
Speed: Fast
Armor: Weak

The workhorse of the Russian Army, the Mi-17 is a multi-role helicopter capable of transport, attack, air support, electronic warfare, and medical evacuation. Originally manufactured as the Mi-8 throughout the 1960s and early 1970s, the helicopter later received extensive upgrades and was renamed the Mi-17 in 1981. It is fitted with state-of-the-art electronics for safe operation in darkness or inclement weather, as well as more cargo space for equipment and personnel.

Mi-17 Armament

Key	Crew Position	Weapon	Countermeasure
F1	Pilot	—	Heat Flares
F2	Passenger 1	Minigun	—
F3	Passenger 2	Minigun	—
F4	Passenger 3	Kit Weapons	—
F5	Passenger 4	Kit Weapons	—
F6	Passenger 5	Kit Weapons	—

Transport Helicopter Tactics

Each transport helicopter is capable of holding six players, making it ideal for quickly transporting squads to any spot on the battlefield. These large choppers are also the best way to capture neutral control points at a battle's start. Load up with teammates and fly over each control point. Instead of taking the time to land, troops should bail out and parachute to the control point. If a squad leader is the pilot, his squadmates can spawn in the chopper. Hover above an enemy-held control point and rain squadmates until they can capture the position—if you fly high enough, troops on the ground won't be able to see the helicopter. But the transport helicopter's impressive troop capacity is also a weakness, and may result in a big score for an enemy fighter pilot who shoots down a full chopper. To avoid falling victim to heat-seeking missiles, pilots should fly low and fast, using hills, trees, and buildings for cover. Flying behind these objects can break a missile lock. You can also deploy heat flares to fool incoming missiles. The miniguns/machine guns mounted on the chopper's port and starboard sides are decent defensive weapons, but are difficult to aim accurately while moving. Slowing down to give the gunners a better shot leaves the helicopter open to ground fire—a slow helicopter is an attractive target for anti-tank troops. Therefore, reserve the air-to-ground duties for the attack helicopters.

ATTACK HELICOPTERS

AH-1Z Super Cobra

Affiliation: USMC
Speed: Fast
Armor: Weak

The AH-1 Super Cobra's lineage traces back to the mid-1960s when the US Army developed it for use in Vietnam. This attack helicopter has since been updated and modified in accordance with the US Marine Corps's need for a frontline fire support helicopter. With its ability for low altitude and high-speed flight, the Super Cobra is tasked with clearing landing zones of enemy troops and armor as well as providing cover for the Marines' advance. The Super Cobra can accomplish these missions day or night during any type of weather.

AH-1Z Armament

Key	Crew Position	Weapon	Weapon 2	Countermeasure
F1	Pilot	Unguided Rockets (56)	—	Heat Flares
F2	Gunner	20mm Auto-cannon (900)	TV-guided Missile (8)	—

Z-10

Affiliation: China
Speed: Fast
Armor: Weak

In contrast to the US and Russia, China had never had a dedicated attack helicopter. Enter the Z-10. In development since the mid-1990s, the helicopter was designed to swiftly eliminate enemy ground forces. Built with radar-absorbent material and bullet-proof glass, the Z-10 can also defend itself.

Z-10 Armament

Key	Crew Position	Weapon	Weapon 2	Countermeasure
F1	Pilot	Unguided Rockets (56)	—	Heat Flares
F2	Gunner	20mm Auto-cannon (900)	TV-guided Missile (8)	—

Mi-28 Havok

Affiliation:	MEC
Speed:	Fast
Armor:	Weak

The Mi-28 Havok is the latest Russian Army Air Force innovation to replace an older aircraft; in this case, the Mi-24 Hind, which has been in service for nearly 25 years. An all-weather, night-capable attack helicopter, the Havok can engage aerial targets in addition to mechanized infantry and main battle tanks, the helicopter's primary foe.

Mi-28 Armament

Key	Crew Position	Weapon	Weapon 2	Countermeasure
F1	Pilot	Unguided Rockets (56)	—	Heat Flares
F2	Gunner	30mm Auto-cannon (450)	TV-guided Missile (8)	—

Attack Helicopter Tactics

The attack helicopters are the most devastating vehicles in the game. But as with the fighter bombers, a two-man crew is necessary for each chopper to live up to its deadly potential. The pilot can fire the chopper's unguided rockets, but it's the gunner who benefits from the awesome firepower offered by the auto-cannon and TV-guided missiles. Similar to the primary weapons found on the APCs and AA vehicles, the attack helicopter's auto-cannon rapidly fires small explosive rounds. This cannon is mounted in a turret beneath the chopper's nose, and is capable of rotating more than 180 degrees. The gunner can use this weapon to rack up dozens of infantry kills as well as shred light armored vehicles. It can also inflict damage on tanks, but the TV-guided missiles are a better option for destroying enemy armor. For best results, the pilot should aim the helicopter toward the enemy target so the gunner can attain visual contact on the TV screen. Once in view, the gunner can launch and guide the missile toward the target for a guaranteed kill. As in the fighter bomber, the attack helicopter's crew should form their own squad and use VOIP to streamline communications. Instead of flying all over the battlefield, and potentially over-flying enemy AA turrets, use the attack helicopter as a stand-off weapon. Because the gunner holds most of the attack chopper's offensive capability, the pilot should constantly orient the helicopter to best deploy the auto-cannon and TV-guided missiles against enemy ground targets. Hover behind trees or above a hill's crest to stay out of sight. This way you can drop behind cover if a threat appears. Hovering is dangerous, but if adequate cover is nearby, a good pilot can use the surroundings to hide from enemy fire. Mastering the pilot and co-pilot positions of an attack helicopter isn't easy, but an experienced crew can dominate the battlefield.

Helicopters: Tester Tips
by Jose Gonzales

- Choppers have an engine start-up delay on the first time they spawn. When starting up the chopper's engines, be on the lookout for the enemy as you are vulnerable to nasty things like enemy AT rounds.

- Make sure to fully man the chopper. The attack chopper gets assistance from a gunner (sits in seat #2 and can direct lethal TV-guided missiles), while the transport chopper gets minigun/50 .cal support and/or small arms fire support from the occupants in exposed passenger positions.

- The transport chopper's high occupant number makes it a great vehicle to use for squads.

- The transport chopper is great to have fully manned to hover low and capture flags. The flag turns faster when more soldiers are in the flag radius.

- Pilots in first-person view can turn their heads in the cockpit by holding down the left Ctrl key and moving the mouse around. This is a great thing to know when trying to get a visual on enemy aircraft in dogfights.

- Helicopter pilots can break a heat-seek lock by throwing flares down.

- On some maps, the out of bounds "red zone" area is extended out, to allow for aircraft occupants to dogfight easier.

- Be aware that you can be shot out of the pilot seat if you decide to hover for too long. The M95 sniper rifle (unlockable kit for sniper class) round can penetrate the cockpit enclosure.

CHAIN OF COMMAND

ORGANIZATION

While the *Battlefield* series of games has always stressed team play, there has never been an inherent capability for organizing a team into a military-type unit. *Battlefield 2* has solved that problem. While players are still free to wander about the map on their own, a new interface allows for you to organize a team into squads, each with a squad leader. A team can even have an overall commander who can help direct the battle and provide support where needed.

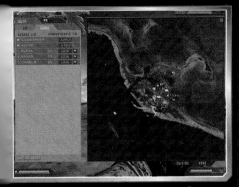

To join a squad, go to the Squad Screen, then click on the Join button for the squad you wish to become a part of. After you join a squad, the squad leader will give you the squad's current orders.

To access the Squad Screen, press Caps Lock. A console will appear on the screen's left side, allowing you to join a squad, create a new squad with you as the squad leader, and apply to be the commander for your team. Joining a squad has several advantages. Squad members can use the squad leader as a spawn point. During a battle, having to respawn at a base away from the action after you are killed is a pain. However, because your squad leader is also a spawn point, you can get back into the action. Another advantage to squad membership is the ability to use voice communications to talk to others in your squad rather than having to type out messages. Furthermore, your squad leader can help focus the soldiers in your squad so you work together.

Communication

For a team to work effectively together, they have to be able to communicate. *Battlefield 2* provides three ways to communicate.

Chat

As with most multiplayer games, you can type out messages to chat with other players in the game.

Key Press	Send Message To:
J	All Players in Game
K	All Players on Your Team
L	All Players in Your Squad

Chat is the only way to send messages to players on the other team. It also allows for you to send detailed messages to players on your own team. The downside to this communication type is that it takes time. While you are typing your message, you are unable to control your character and may get killed while you are communicating. Find a safe place before you type messages and devise a form of shorthand to keep your messages brief. You also don't want the people receiving your message to get killed while they are reading it—at least those on your team.

Commo Rose

A quick way to communicate to your team is via the commo rose. Press Q to open the commo rose, then move your mouse to highlight one of 11 common messages.

- Spotted
- Go, Go, Go
- Need Backup
- Need Pickup (Get In*)
- Roger That
- Negative
- Thank You
- Sorry
- Need Medic (Need Repairs*)
- Need Ammo
- Follow Me (Bail Out*)

* If you are in a vehicle, some of the messages will change to reflect the context of your situation.

Highlight a message, then left-click to send it. Your team will not only receive a text message, but also hear it spoken. Depending on the context, visual cues will also appear on certain players' screens or maps. For example, a "Need Medic" message will show medics where the sender is, while a "Need Ammo" will do the same for support troops. The "Spotted" message is in the commo rose's center. It is meant to be centered over a target before being sent. Placing it over infantry or an empty spot will send an "Infantry Spotted" message, while placing the reticule over a tank or other vehicle will send an appropriate message on the type of target. You can even send messages while using the sight or scope view from your weapon. This ability makes the sniper more valuable as an observer because he can call out enemy vehicles from a distance.

VOIP

VOIP, or Voice Over Internet Protocol, allows you to communicate with other players in your squad as long as you have a headset with a microphone connected to your computer. No additional software is required because VOIP is included in *Battlefield 2*. Using VOIP, squad leaders can talk to the team commander and the commander can talk to the squad leaders.

SQUADS

Squads represent the basic functional unit within the scope of *Battlefield 2*. Each team can have up to nine squads and each squad can contain a maximum of six soldiers. Squads are created by a squad leader who can invite other players to join the squad, or they can join on their own from the Squad Screen. Members of a squad must communicate and work together to achieve a common objective. Because each troop kit has its unique strengths and weaknesses, combining different kits allows for other members to cover your weakness while you make up for theirs.

Types of Squads

A squad should be made up of players with a variety of troop kits. Depending on the squad's task, the composition may vary. However, for most squads, you should have a support soldier, a medic, an Engineer (especially if using vehicles), an anti-tank soldier, and an assault soldier. Not all squads must have six players in them. In fact, for crews of vehicles such as fighter bombers and attack helicopters, the pilot and gunner/weapons officer should form her own squad for VOIP communications. Let's take a look at some sample squad compositions and how they are best deployed.

Assault Squad

| 2 Anti-tank |
| 2 Assault |
| 1 Medic |
| 1 Support |

This squad is designed for capturing a control point. While the support soldier lays down suppressive fire and provides ammo for the rest of the squad, the anti-tank troops can take out defensive positions and vehicles. This allows the assault troops to flank the enemy and approach the flagpole.

Vehicle Squad

| 1 Anti-tank |
| 1 Assault |
| 2 Engineer |
| 1 Medic |
| 1 Support |

Use this squad when using two vehicles, whether it be a tank and an APC or even a couple of jeeps. By having an Engineer in each vehicle, the two vehicles can repair one another while they are close together. Any of the squad can be the drivers except for the assault and anti-tank, because they need to dismount to add additional firepower when engaging the enemy. This squad can also use a single transport helicopter. Place the Engineers in the positions where they use their kit weapons, then they can select their wrenches and repair on the fly.

Defensive Squad

| 2 Anti-tank |
| 3 Assault |
| 1 Engineer |

This squad is intended for defending a control point against an enemy attack. A medic and support soldier are absent. A supply crate provided by the commander can provide healing and ammo, allowing for more firepower to use against enemy assaults. The Engineer should place mines near access points enemy vehicles can use.

Recon Squad

| 1 Sniper |
| 1 Support |

This is a small squad whose purpose is to avoid the enemy as much as possible, and instead observe and report the enemy's actions and positions. The sniper should be the squad leader because the sniper rifle's scope provides a long-range view you can use for setting targets for artillery strikes. The support soldier's job is to cover the sniper's flanks and rear and provide ammo as needed. By keeping this squad small, it is less likely to be detected than a squad of six.

Anti-Vehicle Squad

| 2 Anti-tank |
| 1 Support |

This is another small squad whose main objective is to engage enemy vehicles. It should find a position overlooking a bottleneck on the map such as a bridge or road where you expect a lot of enemy activity. With two anti-tank soldiers, you can take out a tank or several lighter vehicles. The support soldier is there to load them with anti-tank missiles. Because the missiles leave a smoke trail leading to your position, move after every shot or two, or you can expect a competent enemy to call in an artillery strike on you or shoot at your position.

Raiding Squad

2-3 Special Forces
None of the previous squads list special forces as members. This is because you should use this troop's kit for special tasks behind enemy lines. For any other role, there is another kit that works better. Raiding squads can deploy by air—dropping from aircraft by parachute—or by light jeep. The key is to get to their targets quickly and avoid combat. Raid squads should target bridges, artillery, and support structures where their C4 is most useful. Vehicles also make great targets. If they need more ammo or explosives, a supply crate is better than dragging along a support soldier. After destroying the structures, the raiding squad can either move to another target, or hide and wait to take out Engineers sent to repair the damage.

SQUAD LEADERS

Squad leaders have a number of different important functions that encourage and make team play more effective. They can give orders to the squad members, request support from the commander, and serve as a walking spawn point for squad members. To become a squad leader, create your squad from the Squad Screen. You can also be promoted if your squad leader leaves the squad and you are the next in line for your squad.

Squad leaders have their own commo rose. Press [T] to open the squad leader commo rose. While it looks like the normal commo rose, this one has different messages.

- **Attack**
- **Defend**
- **Destroy**
- **Move**
- **Repair Here**
- **Need Artillery**
- **Need Orders**
- **Need Supplies**
- **Need UAV**

The messages use the reticule to show the order or request location. The first four give orders to your squad members. On the map, a colored smoke grenade appears at the designated spot, and your squad has an icon appear on its map and display showing the location where they must perform the order. The Repair order only goes out to Engineers who can repair a targeted vehicle or bridge. The four "Need" requests go to the commander who can provide you with the support as available.

Squad leaders can also give orders and make requests using the map on the Squad Screen. You can zoom in and out on the map using the mousewheel or [N]. By right-clicking on a position, you will bring up a menu where you can then select the order/request with a left click, which will be passed on to your squad or commander.

Squad Leader Tactics

When playing as a squad leader, it is important to realize your role. Don't be the first to rush into enemy fire. The squad leader's spawn point ability is valuable and can help keep up constant pressure on the enemy during an attack. Your main purpose is to support your squad. Use the squad leader commo rose to designate targets for your orders and to keep track of where the members of your squad are. Don't be shy about calling for support from the commander, but realize that other squad leaders may be doing the same. As the squad leader, you will also receive orders for your squad from the commander. The rest of your squad does not get these orders, so it is up to you to pass them on

to your troops. Because combat is second to helping your troops, squad leaders should select troops kits that will complement their squads. If you are using vehicles a lot, be an Engineer. Medics and support troops are also good choices.

Squads: Tester Tips
by Jose Gonzales

- Squad members who communicate with each other are key to capturing or defending CPs. Coordinate via VOIP by holding down [B] when talking—or use chat text within your squad via [L].

- A squad grunt cannot request assistance from the commander directly—he must go through the squad leader. Squad leaders can communicate with the commander via VOIP, holding down [V].

- Any time a squad member is using VOIP, his soldier minimap icon will blink—and a name indicator on the HUD will appear.

- As a squad member, pay close attention to your squad leader's orders. The squad leader is using accurate reconnaissance intel from the commander.

- Don't forget that squad members can use the squad leader as a mobile spawn point (as long as you have at least one control point in your team's possession).

- Defend the squad leader. Do not let him die. He is your mobile spawn point. When he dies, so does your mobile spawn point.

- A squad leader can request the commander for a UAV sweep, supply drop, or artillery bombardment using the Squad menu, or by placing markers using the squad leader commo rose menu.

- The game can handle up to nine squads, six soldiers in each squad (one squad leader and five squad grunts), and one commander.

- Keep squads close together when moving on the ground. Their different classes compliment each other.

COMMANDER

Each team can have a commander. The commander's job is to coordinate the actions of the troops on the team and give orders through the squad leaders. Commanders can also provide support for the troops during battle. To become a commander, go to the Squad Screen at the game's start and apply to be the commander. After a pause which allows other players to apply, the player with the highest rank will be offered the position which they can either accept or reject.

Commanders have access to the commander screen, which you can pull up by pressing [Caps Lock]. Unlike other map views, the commander can zoom in farther to a satellite view where you can see individual vehicles and troops moving around on the ground. To give orders, click on one of your squads on the list to the left, then right-click on the location you want for the order. This brings up a menu where you can select an order with a left click. The order will then go to the selected squad leader. You can also use this method to assign support.

The commander also has a commo rose. There are only three choices here.

Place Artillery
Place Supply Drop
Place UAV

Support

One of the commander's most important functions is to call in support for his team. This can be requested by squad leaders or assigned on the commander's decision. Let's look at the four types of support available to the commander.

Artillery

Artillery is one of the most powerful abilities a commander wields. Strikes can be ordered to attack anywhere on the map. While there is a pause after each bombardment for reloading, artillery attacks are available throughout the game, unless the enemy has destroyed the artillery tubes. However, an Engineer can repair them. Any kills resulting from artillery strikes are credited to the commander. The commander should always have artillery firing. If your squad leaders are not requesting it, hammer enemy-held control points to hit spawning troops as well as vehicles. The zoomed-in view on the commander's screen allows you to target individual vehicles and concentrations of enemy troops.

Scan

The radar scan support is limited. When activated, the scan shows all manned enemy aircraft on the team's mini maps. This is useful for troops manning AA Turrets or AAVs, or flying in jets looking for enemies to shoot down. This support must

recharge after each use. However, if the enemy has aircraft, the commander should use this support when the radar is ready to go. You can prevent the enemy commander from using this support by blowing up the radar dishes.

Supplies

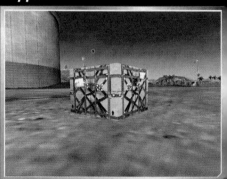

Does one of your squads need ammo and first aid? Drop a supply crate on their position. These crates fall by parachute to the designated location. They can provide health for your troops as well as ammo for both troops and vehicles. Enemy troops can destroy or use supply crates, so be careful where you drop them. Squads should destroy them as they leave to prevent the enemy from using the crates. There is no way to prevent an enemy commander from sending supply drops.

UAV

Along with artillery, UAV support is important. A commander can order a UAV to orbit a targeted location and scan for ground troops and vehicles. All enemies within its search range appear on your troop's mini maps. This is great for seeing where the enemy is hiding before assaulting a control point, as well as for detecting enemy advances along roads or through bottlenecks. Commanders can also use the UAV to find targets for artillery strikes. Destroying a UAV trailer prevents that team from ordering UAV scans.

Commander Tactics

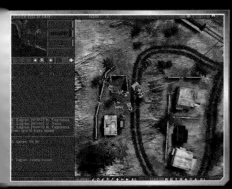

While the commander will have to do some fighting in the 16-player games, in the larger games, use the commander for orders and support. Find a secure location, such as inside buildings or hiding in the grass somewhere, and drop prone. Snipers are a good kit for commanders because their camouflage suit makes them tough to spot, and you can use the claymores to help take out enemies that get too close. Once in position, the commander should bring up the commander screen and stay there. UAVs should orbit over battlefield areas. Order radar scans when the radar recharges from the last scan. Artillery should bombard when the guns are reloaded. If there are no requests for artillery, fire on enemy-held control points. When not assigning support, commanders should monitor the progress of their squads and coordinate their actions. Order squads to hold key control points while guiding other squads to attack the enemy from two directions to capture a control point. Commanders can order pilots to bomb bridges to deny their use to the enemy.

Commanders: Tester Tips
by Jose Gonzales

- Do regular UAV/radar sweeps to spot enemies for your teammates. The recharge time for this commander ability is short, so use it to your advantage.

- You may want to devote some time in 3x zoom mode and do context-sensitive "spotted" actions on the enemy to inform your teammates.

- Be careful when deploying artillery. It is possible to kill your teammates if they are in the vicinity. Also be aware of artillery's slow reload time.

- You can initiate commend/berate/warning actions to your squads by right-clicking on the squads listed in commander mode.

- The commander gets bonus points whenever his team wins a round, so it is in your best interest to lead the team to glory.

- The commander also gets awarded points depending on how well his team is doing. If it is doing a bad job, his score will reflect that.

- The Engineer is the class of choice for battlefield commanders. Commanders can hang out around stations vital to their team use (UAV trailer, radar tower, and artillery cannons), supply commander assistance to squads (UAV sweeps, radar scan, artillery fire, supply drops, and reconnaissance), and defend/repair the stations upon attack/sabotage.

- The commander needs to stay behind (hidden away out of enemy sight) to avoid getting killed. His team is left without artillery or supply drop support if he dies.

- The supply drop can also crush enemy infantry if dropped directly on top of them.

- Commanders have to reapply after a map round ends or the map changes.

- Make sure to deploy a squad near your team's commander stations (UAV trailer, Radar tower, or artillery cannons) to defend/repair them. When the enemy makes a push to your main CP, you will get a lot of enemy special forces soldiers trying to C4 your team's commander stations.

DALIAN PLANT

US Rapid Deployment forces are advancing to capture the Dalian Plant nuclear facility and force disruptions to the electrical grid in northern China. Elements of the Second Army of the People's Republic of China have moved forward to serve as an improvised defensive force. This location is of vital strategic important to both sides, for a major reduction of the generating capacity of the PLA forces would allow rapid consolidation of US units dispersed throughout this vast region.

16-PLAYER

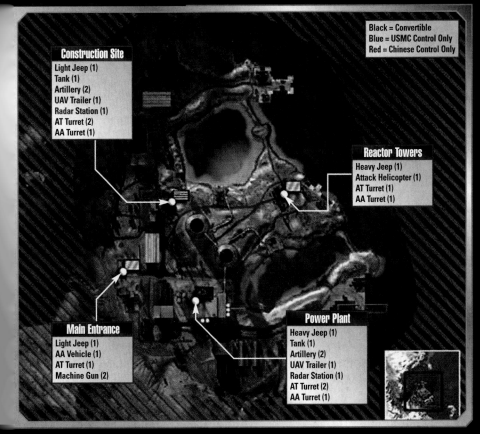

Black = Convertible
Blue = USMC Control Only
Red = Chinese Control Only

Construction Site
Light Jeep (1)
Tank (1)
Artillery (2)
UAV Trailer (1)
Radar Station (1)
AT Turret (2)
AA Turret (1)

Reactor Towers
Heavy Jeep (1)
Attack Helicopter (1)
AT Turret (1)
AA Turret (1)

Main Entrance
Light Jeep (1)
AA Vehicle (1)
AT Turret (1)
Machine Gun (2)

Power Plant
Heavy Jeep (1)
Tank (1)
Artillery (2)
UAV Trailer (1)
Radar Station (1)
AT Turret (2)
AA Turret (1)

Game Type:
Conquest Double Assault
Total Control Points: 4
Convertible Control Points: 4

The Reactor Towers spawn the map's only attack helicopter. Both sides should rush to capture this control point and tilt the odds in their team's favor.

US Strategy

The attack helicopter at the eastern Reactor Towers control point is the key to winning this battle. Fortunately, the Marines have a slight advantage in the race for this critical control point. Using the DPV, rush at least two troops to the Reactor Towers. The DPV is faster than any of the available Chinese vehicles, so the Marines have the best chance of arriving here first. The Chinese will follow, so fight off Chinese attackers using the newly spawned AT turret. Get the Super Cobra into the air, but be careful of flying too close to Chinese AA positions—there's one on the roof of the Power Station, and the Chinese may have a Type 95 roaming around if they took control of the Main Entrance. Instead of flying between the western control points, keep the Super Cobra on the map's periphery with its weapons pointed inward. The helicopter's cannon can inflict enormous casualties. Use the Super Cobra to hold back the Chinese at the Power Station while the M1A2 (from the Construction Site) and DPVs rush in to take the Main Entrance. Isolating the Chinese to the Power Station causes their tickets to bleed away. Use the Super Cobra to pin the Chinese troops as they spawn at the Power Station while Marine ground forces move in for the final capture.

TIP To prevent the other side from capturing the Reactor Towers early, call in an artillery strike on the control point when the battle begins. Enemy troops positioned near the flag will not survive the barrage.

Chinese Strategy

Although the Chinese forces begin with a speed disadvantage, they should still go for the Reactor Towers control point. Move both the Type 98 and NJ 2046 to the control point at the battle's start. But keep some troops back to defend the Power Station, too. If Marines are in place at the Reactor Towers, use the Type 98 to draw their fire while the NJ 2046 rushes in for a close quarter assault. Convert the Reactor Towers control point to gain access to the Z-10 attack helicopter, then use the Z-10 to hammer US troops at the Construction Site—but watch out for the rooftop AA Turret on the northwestern building. Stay low and move the Z-10 to the map's northern end to flank the Construction Site. This gives the helicopter a good view of the M1A2's spawn point, taking it out of the battle. Continue weakening the US at the Construction Site until ground forces can take control of it. With no available tanks, the Marines have a hard time holding the Main Entrance. Use the Type 98 to destroy their M6 Bradley, then move in with Paratrooper Vehicles and the Z-10 to take control of the Main Entrance.

32-PLAYER

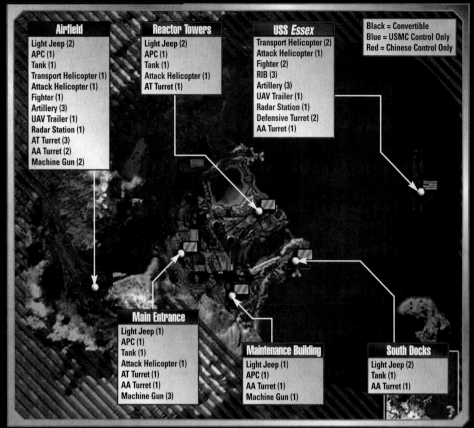

Airfield
Light Jeep (2)
APC (1)
Tank (1)
Transport Helicopter (1)
Attack Helicopter (1)
Fighter (1)
Artillery (3)
UAV Trailer (1)
Radar Station (1)
AT Turret (3)
AA Turret (2)
Machine Gun (2)

Reactor Towers
Light Jeep (2)
APC (1)
Tank (1)
Attack Helicopter (1)
AT Turret (1)

USS Essex
Transport Helicopter (2)
Attack Helicopter (1)
Fighter (2)
RIB (3)
Artillery (3)
UAV Trailer (1)
Radar Station (1)
Defensive Turret (2)
AA Turret (1)

Black = Convertible
Blue = USMC Control Only
Red = Chinese Control Only

Main Entrance
Light Jeep (1)
APC (1)
Tank (1)
Attack Helicopter (1)
AT Turret (1)
AA Turret (1)
Machine Gun (3)

Maintenance Building
Light Jeep (1)
APC (1)
AA Turret (1)
Machine Gun (1)

South Docks
Light Jeep (2)
Tank (1)
AA Turret (1)

Game Type:
Conquest Head-On
Total Control Points: 6
Convertible Control Points: 4

The Chinese must reach the coastal control points, even if it means sacrificing a J-10 fighter.

US Strategy

On this head-on map, it's vital to capture and hold at least two of the mainland control points to prevent a ticket drain. The most crucial control points for the Marines are the Reactor Towers and South Docks. Troops parachuting out of a Seahawk can capture both of these control points early. A second Seahawk loaded with Marines should go after the southern Maintenance Building. The two F-35Bs are responsible for providing air cover throughout the operation. Because the Chinese forces have only one J-10, the Marines have a significant advantage in the air. Instead of attacking ground targets with bombs, the primary focus of the Marine fighters is the Chinese fighter and attack helicopters. Maintaining air superiority throughout the battle allows the Super Cobras to operate without the constant threat of being shot down. Instead, they can focus on holding the three control points while harassing Chinese troops at the Main Entrance. On the ground, the Marines should be in full defensive mode at the Reactor Towers, South Docks, and Maintenance Building. Deploy one squad at each control point to maintain the drain on the Chinese tickets. Do not move in to capture the Main Entrance. Such a move would cause a reduction in troop strength at the other control points. Plus, defenders would face a constant stream of well-armed Chinese attackers approaching from the Airfield. Instead, hold at the three easternmost control points to draw the Chinese attackers toward the coast where the Super Cobras and tanks can engage them.

Chinese Strategy

Establish a defensive line at the coast to prevent the Marines from getting a foothold on the mainland. Load the Z-8 transport helicopter and fly it over the South Docks and Reactor Towers so troops can parachute to these control points and capture them before the Marines arrive. Using the J-10 and the AA Turret at the South Docks, shoot down all approaching Marine aircraft over the sea. While the Chinese can't match the Marines' strength in the air, they can even the odds by taking control of the Main Entrance, Maintenance Building, and South Docks. Each of these control points has an AA Turret useful for shooting down the US helicopters and jets. While you capture the easternmost control points, ground troops in Paratrooper Vehicles should rush toward the plant to take control of the Main Entrance and Maintenance Building. But the bulk of the defensive effort should still be at the coast. If the Marines give up on an air assault, watch the water for incoming boats. The Z-10 attack helicopters are great for engaging incoming RIBs. If the Marines capture the Reactor Towers and South Docks, they'll gain two M1A2s and another Super Cobra. Denying them these assets is crucial to securing a Chinese victory.

64-PLAYER

North Docks
Light Jeep (2)
APC (1)
AA Turret (1)

Warehouse
Light Jeep (2)
APC (1)
Machine Gun (2)

Black = Convertible
Blue = USMC Control Only
Red = Chinese Control Only

Airfield
Light Jeep (2)
APC (1)
Tank (1)
Transport Helicopter (1)
Attack Helicopter (1)
Fighter (1)
Artillery (3)
UAV Trailer (1)
Radar Station (1)
AT Turret (3)
AA Turret (2)
Machine Gun (2)

Reactor Towers
Light Jeep (2)
APC (1)
Tank (1)
Attack Helicopter (1)
AT Turret (1)

Main Entrance
Light Jeep (1)
APC (1)
Tank (1)
Attack Helicopter (1)
AT Turret (1)
AA Turret (1)
Machine Gun (3)

Maintenance Building
Light Jeep (1)
APC (1)
AA Turret (1)

South Docks
Light Jeep (2)
Tank (1)
AA Turret (1)

USS Essex
Transport Helicopter (2)
Attack Helicopter (1)
Fighter (2)
RIB (3)
Artillery (3)
UAV Trailer (1)
Radar Station (1)
Defensive Turret (2)
AA Turret (1)

Game Type:
Conquest Assault
Total Control Points: 8
Convertible Control Points: 6

A Super Cobra and a well-placed artillery strike on the canyon road can prevent the Chinese troops from reaching the Main Entrance from the Airfield.

US Strategy

With speed and some careful coordination, the Marines can use their dominance in the air to capture most of the control points before the Chinese forces can move into position. When the battle begins, move the Super Cobra to the Main Entrance and use it to engage the incoming Chinese vehicles moving along the narrow road to the west. To further delay the Chinese forces, call in an artillery strike on this road. A Seahawk filled with troops should follow the Super Cobra and capture the Main Entrance. Meanwhile, use the F-35Bs to prevent the Chinese aircraft from breaking out of the western valley. The second Seahawk should be used to secure the remaining control points, dropping one player at each. While you must defend all of the control points, most troops are needed at the western control points to maintain a defensive line. The Main Entrance and Warehouse are the most likely to come under attack. Therefore, one Super Cobra should hover near each of these control points and watch for break-out attacks by the Chinese. For added defensive strength, move the M1A2s spawned at the South Docks and Reactor Towers to the west in an effort to keep the Chinese forces isolated to the valley. If the Chinese break out, fall back and shift defensive efforts on holding the three coastal control points as well as the southern Maintenance Building. Holding these four control points will maintain the drain on the Chinese ticket count and ensure a US win.

Chinese Strategy

The Chinese forces must act quickly to break out of the western valley and gain a foothold within the nuclear facility. The Z-8 transport helicopter and J-10 fighter are the quickest ways to do this. Focus on taking the eastern control points. Both the North and South Docks have AA Turrets capable of shooting down the incoming US helicopters and fighters. Ground units from the Airfield need to move west, too, capturing the Main Entrance and branching out to the Warehouse and Maintenance Building. The Chinese need to hold at least four out of the six control points to initiate the drain on the Marine ticket count. If the Marines push their way ashore, fall back into an L-shaped defensive line, holding the Warehouse, Main Entrance, Maintenance Building and South Docks. This partial encirclement of the Reactor Towers and North Docks make it difficult for the Marines to break out. The configuration also gives the Chinese excellent air coverage, with AA Turrets at almost all control points (the exception being the northern Warehouse). Use the Z-10s to keep the Marines pinned at the coast while the J-10 circles the nuclear plant and engages enemy fighters and helicopters. Reinforce front line positions with tanks, APCs, and plenty of anti-tank troops. If opportunities arise, retake any of the Marine coastal positions—all are susceptible to artillery fire. Bleeding the Marine tickets is the best chance the Chinese have at winning this one, so grab control points early and hold onto them.

BASES AND CONTROL POINTS

USS *Essex*

The US assault on the power plant begins on this carrier packed with aircraft and boats. The Marines must use these vehicles to move ashore and establish a foothold at the control points to the west. The northern spawn point on the carrier places troops on the flight deck. This is where most of the team should spawn as the fighters and helicopters are the quickest ways to move inland. Man at least one of the two Phalanx and Sea Sparrow batteries at all times to prevent the Chinese fighters and attack helicopters from attacking the flight deck. The southern spawn point gives players access to the ship's aft, where two RIBs are available for amphibious assaults. While the UAV trailer and radar station are on the carrier, the US artillery is on the southern island. This island also holds an AA Turret and another RIB. There's no need to place a defender on this island, as the carrier's aft Phalanx and Sea Sparrow batteries can protect the island from any air assaults. Still, if the artillery comes under attack, an engineer may be needed to repair them. Because there's no spawn point, anyone heading for the island must find some form of transportation.

Maps: 32- and 64-Player

Adjacent Bases/ Control Points:
- North Docks
- Reactor Towers
- South Docks

USS *Essex* Assets

USMC Control	16-Player	32-Player	64-Player
HH-60H	—	2	2
AH-1Z	—	1	1
F-35B	—	2	2
RIB	—	3	3
Artillery	—	3	3
UAV Trailer	—	1	1
Radar Station	—	1	1
Defensive Turret	—	2	2
AA Turret	—	1	1

North Docks

Its close proximity to the USS *Essex* gives the Marines the best chance of capturing this coastal control point early in 64-player games. There are three ladders on each side of the large concrete pier, allowing troops in RIBs to dock and climb ashore. Once captured, the control point's lack of defensive features can make it difficult to defend. While its AA Turret is great for turning back air strikes, enemy land vehicles approaching from either the Warehouse or Reactor Towers pose a threat. Fortunately, the approaches to the west and south are narrow, making mines effective. Just one or two mines placed on the southern narrow wave breaker is enough to stop vehicle attacks from the Reactor Towers. Defenders can take cover in the concrete building south of the flagpole. You can also use this building's back door to watch the southern approach and Reactor Towers.

Maps: 64-Player Only

Adjacent Bases/ Control Points:
- USS *Essex*
- Reactor Towers
- Warehouse

North Docks Assets

USMC Control	Chinese Control	16-Player	32-Player	64-Player
DPV	Paratrooper Vehicle	—	—	2
LAV-25	WZ 551	—	—	1
AA Turret	AA Turret	—	—	1

Reactor Towers

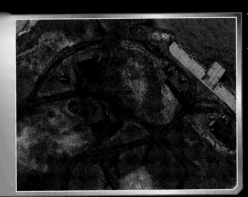

The Reactor Towers are a crucial control point for the Marines, regardless of map size. On the 16-player map, this control point serves up the only attack helicopter for both the US and Chinese forces. But on the 32- and 64-player maps, a Super Cobra and M1A2 spawns here when held by the Marines—the Chinese only get an APC if they hold it. Because the Marines need all the firepower they can get to push inland, they need to hold the Reactor Towers at all costs. US troops can land their RIBs on the eastern dock or drop in by helicopter. The main attack path is to the west, where three roads converge on the control point. The AT Turret has a good view of the center road, but the northern and southern roads are on lower terrain, making it difficult to spot attackers until they're at close range. Use mines or positioning anti-tank troops on the flanks to cover these roads. The Super Cobra can also be used to defend this control point. By hovering above its helipad, it can pick off any approaching attackers with its guided missiles or cannon.

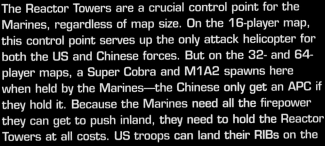

Maps: All

Adjacent Bases/ Control Points:
- USS *Essex*
- North Docks
- South Docks

Reactor Towers Assets

USMC Control	Chinese Control	16-Player	32-Player	64-Player
HMMWV	NJ 2046	1	—	—
DPV	Paratrooper Vehicle	—	2	2
N/A	WZ 551	—	1	1
M1A2	N/A	—	1	1
AH-1Z	Z-10	1	1*	1*
AT Turret	AT Turret	1	1	1
AA Turret	AA Turret	1	—	—

* = USMC Control Only

South Docks

Like the other eastern control points, the South Docks are most valuable to the Marines, providing them with another M1A2. The dominating feature of this control point is the huge shipping container lift. You can access the top of this lift via a ladder on the south side, allowing defenders to fire down on attackers at long range. Both snipers and anti-tank troops are effective here, and can engage targets as far away as the Reactor Towers and Maintenance Building. The control point's AA Turret is also a huge asset for either side. The Marines may need to help defend the Reactor Towers from air strikes while the Chinese can use it to engage incoming aircraft from the USS *Essex*. Like the North Dock's flagpole, this one is also out in the open, making it easy to capture—especially for fast moving vehicles. Defenders should mine the western main road. Chinese defenders should also watch the three ladders leading up from the sea—Marines may attempt to sneak up on the control point using RIBs.

Maps: 32- and 64-Player

Adjacent Bases/ Control Points:
- USS *Essex*
- Reactor Towers
- Maintenance Building

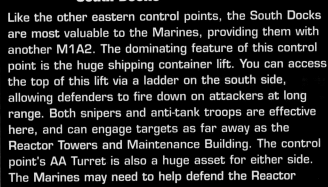

South Docks Assets

USMC Control	Chinese Control	16-Player	32-Player	64-Player
DPV	Paratrooper Vehicle	—	2	2
M1A2	Type 98	—	1	1
AA Turret	AA Turret	—	1	1

TIP The South Docks can be converted/contested from the northern ladder on the pier's eastern edge. A Marine in an RIB can sit here and capture the control point.

Maintenance Building

Filled with only a few crates, this large storage building is the map's only interior control point. The flagpole sits inside the southern large open door. Another entry point is to the north. While these huge doors are hard to miss, defenders often forget the western open side door. Although the flagpole is inside the building, the northern and southern entry points are large enough for vehicles to drive through. The best way to defend against such vehicle rushes is by placing mines at these doorways. Defenders should also use the height advantage offered by the various catwalks. One of the best defensive positions is on the upper level platform in the southeast corner. From this spot, defenders can cover all three entry points as well as the flagpole. Hiding claymores around the crates surrounding the flagpole is also a good way to catch attackers by surprise. The control point's AA Turret is outside the southern building and can be used to shoot down enemy aircraft attempting to avoid the map's chaotic center. Its remote location makes this AA Turret one of the safest on the map—unless enemy snipers are active at the South Docks.

Maps: 32- and 64-Player

Adjacent Bases/ Control Points:
- South Docks
- Main Entrance

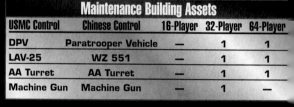

Maintenance Building Assets

USMC Control	Chinese Control	16-Player	32-Player	64-Player
DPV	Paratrooper Vehicle	—	1	1
LAV-25	WZ 551	—	1	1
AA Turret	AA Turret	—	1	1
Machine Gun	Machine Gun	—	1	—

Power Plant

On the 16-player map, the Power Plant is the starting spawn point for the Chinese. As such, it's also home to their commander's assets as well as their only tank spawn point—if the Marines capture the Power Plant, a tank won't spawn here. Vehicle rush attacks are the biggest threat here, therefore place mines at the access points to the flagpole's west and northeast. Should the enemy capture the Reactor Tower's control point and gain access to the only attack helicopter, a defender at the Power Plant should take to the roof south of the flagpole. Access the roof by a ladder on the building's south side. The control point's AA Turret sits on this rooftop, offering an awesome view of the whole battlefield, making it difficult for the enemy attack helicopter to hide. On the ground, the two AT Turrets have a clear view of approaches from the surrounding control points. But because they're in the open, the operators are susceptible to sniper fire. More safety and concealment is offered by the dark tunnel-like feature east of the flagpole.

Maps: 16-Player Only

Adjacent Bases/ Control Points:
- Main Entrance
- Reactor Towers

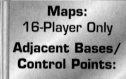

Power Plant Assets

USMC Control	Chinese Control	16-Player	32-Player	64-Player
HMMWV	NJ 2046	1	—	—
N/A	Type 98	1	—	—
N/A	Artillery	2	—	—
N/A	UAV Trailer	1	—	—
N/A	Radar Station	1	—	—
AT Turret	AT Turret	2	—	—
AA Turret	AA Turret	1	—	—

Main Entrance

In terms of assets, the Main Entrance is a near mirror image of the Reactor Tower's control point, except this one benefits the Chinese more than it does the Marines. On the 16-player map, both sides share similar gear when capturing this control point, including the map's only AA vehicle. But on the 32- and 64-player versions, the Chinese gain a Z-10 and a Type 98 when holding this control point, while the Marines only get an LAV-25. This control point also has a number of useful defensive assets. The two eastern facing machine guns and AT Turret are effective at engaging enemy units in the map's center. The partially constructed building is a great spot for snipers and other defenders covering the flagpole. Defenders and attackers should note that the control point can be converted from within the guard post building to the west. It can also be converted by standing outside the western perimeter fence.

Maps: All

Adjacent Bases/Control Points:
- Airfield
- Construction Site
- Power Station

Main Entrance Assets

USMC Control	Chinese Control	16-Player	32-Player	64-Player
DPV	Paratrooper Vehicle	1	1	1
LAV-25	N/A	—	1	1
M6 Bradley	Type 95	1	—	—
N/A	Type 98	—	1	1
N/A	Z-10	—	1	1
AT Turret	AT Turret	1	1	1
AA Turret	AA Turret	—	1	1
Machine Gun	Machine Gun	2	3	3

Construction Site

The Construction Site is the Marine starting position on the 16-player map, and there's no reason why they should lose it. The flagpole is surrounded by three partially constructed building, providing perfect positions for defenders. The building north of the flagpole contains an AT Turret on the third floor. A sniper positioned here can cover the southern approach and engage enemies as they spawn at the Power Station. By switching between the AT Turret and sniper rifle, one player can single-handedly hold this control point. One player can even drop grenades on enemy troops attempting to convert the flag below. More defensive options are provided by the AT and AA Turrets on the building rooftop west of the flagpole. These rooftop positions offer less concealment and a more restrictive view, but they come in handy when facing an enemy siege.

Maps:
16-Player Only

Adjacent Bases/Control Points:
- Main Entrance
- Reactor Towers

Construction Site Assets

USMC Control	Chinese Control	16-Player	32-Player	64-Player
DPV	Paratrooper Vehicle	1	—	—
M1A2	N/A	1	—	—
Artillery	N/A	2	—	—
UAV Trailer	N/A	1	—	—
Radar Station	N/A	1	—	—
AT Turret	AT Turret	2	—	—
AA Turret	AA Turret	1	—	—

TIP The DPV spawned at the Construction Site gives the Marines an early advantage. Use its speed to capture the Reactor Towers before the Chinese can reach them in their slower moving NJ 2046 spawned at the Power Station.

Warehouse

The Warehouse is identical to the Maintenance Building, except this time the flagpole is outside, along the structure's eastern side. With nothing more than a couple of machine guns facing south and east, defenders have their work cut out here. The simplest solution to stop vehicle attacks is by mining the main approaches to the north and south. But the control point can be converted from within the eastern side of the Warehouse too, by either infantry or vehicles. Therefore, place mines at the entrances of the building, too. The northern building is the ideal sniper position to cover the flagpole, but there's no ladder. So any rooftop defenders here will need a helicopter's assistance to reach their destination. Fast-moving DPV or Paratrooper Vehicle assaults are the most likely, so position anti-tank troops facing east and south, behind the cover near each machine gun position.

Maps:
64-Player Only

Adjacent Bases/ Control Points:
- North Docks
- Main Entrance

Warehouse Assets

USMC Control	Chinese Control	16-Player	32-Player	64-Player
DPV	Paratrooper Vehicle	—	—	2
LAV-25	WZ 551	—	—	1
Machine Gun	Machine Gun	—	—	2

Airfield

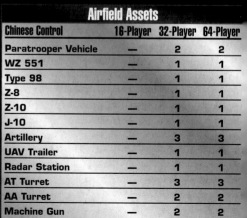

This fortified Airfield, tucked away in a western narrow valley, serves as the Chinese base and cannot be captured. The Marines have little to gain and much to lose by attacking this area—especially if the Airfield is well defended. If the steep mountains aren't enough of a deterrent to Marine pilots, the two AA Turrets will be. Like the USS *Essex*, the Airfield has two spawn points. The northern spawn point drops Chinese troops near the Z-10 and J-10—a Paratrooper Vehicle is also parked nearby. You can access the rest of the vehicles (including the Z-8 transport helicopter) by using the southern spawn point. There are three main roads exiting the Airfield. The main paved road leads into the Main Entrance, allowing for a quick capture at each battle's outset. Two mountainous dirt roads flank the central paved road, the northern one leading to the Warehouse and the southern one ending near the southern side of the Main Entrance. Although Marine capture is impossible, the Chinese should still leave a few defenders behind to prevent vehicle theft and sabotage of the artillery and other commander assets. The three AT Turrets are well-positioned to engage any intruding vehicles. If extra manpower is available, use the Z-8 to drop a sniper or anti-tank soldier on the shallow mountain slope west of the Airfield's entrance.

Maps: 32- and 64-Player

Adjacent Bases/ Control Points:
- Main Entrance

Airfield Assets

Chinese Control	16-Player	32-Player	64-Player
Paratrooper Vehicle	—	2	2
WZ 551	—	1	1
Type 98	—	1	1
Z-8	—	1	1
Z-10	—	1	1
J-10	—	1	1
Artillery	—	3	3
UAV Trailer	—	1	1
Radar Station	—	1	1
AT Turret	—	3	3
AA Turret	—	2	2
Machine Gun	—	2	2

DALIAN PLANT TACTICS

Amphibious Assault

The RIBs aren't the quickest way for the Marines to make it onto dry land, but attacking by sea gives the US troops the element of surprise they need to assault the coastal control points. When attacking the Reactor Towers, drive the boat up onto this ramp—APCs can use the same ramp.

The high concrete piers of the South and North Docks aren't as easy to access. But there are ladders on each side of the pier. Troops will have to exit the boat, then climb the ladders to make it ashore.

You can also access the two pumping stations west of the Reactor Tower's control point by sea. Here troops can enter a tunnel and climb a ladder to reach land.

Construction Site Kill Zone

On the 16-player map, the Construction Site is a key Marine position, producing the Marines' only M1A2. Therefore, defend it at all times. An AT Turret is on the third floor of the building north of the flagpole. The elevation and darkened surroundings make this an ideal defensive position. Use the AT Turret to blast approaching vehicles as far away as the Power Station.

Choose the sniper when defending here. When you're not firing at vehicles with TOW missiles, switch to the rifle and pick off enemy infantry at long range. Should enemies sneak up on the flag below, drop a grenade or two on them. With the aid of the AT Turret, one sniper positioned here can inflict massive casualties on the enemy.

Fly Smart

On each map size, the nuclear facility is well defended against air attacks, with AA Turrets at most of the control points. This makes flying through the map's center an extremely risky move. Instead, stick to the map's perimeter, especially when flying slow-moving transport helicopters.

Attack helicopters should make use of the various buildings for cover. The huge cooling towers in the map's center are a good way to stay out of the sights of an enemy AA Turret. Either slide left or right to peek around them or pop up over the top of them.

Both the AH-1Z and Z-10 are devastating against ground targets. Hover at a safe distance and allow the gunner to mow down enemy troops with the cannon. Their guided missiles are also the quickest way to demolish enemy armor.

The F-35B can hover, too. Hover to the north or south and engage air traffic in the center of the map with heat-seeking missiles.

Avoid flying over the enemy base at the Airfield or USS *Essex*. Each site is packed with juicy stationary targets, but their air defenses (if manned) are deadly. Also, each target you destroy will respawn a few seconds later.

Cooling Tower Advance

Crossing the map's center on foot can be made less risky by using the covered walkways circling the large cooling towers. The low walls surrounding each walkway provide some cover, allowing for a safe defensive position if the advance is stalled by incoming fire.

Using the large cooling tower as a backdrop minimizes the visibility of your silhouette, making it difficult for enemies to spot movement.

DAQING OILFIELDS

American forces striking south are now poised to seize this crucial logistic component in China's ongoing war effort, seeking to both divert petroleum resources while simultaneously hindering PLA mechanized efforts in this sector. The stakes are high in this head-on collision between advancing US brigades and the defending Chinese forces, with both sides advised to cautiously advance through this volatile landscape.

16-PLAYER

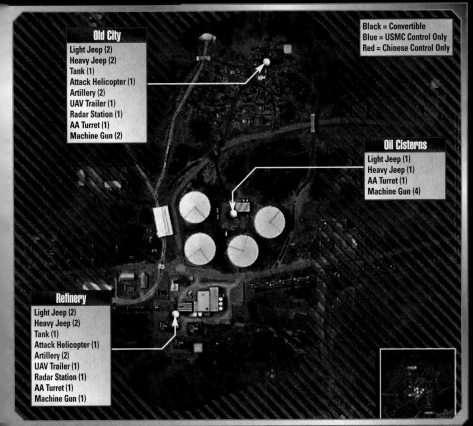

Black = Convertible
Blue = USMC Control Only
Red = Chinese Control Only

Old City
Light Jeep (2)
Heavy Jeep (2)
Tank (1)
Attack Helicopter (1)
Artillery (2)
UAV Trailer (1)
Radar Station (1)
AA Turret (1)
Machine Gun (2)

Oil Cisterns
Light Jeep (1)
Heavy Jeep (1)
AA Turret (1)
Machine Gun (4)

Refinery
Light Jeep (2)
Heavy Jeep (2)
Tank (1)
Attack Helicopter (1)
Artillery (2)
UAV Trailer (1)
Radar Station (1)
AA Turret (1)
Machine Gun (1)

Game Type:
Double Assault
Total Control Points: 3
Convertible Control Points: 3

Always attack the Oil Cisterns with full squads to overwhelm any defenders gathered near the flag.

US Strategy

To impose a ticket drain on the Chinese, all the Marines need to do is capture the Oil Cisterns while holding onto the Refinery. But even with this advantage the battle can carry on much longer than necessary. Instead, try to capture the Oil Cisterns and Old City at the outset of the battle to bring the fight to a quick conclusion. Split the team into three squads, one assigned to each control point. The first squad must move out quickly (preferably in a DPV) to capture the Oil Cisterns before the Chinese do. A couple of squad members should follow behind in the Super Cobra and help defend the Oil Cisterns from attack. The second squad needs to hold at the Refinery and should consist of at least one sniper and an anti-tank soldier. Capturing the Old City falls to the third squad. Using a DPV or Humvee, this squad should sneak along the eastern dirt road and assault the Old City from the east. Before arriving, call in an artillery strike on the control point and request a UAV or radar scan to spot any defenders hiding near the flagpole. Chances are most of the Chinese troops are attacking the Refinery or Oil Cisterns. Leave the vehicle behind and approach the flagpole on foot. Three or four troops can convert the control point within a few seconds. If the other two control points are held, the Chinese will have nowhere left to spawn. Hold strong at all three control points till the remaining enemy troops are wiped out.

Chinese Strategy

The Chinese should follow the same basic strategy as the Marines but with a few variations. As soon as the battle begins, call in an artillery strike on the Oil Cisterns in an attempt to stifle the Marine advance. If the timing is right, the shells should slam down just as the first group of Marines enter the facility. Meanwhile, use the Z-10 to hold off further attacks on the Oil Cisterns while a squad of ground troops rushes in from the north for the capture. While holding at the Oil Cisterns and Old City, move another squad toward the Refinery following the railroad tracks to the west. Instead of rushing in through the Refinery's southern main entrance, move along the western perimeter fence and look for a patched hole near the south-western smokestack. To preserve stealth, shoot it open with a few rounds from a silenced pistol. Rush through the hole in the fence and sneak toward the flag by moving beneath the south-western smokestack's platform. The flag can be converted by holding near the red shipping container next to the southwest smokestack. Once the Refinery is in Chinese hands, destroy the artillery and other commander elements. If it's still airborne, try to shoot down the Super Cobra too, as it's likely to counter-attack. Even if the Oil Cisterns falls to the Marines, by holding the Old City and Refinery you deny the US their Super Cobra and M1A2, making a Chinese victory much easier.

32-PLAYER

Chinese HQ
Light Jeep (3)
Heavy Jeep (2)
AA Vehicle (1)
Tank (1)
Transport Helicopter (1)
Attack Helicopter (1)
Fighter (1)
Fighter Bomber (1)
Artillery (4)
UAV Trailer (1)
Radar Station (1)
AT Turret (2)
AA Turret (2)
Machine Gun (3)

Power Station
Light Jeep (1)
Heavy Jeep (2)
Tank (1)
Machine Gun (1)

Refinery
Light Jeep (2)
Heavy Jeep (1)
AA Vehicle (1)
Tank (1)
Machine Gun (1)

Oil Cisterns
Light Jeep (1)
Heavy Jeep (3)
AA Turret (1)
Machine Gun (4)

Old City
Light Jeep (1)
Heavy Jeep (1)
AA Vehicle (1)
Tank (1)
Machine Gun (2)

Gas Station
Light Jeep (2)
Tank (1)
AT Turret (1)

US Town
Light Jeep (3)
Heavy Jeep (2)
AA Vehicle (1)
Tank (1)
Transport Helicopter (1)
Attack Helicopter (1)
Fighter (1)
Fighter Bomber (1)
Artillery (4)
UAV Trailer (1)
Radar Station (1)
AT Turret (3)
AA Turret (1)
Machine Gun (4)

Black = Convertible
Blue = USMC Control Only
Red = Chinese Control Only

Game Type:
Conquest Head-On
Total Control Points: 7
Convertible Control Points: 5

Use supply drops to keep defenders healed and stocked with ammo. Anti-tank troops need a constant source of ammo to repel enemy vehicle attacks.

US Strategy

To avoid spreading the team too thin, the Marines should try to capture and hold three out of five control points to bleed the Chinese ticket count. To pull off this strategy, the team should be split into four separate squads, three responsible for capturing and defending control points and a fourth to provide close air support in the aircraft. Using DPVs, two of the squads should take off immediately, heading for the Refinery and Gas Station. Another squad should board the Seahawk and fly to the Power Station. By holding these three control points, the Marines initiate the drain on the Chinese tickets. Instead of attacking, simply hold back and defend. With an M1A2 at each control point, defenders should have little problem repelling ground attacks. Air strikes, however, are a different issue. Move the M6 Bradleys spawned at the US Town and Refinery to the Gas Station and Power Station for air protection. The F-15 and F-18 must fill in any gaps in your air defenses—shooting down enemy aircraft is their first priority. At each forward control point, the squad leaders should defend from a distance, providing squad members with a nearby spawn point should the position fall into enemy hands. If necessary, request artillery and air support when counterattacking a fallen control point. Once a Marine victory is at hand, move in on the Oil Cisterns and Old City while maintaining defensive units at the other control points.

Chinese Strategy

Like the Marines, the Chinese should capture and hold three key control points instead of trying to dominate the whole map. Using three squads of ground troops, go for the Old City, Power Station, and Gas Station early in the battle. The squad going for the Gas Station should use the Z-8, but ground transportation is fast enough for the other two squads to get in position. The rest of the team should take to the skies in the Z-10, J-10, and SU-30. Use the jets to provide air cover over the Gas Station and Power Station until the Type 95s (from the Chinese HQ and Old City) can be moved into place. Hold at these three control points until a clear ticket advantage is held over the Marines. If defenses are solid at the control points, consider an attack on the Oil Cisterns. Combined with the relocated Type 95s at the Gas Station and Power Station, attaining the AA turret at the Oil Cisterns completes a solid air defense line across the center of the map, greatly hindering US air operations. But don't get too greedy—holding the Power Station, Old City, and Gas Station is still the main priority. Only branch out if an opportunity presents itself. Use the UAV and radar scans to monitor enemy strength at the Oil Cisterns before attempting an attack. If an assault is deemed too risky, simply hold out at the three control points until the Marines run out of tickets.

64-PLAYER

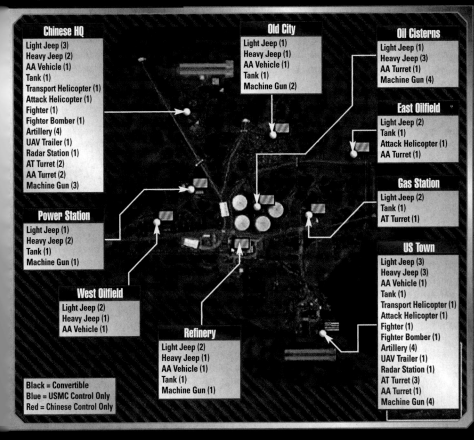

Chinese HQ
Light Jeep (3)
Heavy Jeep (2)
AA Vehicle (1)
Tank (1)
Transport Helicopter (1)
Attack Helicopter (1)
Fighter (1)
Fighter Bomber (1)
Artillery (4)
UAV Trailer (1)
Radar Station (1)
AT Turret (2)
AA Turret (2)
Machine Gun (3)

Power Station
Light Jeep (1)
Heavy Jeep (2)
Tank (1)
Machine Gun (1)

West Oilfield
Light Jeep (2)
Heavy Jeep (1)
AA Vehicle (1)

Old City
Light Jeep (1)
Heavy Jeep (1)
AA Vehicle (1)
Tank (1)
Machine Gun (2)

Refinery
Light Jeep (2)
Heavy Jeep (1)
AA Vehicle (1)
Tank (1)
Machine Gun (1)

Oil Cisterns
Light Jeep (1)
Heavy Jeep (3)
AA Turret (1)
Machine Gun (4)

East Oilfield
Light Jeep (2)
Tank (1)
Attack Helicopter (1)
AA Turret (1)

Gas Station
Light Jeep (2)
Tank (1)
AT Turret (1)

US Town
Light Jeep (3)
Heavy Jeep (3)
AA Vehicle (1)
Tank (1)
Transport Helicopter (1)
Attack Helicopter (1)
Fighter (1)
Fighter Bomber (1)
Artillery (4)
UAV Trailer (1)
Radar Station (1)
AT Turret (3)
AA Turret (1)
Machine Gun (4)

Black = Convertible
Blue = USMC Control Only
Red = Chinese Control Only

Game Type:
Conquest Head-On
Total Control Points: 9
Convertible Control Points: 7

Defending the Oil Cisterns requires some heavy firepower. Use tanks and other vehicles from the surrounding control points to help reinforce this position.

US Strategy

The Marines must move quickly to build a solid defensive line across the center of the map. Dispatch squads in DPVs toward the Gas Station, Refinery, and West Oilfield as soon as the battle begins. Using the Seahawk, drop more troops at the Oil Cisterns and Power Station. Although you only need four control points to bleed the Chinese ticket count, it's important to hold a firm line across the map's center at the Power Station, Oil Cisterns, and Gas Station. Use vehicles spawned at the Refinery and West Oilfield to strengthen defenses at the front line positions, and fill gaps in the front line with infantry. Keep an eye on the roads and railroad tracks. Allowing the Chinese to capture the East Oilfield gives them an extra attack helicopter, so make sure all control points are well protected from air strikes. The M6 Bradley spawned at the West Oilfield is adequate to cover the western side of the map, and the AA turret at the Oil Cisterns can cover the center. But the Gas Station needs some help. Drive the M6 Bradley from the Refinery to the Gas Station to solidify AA coverage on the front line. As usual, the F-15 and F-18 should patrol the skies for enemy aircraft while the Super Cobra provides close air support. Hold strong at the front line control points while defending the rear from breakthrough attacks. By holding five control points, the Marines can maintain the drain on the Chinese tickets even if one control point temporarily falls. Stay on the defensive until the enemy's collapse is imminent, then move on the East Oilfield and Old City to guarantee a win.

Chinese Strategy

Instead of getting bogged down in the center of the map, the Chinese should look to the perimeter. Immediately move ground troops to the West Oilfield, Power Station, and Old City while troops in the Z-8 are dropped at the East Oilfield. Capturing and holding these perimeter control points is just enough to initiate the drain on the US ticket count. Plus, each area has its own air defenses in place, so there's no need to juggle AA assets. Capturing the East Oilfield also gives the Chinese an extra Z-10 attack helicopter. Use this Z-10 to help defend the Old City and East Oilfield while the one from the Chinese HQ defends the Power Station and West Oilfield. Meanwhile, the J-10 and SU-30 should patrol for enemy aircraft. There are no native air defenses at the Gas Station, so instead of capturing it, consider just bombing the Marines there with your jets; harassing US troops and vehicles here relieves some pressure on your ground forces at the East Oilfield. The Marines are likely to stage numerous vehicle rush attacks given the number of heavy and light jeeps in their arsenal. To prevent these attacks from succeeding, consider positioning some well concealed anti-tank troops around the periphery of each control point. It's much easier to wipe out the attackers before they exit the vehicle and disperse. Engineers can also have an impact by placing mines at the main entries of each control point. With careful coordination on the ground and in the air, the Chinese have an excellent chance of holding out for a victory.

BASES AND CONTROL POINTS

US Town

On the 32- and 64-player maps, the US Town is the Marine's base, providing the bulk of their vehicles. Since both are head-on maps, this site cannot be captured by Chinese troops. But the Marines should still ready to fight off sporadic Chinese attacks. The base's AA turret (located near the two bridges) should be enough to deter enemy pilots from making bombing and strafing runs while the three AT turrets (at the main entrance to north) can deal with incoming vehicles. Like most large bases, the US Town has two spawn points. The southern spawn point drops troops near the airfield, allowing them quick access to the helicopters and jets. Those looking for a ground vehicle should spawn at the northern control point, within the town itself. Using the two roads to the north, Marines spawning here can quickly capture the Refinery and Gas Station control points. To maximize speed, stick to the roads whenever possible. Driving through the nearby marshes and rice fields may seem like a quicker route, but the soggy and uneven terrain makes for a slow and potentially hazardous journey.

Maps: 32- and 64-Player

Adjacent Bases/ Control Points:
- Refinery
- Gas Station

TIP The two bridges in the center of the US Town can be destroyed with C4 or bombs. However, their demolition has little impact on the Marine advance, since most of the ground vehicles spawn on the northern side of the bridges. In fact, the Marines might want to destroy these bridges themselves to prevent Chinese ground troops from racing in and stealing their air vehicles.

US Town Assets

USMC Control	16-Player	32-Player	64-Player
DPV	—	3	3
HMMWV	—	2	3
M6 Bradley	—	1	1
M1A2	—	1	1
HH-60H	—	1	1
AH-1Z	—	1	1
F-18 E/F	—	1	1
F-15E	—	1	1
Artillery	—	4	4
UAV Trailer	—	1	1
Radar Station	—	1	1
AT Turret	—	3	3
AA Turret	—	1	1
Machine Gun	—	4	4

Gas Station

Located just east of the giant Oil Cisterns, the Gas Station provides occupiers with a tank, making this control point well worth fighting for. The flagpole sits outside the service station building. The interior of this building is accessible from front and backdoors on the western and eastern sides. Its roof can also be accessed via a ladder on the eastern wall. Both attackers and defenders should realize that the control point can be converted/contested from within the building as well as from its rooftop. As such, defenders should consider placing a few claymores in the dark halls and near the ladder to prevent stealthy capture attempts. Snipers or other defenders can watch the flagpole from the top of the three large cylindrical storage tanks to the north. These tanks are also useful for covering the woods to the north. The control point's AT turret is tucked in the facility's northeast corner, making it most useful for engaging approaching vehicles from the west and south. But attackers moving through the nearby north entrance

Maps: 32- and 64-Player

Adjacent Bases/ Control Points:
- US Town
- Refinery
- Oil Cisterns
- East Oilfield

Gas Station Assets

USMC Control	Chinese Control	16-Player	32-Player	64-Player
DPV	Paratrooper Vehicle	—	2	2
M1A2	Type 98	—	1	1
AT Turret	AT Turret	—	1	1

can effectively blindside the AT turret at point blank range. With no anti-aircraft protection, the Gas Station is extremely vulnerable to air strikes and helicopter raids. Due to the surrounding terrain and structures, friendly AA turrets at the Oil Cisterns, East Oilfield, or Refinery won't be much of a help either. If necessary, move an AA vehicle here to deter air attacks.

Refinery

This sprawling industrial complex is a key control point on each map. On the 16-player map, the Refinery is the starting position for the Marines and home to their commander elements. The control point is neutral in the larger maps, but produces a variety of ground vehicles for both sides including a tank and an AA vehicle. Its close proximity to the US Town gives the Marines the best chance of capturing the Refinery early. When moving in on the Refinery, always use the rear entrances to avoid the potentially high traffic areas along the road to the north. Regardless of who captures it, this control point must be defended. If resources allow, hold enemy attackers at the perimeter fence. But with openings to the north, east, and west, such a strategy is difficult to pull off with only a handful of defenders. Instead, consider using the elevated catwalks ringing the three large southern smokestacks. While perched here, snipers and anti-tank troops can engage infantry and vehicles at long range from all approachable directions. Most importantly, they can target enemy troops gathered around the flagpole. The northern smokestack's walkway is higher, offering an even better view of the Refinery as well as the West Oilfield, Power Station, and even parts of the Oil Cisterns.

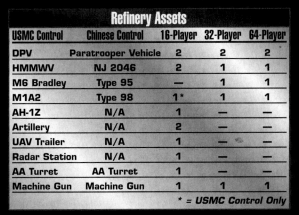

Maps: All

Adjacent Bases/ Control Points:
- US Town
- Gas Station
- Oil Cisterns
- West Oilfield

Refinery Assets

USMC Control	Chinese Control	16-Player	32-Player	64-Player
DPV	Paratrooper Vehicle	2	2	2
HMMWV	NJ 2046	2	1	1
M6 Bradley	Type 95	—	1	1
M1A2	Type 98	1*	1	1
AH-1Z	N/A	1	—	—
Artillery	N/A	2	—	—
UAV Trailer	N/A	1	—	—
Radar Station	N/A	1	—	—
AA Turret	AA Turret	1	—	—
Machine Gun	Machine Gun	1	1	1

* = USMC Control Only

West Oilfield

Compared to its eastern counterpart, the West Oilfield's assets are relatively light. However, the AA vehicle spawned here is useful for defending the nearby Refinery and Power Station from air strikes. Located on the western outskirts of the map, this control point probably won't see much action. Still, defenders should prepare for attacks in every direction. The perimeter fence isn't much use, with entry points to the north, east, and south. Instead of predicting the enemy's avenue of attack, concentrate on the flag. Placing mines near its base can prevent vehicle rush attacks. Infantry should take cover in the surrounding sheds or within the two L-shaped buildings to the north and south. Attackers who breach the perimeter fence should rush for the red and blue dumpsters near the flagpole. The control point can be converted from within either dumpster. As such, defenders may want to booby trap each dumpster with a claymore.

Maps: 64-Player Only

Adjacent Bases/ Control Points:
- Refinery
- Power Station

West Oilfield Assets

USMC Control	Chinese Control	16-Player	32-Player	64-Player
DPV	Paratrooper Vehicle	—	—	2
HMMWV	NJ 2046	—	—	1
M6 Bradley	Type 95	—	—	1

Power Station

The Power Station is located on a slight hill just north of the West Oilfield. Its key asset is the tank, but the light and heavy jeeps are also useful for staging fast-moving assaults on the surrounding control points. The lack of defensive weaponry and cover can make the Power Station difficult to hold. There are no building interiors for infantry to hide in, leaving defenders vulnerable to artillery and air strikes. The eastern facing machine gun covers the approach from the Oil Cisterns, but the roads to the north and south are open. The perimeter fence doesn't make much of a barrier either, with wide openings to the north, east, and south. However, the flag is somewhat protected with a tall stack of crates to its south, a red shipping container to its north, and the Power Station itself to the east. If the control point's tank is off fighting elsewhere, troops should consider defending from this enclosed area around the flag. Add a machine gun to the area by parking a heavy jeep nearby. The better solution is to defend from a distance by positioning snipers and other troops in the forest to the west. This is the best way to watch the flag while staying away from the hazards caused by falling bombs, missiles, and shells.

Maps: 32- and 64-Player

Adjacent Bases/ Control Points:
- Chinese HQ
- Oil Cisterns
- West Oilfield

Power Station Assets

USMC Control	Chinese Control	16-Player	32-Player	64-Player
DPV	Paratrooper Vehicle	—	1	1
HMMWV	NJ 2046	—	2	2
M1A2	Type 98	—	1	1
Machine Gun	Machine Gun	—	1	1

Oil Cisterns

The popularity of the Oil Cisterns is not dictated by its assets, but more by its geography. On each map size, this control point is often the center of all the action due to its central location. Troops spawning here can stage assaults on almost every other control point on the map. But this advantage is also the Oil Cisterns' greatest weakness, as the control point can be easily surrounded and attacked from every direction. Fortunately the site is equipped with several defensive features to help keep attackers at bay. The factory building has four machine guns along the railing of its upper level walkway, each covering a different direction. These are great for engaging infantry as well as light vehicles. The control point's AA turret can only be accessed from the ladder on the north side of the factory. From this elevated position the AA turret can engage enemy aircraft in all directions. Plus it can tilt downward and used to blast incoming infantry and vehicles—but not very accurately.

Maps: All

Adjacent Bases/ Control Points:
- Old City
- Power Station
- Refinery
- Gas Station

Oil Cisterns Assets

USMC Control	Chinese Control	16-Player	32-Player	64-Player
DPV	Paratrooper Vehicle	1	1	1
HMMWV	NJ 2046	1	3	3
AA Turret	AA Turret	1	1	1
Machine Gun	Machine Gun	4	4	4

The flag is located within the center of a factory building, surrounded by four tall cylindrical tanks. It can be converted/contested by troops gathered either near its base or on the upper level walkway surrounding it. In most cases, attackers should enter the structure at ground level as the interior provides more cover, forcing defenders to engage at close range. Defenders can prevent such attacks by simply placing claymores at the three ground level entrances. Troops hiding below can also be eliminated by attacking from the upper level walkway using automatic fire and grenades. Therefore attackers may want to position snipers around the periphery of the control point before moving in for the capture. The cistern to the east is great sniper perch and is the only one that has a ladder leading to the top. All upper-level defenders should be eliminated before moving troops inside the factory. For best results, attack from multiple directions to keep the defenders on their toes. Initiating the assault with an artillery strike is also a great way to keep the defenders off balance.

East Oilfield

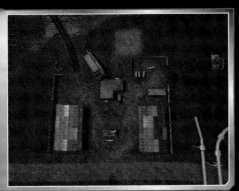

The East Oilfield is one of the most valuable control points on the 64-player map. Both sides should rush here as quickly as possible to gain access to its tank and attack helicopter. In a tight battle, gaining an extra attack helicopter can make a huge difference. The AA turret is also a valuable asset, helping curtail enemy air operations on the eastern side of the map. The main entry points to this facility are to the east and west. Both of these narrow openings can be mined to prevent vehicle rush attacks. Another opening is located to the east. Defenders can take cover in the building just north of the flag. The control point can also be converted from within this building. The surrounding hills can also be used by attackers and defenders to clear out enemy troops around the flagpole. The

Maps:
64-Player Only

**Adjacent Bases/
Control Points:**
- Old City
- Oil Cisterns
- Gas Station

East Oilfield Assets

USMC Control	Chinese Control	16-Player	32-Player	64-Player
DPV	Paratrooper Vehicle	—	—	2
M1A2	Type 98	—	—	1
AH-1Z	Z-10	—	—	1
AA Turret	AA Turret	—	—	1

large hill to the northwest has a good view of the entire facility, making it a great spot for snipers and anti-tank troops. Since the helipad sits to the north, outside the facility's fence, defenders should look out for thieves attempting to steal the attack helicopter. If an enemy manages to get in the chopper, an anti-tank soldier should destroy it before it can take off.

> **TIP** The East Oilfield's helipad can be used by helicopters for repairs and rearmament on the 32-player map.

Old City

This abandoned urban center is one of the deadliest control points on the map. On each map size, the Chinese have the best chance of taking this control point early—this is their starting spawn point on the 16-player map. Once captured, the Old City must be held at all costs, as retaking it is often a costly endeavor. There are four main direct roads running through the Old City: one to the west, one to the east, and two to the south. Vehicle and troops moving along these roads must pass numerous buildings on the way to the flagpole, which allows for many

Maps: All

**Adjacent Bases/
Control Points:**
- Chinese HQ
- Oil Cisterns
- East Oilfield

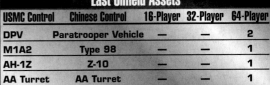

ambush opportunities. Defenders can halt most vehicle advances with mines and anti-tank troops. Attackers are better off moving in on foot and using the various building interiors for concealment and cover. But even these can be booby trapped with claymores by defenders. The flagpole is located in a courtyard on the northern edge of the Old City. This is a regular kill zone for defenders camped on the courtyard's perimeter. The building to the

Old City Assets

USMC Control	Chinese Control	16-Player	32-Player	64-Player
DPV	Paratrooper Vehicle	2	1	1
HMMWV	NJ 2046	2	1	1
M6 Bradley	Type 95	—	1	1
M1A2	Type 98	1*	1	1
N/A	Z-10	1	—	—
N/A	Artillery	2	—	—
N/A	UAV Trailer	1	—	—
N/A	Radar Station	1	—	—
AA Turret	AA Turret	1	—	—
Machine Gun	Machine Gun	2	2	2

* = Chinese Control Only

south is a popular spot for defenders as its interior and rooftop are accessible. Defenders on the hill to the north can also cover the flagpole, using the low stone wall for cover. Needless to say, attackers should approach cautiously and scan the surroundings for enemies before rushing in for the capture—this is where the UAV comes in handy.

Chinese HQ

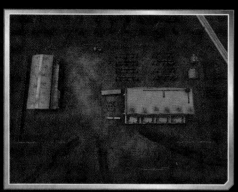

Like the US Base, the Chinese HQ cannot be captured and is divided into two distinct areas, each with its own spawn point. The southern portion of the HQ sits on a large hill and is surrounded by a perimeter fence. This is where most of the ground vehicles and transport helicopter appear. The main gate to the south is flanked by two guard posts, each equipped with a machine gun. If that's not deterrence enough, the two AT turrets nearby should dissuade Marine attackers from using this entrance. The eastern entrance also has a guard post, but there are no machine guns or AT turrets covering this road. Still, defenders positioned in the guard post have a great view of the eastern road and can even see the western outskirts of the Old City. Enemy aircraft can be countered with the AA turret in the northwest corner. A second AA turret is located in the valley to the north, right next to the two runways. Chinese troops wanting to fly the Z-10, J-10, or SU-30 should spawn here. Although a frontal assault is unlikely, defenders should watch the railroad tracks to the west for US infiltrators. Using these tracks as a road, US attackers can bypass the HQ and attack the airfield, potentially stealing aircraft or sabotaging the commander elements.

Maps: 32- and 64-Player

Adjacent Bases/ Control Points:
- Old City
- Power Station

Chinese HQ Assets

Chinese Control	16-Player	32-Player	64-Player
Paratrooper Vehicle	—	3	3
NJ 2046	—	2	2
Type 95	—	1	1
Type 98	—	1	1
Z-8	—	1	1
Z-10	—	1	1
J-10	—	1	1
SU-30	—	1	1
Artillery	—	4	4
UAV Trailer	—	1	1
Radar Station	—	1	1
AT Turret	—	2	2
AA Turret	—	2	2
Machine Gun	—	3	3

DAQING OILFIELDS TACTICS

Cooling Tower Advance

Most of the control points on this map are fenced off, with only a few main entry points that are likely to be defended. But you can usually find a patched hole in a fence like this.

Only a few rounds fired from any weapon is enough to open the hole in the fence. To remain stealthy, use a silenced pistol. These fence breaches are the best way to sneak up on a control point.

Take the High Ground

The northern smokestack at the Refinery is the tallest accessible point on the map, making it an ideal perch for snipers and anti-tank troops. From this high position they can cover the flag below as well as the areas around the West Oilfield, Oil Cisterns, and even the Gas Station.

Although they lack cover and concealment, the huge cisterns at the center of the map are another popular sniper position, useful for covering all surrounding control points. Although the eastern cistern is the only one accessible by a ladder, helicopters can drop troops on the other three.

A less conspicuous sniper position is the railroad depot's roof just west of the Oil Cisterns. Troops need a lift to reach this rooftop, but it's worth the effort. Snipers here can engage enemy troops at the Refinery, West Oilfield, Power Station, and the Old City.

The western road and rail line are popular avenues of attack. Consider ambushing vehicles moving along these paths by hiding on (or in) the boxcars just north of the railroad depot.

There are a few more hills on the northern side of the map. Use these hilltops to cover control points from a distance. The steep hill northwest of the East Oilfield is a good spot for both snipers and anti-tank troops. Take advantage of the nearby forests for cover too.

Old City Assault

The Old City is one of the most dangerous control points to assault. But attackers can bypass some of its hazards by approaching from the eastern side. Load a squad up in a heavy or light jeep and use the dirt road running between the Oil Cisterns and Gas Station to quickly reach the Old City's perimeter.

When you reach the Old City's eastern flank, leave the vehicle behind and move in on foot. Setup a mini-fire base at the crater caused by a crashed F-15—look for the rising smoke. The squad leader should take cover here and serve as a spawn point while the squad moves in to attack.

Before moving into the Old City, always request a UAV over the control point. This reveals the locations of defenders camped around the flagpole. Use this info to take the enemy by surprise.

When the area around the flagpole is clear, the whole squad should rush in to quickly neutralize and capture the control point.

Vehicle Jumps

There are a number or ramps on this map ideal for jumping light and heavy jeeps. Use this one on the south side of the Oil Cisterns to clear the perimeter fence. There's little tactical or strategic worth to these jumps, but they're fun. Just make sure your vehicle as sufficient health to survive a rough landing.

BATTLEFIELD 2

DRAGON VALLEY

Ancient legends of this "fairyland on earth" tell of a yellow dragon that helped the king channel flood waters into the sea. Currently, American military forces are converging upon this idyllic valley, to secure a foothold in the Minshan mountain range. Elements of the US Marines are on the offensive in this sector, while the forces of the People's Republic of China are called upon to defend ancient ancestral lands, in what promises to be a bitter engagement.

16-PLAYER

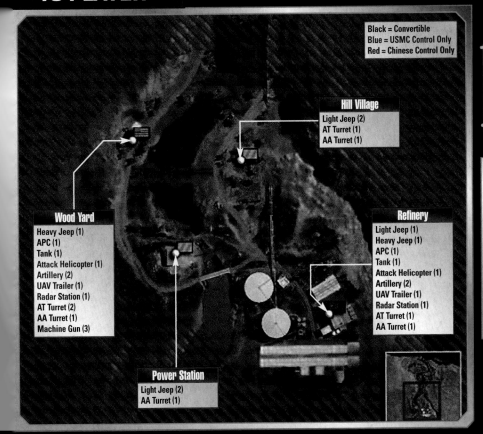

Black = Convertible
Blue = USMC Control Only
Red = Chinese Control Only

Hill Village
Light Jeep (2)
AT Turret (1)
AA Turret (1)

Wood Yard
Heavy Jeep (1)
APC (1)
Tank (1)
Attack Helicopter (1)
Artillery (2)
UAV Trailer (1)
Radar Station (1)
AT Turret (2)
AA Turret (1)
Machine Gun (3)

Refinery
Light Jeep (1)
Heavy Jeep (1)
APC (1)
Tank (1)
Attack Helicopter (1)
Artillery (2)
UAV Trailer (1)
Radar Station (1)
AT Turret (1)
AA Turret (1)

Power Station
Light Jeep (2)
AA Turret (1)

Game Type:
Conquest Double Assault
Total Control Points: 4
Convertible Control Points: 4

When possible, try to isolate the enemy to the Power Station, then use an attack helicopter to pound them into submission.

US Strategy

This double assault battle is very balanced, but with some skill and teamwork, the Marines can tilt the odds in their favor. Start by assigning a squad to defend the Wood Yard. Achieving a victory hinges entirely on holding this starting control point—it spawns the team's only Super Cobra. While one squad takes up defensive positions around the Wood Yard, rush another small squad across the nearby river ford in the Humvee to capture the Hill Village. Holding these two northern control points gives the Marines access to two AA turrets, allowing them to blow the Chinese Z-10 out of the sky. Use the Super Cobra to help defend the Hill Village and Wood Yard from incoming attacks. At the Hill Village form another special forces attack squad and use one of the DPVs to rush the Refinery. If the Refinery's entrance appears to be guarded, ditch the DPV and infiltrate the facility through one of the holes in the perimeter fence on the eastern side. A squad of three can convert the Refinery within a few seconds. Holding three control points causes the Chinese tickets to drain away slowly. Speed up the process by cornering them at the Power Station. By using the Super Cobra and the tanks from the Refinery and Wood Yard, you can contain the Chinese forces while inflicting heavy casualties. Rush into the Power Station facility with a DPV as soon a capture opportunity presents itself. The Super Cobra can provide cover while the ground assault squad huddles around the flagpole. Wiping out the Chinese spawn points ensures a US victory.

Chinese Strategy

Like the US, the Chinese need to figure out where they want to corner the Marines. The Power Station is ideal because it has no AA turrets, and therefore no way to defend against attack helicopters. But the Hill Village can work well too. Move all of your ground forces west to the Power Station. Meanwhile, use the Z-10 to defend the Refinery from any rush attacks. After quickly dropping some troops off at the Power Station to convert and defend it, keep moving the Type 98 and WZ 551 north toward the Wood Yard. Anti-tank troops at the Power Station can help support the assault by firing missiles down at Marine targets parked at the Wood Yard. An artillery strike can help soften up the defenses too. Blast your way into the Wood Yard with the tank and APC to convert the control point before the Marines can respond. Now focus on holding the three control points while containing the Marines to the Hill Village. Keep the Z-10 near the Refinery and Power Station to prevent breakthrough attacks on these southern control points. Continuously pound the Hill Village with artillery while closing in on the control point with tanks from the Refinery and Wood Yard. Overwhelm the control point with armor until the Hill Village is secured and the Marines have nowhere left to spawn.

32-PLAYER

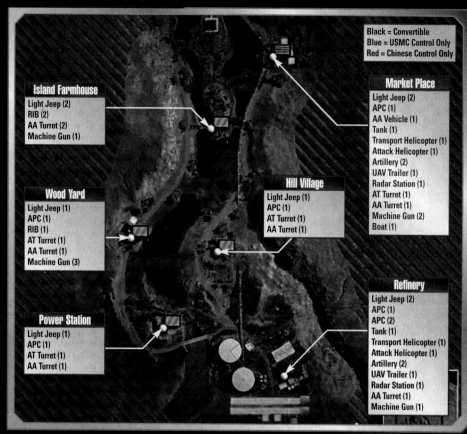

Black = Convertible
Blue = USMC Control Only
Red = Chinese Control Only

Island Farmhouse
Light Jeep (2)
RIB (2)
AA Turret (2)
Machine Gun (1)

Wood Yard
Light Jeep (1)
APC (1)
RIB (1)
AT Turret (1)
AA Turret (1)
Machine Gun (3)

Power Station
Light Jeep (1)
APC (1)
AT Turret (1)
AA Turret (1)

Hill Village
Light Jeep (1)
APC (1)
AT Turret (1)
AA Turret (1)

Market Place
Light Jeep (2)
APC (1)
AA Vehicle (1)
Tank (1)
Transport Helicopter (1)
Attack Helicopter (1)
Artillery (2)
UAV Trailer (1)
Radar Station (1)
AT Turret (1)
AA Turret (1)
Machine Gun (2)
Boat (1)

Refinery
Light Jeep (2)
APC (1)
APC (2)
Tank (1)
Transport Helicopter (1)
Attack Helicopter (1)
Artillery (2)
UAV Trailer (1)
Radar Station (1)
AA Turret (1)
Machine Gun (1)

Game Type:
Conquest Assault
Total Control Points: 6
Convertible Control Points: 5

Anti-tank troops are the best defenders against vehicle assaults. Find a good spot with views of more than one control point, then request a supply crate to stay stocked on ammo.

US Strategy

On this assault map, the Marines are the attackers and must capture a control point to stop the drain on their tickets. Unfortunately, the valley is packed with AA turrets, making the Super Cobra and Seahawk almost useless. Therefore, the Marines must use their ground assets to break out of the Market Place. As soon as the battle begins, call in an artillery strike at the Island Farmhouse and follow up by throwing all of your ground vehicles (including the M1A2 and Bradley) at this central control point. Unless the Chinese counter with tons of anti-tank troops, the defenders at the Island Farmhouse simply don't have the firepower to turn back such a heavy armor assault. Capturing this control point also takes two AA turrets away from the Chinese and allows for greater flexibility in the air. Now put the Super Cobra to work by defending the Island Farmhouse while the ground forces launch a new offensive against the Wood Yard. Consider flying some troops to the south in the Seahawk for some sneak attacks on the Power House or the Refinery. If the Marines can take the Refinery and hold it, the Chinese will have little chance to recuperate, having lost their only source of a tank and an attack helicopter, not to mention their artillery. But don't expect the Chinese to give up the Refinery without a fight. If sneaking in doesn't work, hold off the assault until the Hill Village is under Marine control, then move into the Refinery with ground vehicles. Even if other control points fall, the Refinery must be captured and held if the Marines hope to gain an upper hand.

Chinese Strategy

The Chinese begin this battle with an enormous advantage, but steps must be taken immediately to maintain this edge. First, AA turrets at the Island Farmhouse, Hill Village, Wood Yard, and Power Station must be manned to prevent the US Super Cobra and Seahawk from sneaking out of the Market Place and staging sneak attacks on the southern control points. Next, send a large contingent of anti-tank troops to the Island Farmhouse to halt the incoming onslaught of Marine vehicles approaching from the Market Place. Call in an artillery strike on the Market Place as soon as the battle begins to slow down their mobilization efforts. The Z-10 also needs to respond to the central valley to help halt any breakthroughs by the Marines—just stay clear of the Market Place's AA turret as well as the M6 Bradley. Hold out at the Island Farmhouse as long as possible. This allows the Chinese forces to consolidate their strength at one position while the Marine tickets slowly dwindle. If the Marines push past the Island Farmhouse, beware. The direction of their advance becomes more unpredictable, requiring the Chinese to spread their defensive coverage between the Hill Village and Wood Yard. The Chinese also lose the AA turrets on the island, giving the Marine helicopters a better chance of breaking out and attacking in more non-linear fashion.

Even more important than defending the Island Farmhouse is holding the Refinery. The loss of this key control point would be disastrous, so make sure its flagpole is defended by at least one competent player—the two smoke stacks are awesome sniper posts.

64-PLAYER

Black = Convertible
Blue = USMC Control Only
Red = Chinese Control Only

Docks
Light Jeep (2)
Light Jeep (3)
APC (2)
Tank (1)
RIB (2)
Transport Helicopter (1)
Artillery (3)
UAV Trailer (1)
Radar Station (1)
Machine Gun (1)

Island Farmhouse
Light Jeep (2)
RIB (2)
AA Turret (3)
Machine Gun (1)

Wood Yard
Light Jeep (1)
APC (1)
RIB (1)
Attack Helicopter (1)
AT Turret (2)
AA Turret (1)
Machine Gun (3)

Power Station
Light Jeep (2)
Tank (1)
AA Turret (1)
Machine Gun (2)

Temple
RIB (1)
AT Turret (1)

River Village
Light Jeep (1)
APC (1)
AA Vehicle (1)
RIB (2)
Machine Gun (1)

Hill Village
Light Jeep (1)
APC (1)
AA Vehicle (1)
AT Turret (1)
AA Turret (1)

USS Essex
RIB (2)
Attack Helicopter (2)
Fighter (2)
Defensive Battery (2)

Vista Point
Light Jeep (1)
AT Turret (1)

Market Place
Light Jeep (1)
APC (1)
Attack Helicopter (1)
AT Turret (1)
AA Turret (1)
Machine Gun (3)

Refinery
Light Jeep (2)
APC (1)
APC (1)
Tank (1)
Transport Helicopter (1)
Attack Helicopter (1)
Fighter (2)
Artillery (3)
UAV Trailer (1)
Radar Station (1)
AA Turret (1)
Machine Gun (1)

Game Type:
Conquest Assault
Total Control Points: 11
Convertible Control Points: 10

Use the various river fords to access both river banks. Unlike the bridges, they're wider and less likely to be booby trapped.

US Strategy

The addition of several new control points, fighter aircraft, and twice the manpower makes the 64-player map look much more complicated, but the Marines should actually have a much easier time breaking out. This time they can put their Super Cobras to work at the outset, using them to strike Chinese troops at the Vista Point, River Village, and Temple control points while ground units move in for the capture. Use the F-35Bs to shoot down the Chinese fighters and helicopters while operations wrap up in the northern valley. Due to the high concentration of AA turrets in the central valley, ground forces should spearhead the next phase of the offensive as Marines move against the Market Place and Island Farmhouse. Attack the Market Place from the mountain road to the east while swarming the Island Farmhouse with RIBs and infantry attacks from the Temple. While advancing, defenders need to be posted at each newly captured control point; the Chinese are likely to attempt counterattacks, possibly by using their Z-8 transport helicopter. Consider running a few aerial raids of your own with the Seahawks. Use them to ferry a squad or two south toward the Refinery. Hit the Refinery from the east or west, with the squad leader holding back to serve as a spawn point. If possible, use any Chinese vehicles to your advantage while converting the flag. Taking over the Refinery makes securing the remaining control points much easier to capture. Pressure the Power Station, Wood Yard, and Hill Village from the north and south until the Chinese tickets are depleted or until all control points are captured and they have nowhere else to spawn.

Chinese Strategy

As the defenders, the Chinese need to hold onto their starting positions as long as possible to maintain the drain on the US ticket count. The shortage of anti-aircraft capability in the north valley is a serious problem at the start of the battle and must be remedied before Marine helicopters and fighters make an impact. At the Refinery, get the J-10s up into the air as soon as possible to combat the influx of US air power. The Type 95 spawned at the Hill Village should also move north. Consider parking it on the central island just south of the Temple. In any case, make sure it's somewhat concealed and can cover the air space over the Vista Point, River Village, and Temple control points. Instead of attacking the Docks, troops positioned in the north valley should focus on holding the nearby control points. Deploy anti-tank troops and engineers at the three northern most control points, using mines and missiles to engage the approaching Marine vehicles. The Z-10s are also crucial in halting the Marine advance. Use them to chase down any DPVs or RIBs that manage to breakthrough the front line positions. If the Marines manage to capture one of the northern control points, consider falling back to the central valley where anti-aircraft protection is more concentrated. Hold at the Market Place and Island Farmhouse while using the J-10s and Z-10s to harass the attackers on the eastern and western roads. While defending, try to maintain a presence on both banks of the river in an effort to form an east-west defensive line across the valley. Otherwise the Marines will flank, making it difficult to hold control points. As on the smaller maps, defend the Refinery at all costs. Losing access to its fighters would give the Marines a huge advantage in the air, effectively sealing your team's fate. If necessary, always fall back the Refinery to make your last stand.

BASES AND CONTROL POINTS

USS *Essex*

Not only does the USS *Essex* provide the bulk of the Marine's aerial assets, it also helps make the northern edge of the map an enemy no-fly zone thanks to its devastating Phalanx and Sea Sparrow batteries. Both of these batteries should be manned at all times to defend the carrier from air strikes. The aft turret can even help cover the Docks to the west and Vista Point to the south. The extra air protection allows the Marines to advance without worrying about being harassed by Chinese fighters and attack helicopters. There are two separate spawn points on the carrier, dropping troops in two distinct areas. The eastern spawn point places troops on the flight deck where they can take control of an F-35B or Super Cobra. A pair of RIBs awaits the Marines at the western spawn point, allowing for immediate amphibious assaults via the river mouth. Although the USS *Essex* can't be captured, moving troops ashore can be extremely difficult if the Chinese capture the nearby Docks. Use at least one of the Super Cobras spawned here to help protect the Docks from being overrun by Chinese troops.

Maps:
64-Player Only

Adjacent Bases/ Control Points:
• Docks

USS *Essex* Assets

USMC Control	16-Player	32-Player	64-Player
RIB	—	—	2
AH-1Z	—	—	2
F-35B	—	—	2
Defensive Battery	—	—	2

Docks

At the start of the battle, the Docks are the only foothold the Marines have on the mainland, making it a critical control point for both sides. The Marines need this control point to stage deeper incursions into the valley, which is why the Chinese need to contain the Marines to the north coast—the longer they keep the Marines from capturing more control points, the more tickets the US will lose. It's not totally necessary for the Chinese to attack the Docks, but if they do, they should approach from the mountain roads just south of the control point. The Docks have no air defenses, but the nearby USS *Essex* has a surprisingly long reach, especially if its fighters are patrolling the area.

Marines spawned at the Docks have a few different options to approach the Chinese-controlled valley. The road on the western side of the facility climbs up the large mountain to the south and leads to the River Village. This is a good way to sneak up on the control point. The road to the south of the Docks branches east and west. The western branch winds up the mountain and leads to Vista Point. Due to the steep terrain, consider using DPVs when taking this road. The eastern branch of the southern road bypasses the mountain and sticks close to the river. By using bridges or river fords, vehicles moving along this road can cross over to the eastern side of the valley. The flat terrain of the eastern road makes for faster movement, but there is also less cover. Since these same roads can be used by Chinese attackers, consider using the Super Cobra to patrol the area around the mountain for incoming surprises.

Maps:
64-Player Only

Adjacent Bases/ Control Points:
• USS *Essex*
• Vista Point
• River Village

Docks Assets

USMC Control	Chinese Control	16-Player	32-Player	64-Player
DPV	Paratrooper Vehicle	—	—	2/3*
LAV-25	N/A	—	—	2
M1A2	N/A	—	—	1
RIB	RIB	—	—	2
HH-60H	N/A	—	—	1
Artillery	N/A	—	—	3
UAV Trailer	N/A	—	—	1
Radar Station	N/A	—	—	1
Machine Gun	Machine Gun	—	—	1

* = Chinese Control Only

Vista Point

This mountain-top control point is a front-line position in the battle for the valley. Located just south of the Docks, it's likely to come under Marine attack during the first few seconds of the battle. Chinese defenders should hold back in the nearby woods and cover the flagpole from a distance. Don't be surprised if a Marine Super Cobra tries to land nearby and capture the control point by either landing or hovering. An anti-tank soldier hiding in the trees can make quick work of any such attempts. The winding mountain road to the north should also be defended. Engineers can halt incoming vehicles by dropping mines across the road. The elevation also makes this mountain a good sniping spot. Snipers positioned here can fire down on the River Village and Temple. Whoever holds Vista Point has an easier time defending or attacking the surrounding control points in the valley.

Maps:
64-Player Only

Adjacent Bases/ Control Points:
- Docks
- River Village

Vista Point Assets

USMC Control	Chinese Control	16-Player	32-Player	64-Player
DPV	Paratrooper Vehicle	—	—	1
AT Turret	AT Turret	—	—	1

River Village

While the assets offered by the River Village are relatively modest, vehicles don't play a huge role in either capturing or defending this control point—this is largely an infantry fight. Marine attackers should use vehicles to rush the village from the nearby mountain road to the northwest, but infantry are needed to convert the control point. The flagpole sits in a courtyard surrounded by a perimeter wall with narrow, arched entry points to the north, east, and south. Infantry positioned on the eastern side of the courtyard can cover all entry points while using the nearby house for cover and concealment. Therefore, savvy attackers should lob grenades over the wall before entering the courtyard in an attempt to blast hidden defenders. But attackers can also contest the control point by standing outside the courtyard on the southern side of the perimeter wall, near the cluster of birch trees. Even the courtyard's southern-facing machine gun may have a difficult time spotting attackers hiding here. To prevent such a stealthy capture attempt, defenders should place a claymore or two around these trees. If the Marines capture the River Village, they'll have access to an M6 Bradley, hindering Chinese air operations over the northern valley control points. This allows the Marine advance to gather some much needed momentum for the push south.

Maps:
64-Player Only

Adjacent Bases/ Control Points:
- Docks
- Vista Point
- Temple

River Village Assets

USMC Control	Chinese Control	16-Player	32-Player	64-Player
DPV	Paratrooper Vehicle	—	—	1
LAV-25	WZ 551	—	—	1
M6 Bradley	N/A	—	—	1
RIB	RIB	—	—	2
Machine Gun	Machine Gun	—	—	1

Temple

Sitting on the northern end of an island in the middle of the river, the Temple can be a tough control point to capture, especially if it's well defended. Most attackers make the mistake of going right for the northern dock in an RIB. Not only is it difficult to physically step out onto the dock, but it's covered by an AT turret. It's better to land on the eastern or western slopes of the island. Even then, there's only one accessible entry point into the Temple facility, via the steps to the south. Support troops within the Temple compound can simply train their machine guns on this chokepoint to mow down attackers. Claymores can also be a useful defensive measure near this entry point. Since it's so easy for defenders to lock down this control point, attackers may want to consider an airborne assault using helicopters and parachutes. While holding this control point, defenders can also help out at the River Village, Vista Point, and the Market Place—snipers and anti-tank troops are very effective at covering the surrounding control points. The AT turret on the docks is also extremely useful for covering the roads along both river banks as well as blasting incoming enemy RIBs.

Temple Assets

USMC Control	Chinese Control	16-Player	32-Player	64-Player
RIB	RIB	—	—	1
AT Turret	AT Turret	—	—	1

Maps:
64-Player Only

Adjacent Bases/ Control Points:
• River Village
• Market Place

Market Place

On the 32-player map, the Market Place serves as the Marine base and cannot be captured by the Chinese. In these games, the Marines need to use the vehicles provided here to quickly capture the control points to the south. The Seahawk and Super Cobra are the quickest way to transport troops. On the 64-player map, the Market Place is just another central control point, and can be captured by both sides. Its transport helicopter is useful for staging air assaults on the surrounding control points. This is also home to the northernmost AA turret, a valuable asset for both sides. Use it to defend the northern and central valley from enemy air strikes. On the ground, the most likely avenue of attack is from the main road running along the western side of the control point. Accordingly, the Market Place's machine guns and AT turret are lined up along the western wall to cover the road. However, another road runs along the hill to the east and may be used by Marine attackers approaching from the Docks. Chinese defenders should place mines on this road and position anti-tank troops nearby to prevent a rear sneak attack.

Maps: 32- and 64-Player

Adjacent Bases/ Control Points:
• Temple
• Island Farmhouse

Market Place Assets

USMC Control	Chinese Control	16-Player	32-Player*	64-Player
DPV	Paratrooper Vehicle	—	2	1
LAV-25	WZ 551	—	1	1
M6 Bradley	N/A	—	1	—
M1A2	N/A	—	1	—
HH-60H	Z-8	—	1	1**
AH-1Z	N/A	—	1	—
Artillery	N/A	—	2	—
UAV Trailer	N/A	—	1	—
Radar Station	N/A	—	1	—
AT Turret	AT Turret	—	1	1
AA Turret	AA Turret	—	1	1
Machine Gun	Machine Gun	—	2	3
RIB	N/A	—	1	—

* = USMC Control Only
** = Chinese Control Only

In general, attackers should initiate an artillery strike on the Market Place just before they arrive. With no accessible building interiors, the defenders have no way to protect themselves from the incoming shells.

Island Farmhouse

It may not look like much, but the Island Farmhouse is one of the most critical control points on both the 32- and 64-player maps. Sitting on the southern tip of the same island as the Temple, this control point doesn't produce much in terms of vehicles, but its multiple AA turrets play a huge part in controlling the skies over the central valley. On the 64-player map, the Chinese should man these turrets early to prevent Marine aircraft from reaching the southern control points.

While relatively safe from air attack, the Island Farmhouse is open to ground assaults from multiple directions. There are two river fords at the island's center (to the north) allowing vehicles from the eastern and western banks to move in on the control point. Though it's possible to mine these fords, it's better to position anti-tank troops on the nearby hill. Near the control point itself are two more crossings. To the east is another river ford and to the west is a wooden bridge. The bridge can be blown with C4, but the eastern river ford needs to be covered by more infantry. Amphibious assaults (by APC or RIB) are also a threat. Since the control point can be hit from so many different angles, focus on simply defending the flagpole, preferably from the hilltop to the north. A few mines and claymores clustered around the flag can buy defenders a bit more time.

> **Maps: 32- and 64-Player**
>
> **Adjacent Bases/ Control Points:**
> - Temple
> - Market Place
> - Hill Village
> - Wood Yard

Island Farmhouse Assets

USMC Control	Chinese Control	16-Player	32-Player	64-Player
DPV	Paratrooper Vehicle	—	2	2
RIB	RIB	—	2	2
AA Turret	AA Turret	—	2	3
Machine Gun	Machine Gun	—	1	1

> **TIP** When piloting a plane or helicopter, always be aware of who controls the Island Farmhouse. If it's held by the enemy, avoid flying over it—its AA turrets are a huge threat to any aircraft.

Wood Yard

The Wood Yard is another control point open to attack from various directions. However, its well-balanced and well-positioned defensive features make an assault on this control point a challenge. Attackers most likely will use the main road running along the western bank of the river, but the road can be covered by the two AT turrets on the northern and southern edges of the control point. The open terrain to the north and south make for some intense long-range engagements. Defenders should also watch for vehicles moving across the river ford to the southeast. Enemies attacking from the Hill Village are likely to use this crossing. Air strikes can be thwarted with the AA turret to the north. On the 16-player map the Wood Yard is the Marine starting position. As their only source of a Super Cobra they should take great measures to defend this control point. On the larger maps, the Wood Yard plays a smaller role, but its strong defensive features still make it a valuable control point for both sides. The Chinese gain a Z-10 when holding this control point on the 64-player map.

> **Maps: All**
>
> **Adjacent Bases/ Control Points:**
> - Island Farmhouse
> - Hill Village
> - Power Station

Wood Yard Assets

USMC Control	Chinese Control	16-Player	32-Player	64-Player
DPV	Paratrooper Vehicle	—	1	1
HMMWV	NJ 2046	1	—	—
LAV-25	WZ 551	1	1	1
M1A2	Type 98	1	—	—
RIB	RIB	—	1	1
AH-1Z	Z-10	1*	—	1**
Artillery	N/A	2	—	—
UAV Trailer	N/A	1	—	—
Radar Station	N/A	1	—	—
AT Turret	AT Turret	2	1	2
AA Turret	AA Turret	1	1	1
Machine Gun	Machine Gun	3	3	3

*= USMC Control Only
** = Chinese Control Only

Hill Village

Just across the river from the Wood Yard is the Hill Village. Although there are two village centers here, the flagpole and all of the vehicles and defensive assets are positioned in the village courtyard to the north. That doesn't mean the southern village courtyard should be ignored, though. It sits on a higher hill and can be used to either attack or defend the control point from a distance—enemies approaching from the Refinery usually attack from this direction. Other attackers will most likely approach from the main road on the river's east bank. Defensive efforts should be focused around the flag first and expand outward as more manpower is available. Infantry can cover the flag from within either the southern or northern courtyard. The wooden structure just north of the flag is a good hiding spot, with its shadow providing great concealment but not great cover. The nearby AT turret is

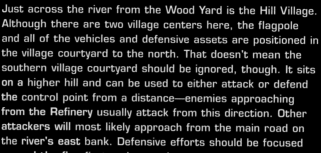

Maps: All

Adjacent Bases/ Control Points:

- Wood Yard
- Power Station
- Refinery

also useful for surprising enemy vehicles that rush into the courtyard. On all maps this control point is also an important anti-aircraft site, with an AA turret positioned right next to the flag. On the 64-player map, the Chinese get a Type 95 here too. Instead of leaving it here, it should be driven to the north and used to defend the north valley control points from air strikes.

Hill Village Assets

USMC Control	Chinese Control	16-Player	32-Player	64-Player
DPV	Paratrooper Vehicle	2	1	1
LAV-25	WZ 551	—	1	1
N/A	Type 95	—	—	1
AT Turret	AT Turret	1	1	1
AA Turret	AA Turret	1	1	1

Power Station

The Power Station is located at the north end of the valley, sitting on the Refinery's western flank. This large facility has two main entrances to the north and south. The road to the north branches just outside the gate and leads to either the Wood Yard or across the wooden bridge toward the Hill Village or Refinery. On the southern end of the Power Plant is a small concrete dam. Taking this road also leads to the Refinery. The wooden bridge to the north can be demolished with C4 or bombs, but the dam can't be destroyed. Keep this in mind, especially if the enemy holds the Refinery or Hill Village. Two more less-visible entrances are located to the north and west, through holes in the perimeter fence. Defenders should watch for infantry infiltrating the facility at these points. Placing a claymore at each breach point is a nice hands-off approach to defending these areas. On the 16- and 32-player maps, the AT turret can

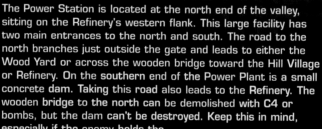

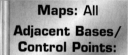

Maps: All

Adjacent Bases/ Control Points:

- Wood Yard
- Hill Village
- Refinery

cover all entry points—it can even fire through the hole in the western fence. An AA turret is available here in the 32- and 64-player maps, positioned outside the main gate to the north, overlooking the valley. Defenders are safest when taking cover in the small concrete building at the facility's southeast corner. From here they can fire out the windows at any attackers rushing toward the flag. It also protects them from artillery strikes. The Power Station's roof can also be accessed via a ladder on the north side. Snipers and anti-tank troops can use the boost in altitude to pick off enemies at long range.

Power Station Assets

USMC Control	Chinese Control	16-Player	32-Player	64-Player
DPV	Paratrooper Vehicle	2	1	2
LAV-25	WZ 551	—	1	—
M1A2	Type 98	—	—	1
AT Turret	AT Turret	1	1	—
AA Turret	AA Turret	—	1	1
Machine Gun	Machine Gun	—	—	2

Refinery

On all map sizes, this sprawling industrial facility serves as the Chinese base. But remember, since these are assault maps, the Refinery can always be captured by the Marines. Due to its size, the Refinery has two spawn points allowing troops easy access to the control point's two distinct areas. The northern spawn point places troops near the airfield where they can board a fighter, helicopter, or man the AA turret north of the runways. Most of the ground vehicles can be accessed quickly by spawning at the southern control point. The large warehouse building just north of the flagpole houses a couple of vehicles.

Maps: All

Adjacent Bases/ Control Points:
- Hill Village
- Refinery

Since the main road to the south is the most likely avenue of attack, defensive efforts should focus on securing the facility's front gate. If necessary, use mines or C4 charges to deny entry to enemy vehicles. Use anti-tank troops and vehicles to fire on incoming enemies at the lower elevations to the south before they can even reach the main gate. While it's relatively easy to close the Refinery to enemy vehicles, infantry can still break through by taking advantage of the porous perimeter fence. There are holes in the fence on the eastern and western sides. To prevent the flag from being converted by such stealthy attacks, position snipers on the two huge smokestacks. From their elevated circular walkways, snipers can pick off any troops loitering near the flagpole. If enemy vehicles are a problem, the defenders should position anti-tank troops on these smokestacks too.

Refinery Assets

USMC Control	Chinese Control	16-Player	32-Player	64-Player
DPV	Paratrooper Vehicle	1	2	2
HMMWV	NJ 2046	1	—	—
LAV-25	WZ 551	1	1*/2**	1*/1**
M1A2	Type 98	1	1**	1**
HH-60H	Z-8	—	1	1
N/A	Jian J-10	—	—	2
N/A	Z-10	1	1	1
N/A	Artillery	2	2	3
N/A	UAV Trailer	1	1	1
N/A	Radar Station	1	1	1
AT Turret	AT Turret	1	—	—
AA Turret	AA Turret	1	1	1
Machine Gun	Machine Gun	—	1	1

* = USMC Control Only
** = Chinese Control Only

DRAGON VALLEY TACTICS

Helicopter Takedown

For defenders and attackers alike, attack helicopters pose a huge threat. Manning one of the many AA turrets available on this map is the quickest way to deal with these threats. Wait until the targeted helicopter has dropped its flares before firing a missile. Once the flares are out of view, wait for a new lock, then fire a couple of missiles to knock the chopper out of the sky.

In a pinch, anti-tank troops can use their guided missiles to shoot down helicopters too. For best results, wait until the chopper is moving away from you before firing—you don't want to give away your position. The slower the helicopter moves the easier it will be to hit. A hovering helicopter is a sitting duck.

On the 16- and 32-player maps, fighter aircraft are not available, so consider using your own attack helicopter to shoot down the enemy's. It's the pilot's job to get on the enemy helicopter's tail while the gunner shreds it with the cannon.

Incoming!

Since most of the control points are open, with little overhead cover, both sides should use artillery as frequently as possible. This is the best way to soften up a control point before an assault.

If you find yourself on the business end of an art forget whatever you were doing and find some fo shelter. Drop prone when you have a roof over y wait out the storm of exploding shells.

Bridge Booby Trap

Your enemies are less likely to cross a bridge if they spot C4 charges stuck to its surface, so try hiding the charges underneath the bridge. You'll need either an APC or a boat, as well as a buddy. Make sure you climb on top of the vehicle before you and your teammate take off—once you're out on the water, you can't climb up on top of your vehicle; you'll just exit into the water. Have your buddy park right beneath a bridge so you can place the charges.

Depending on the height of the bridge, you may jump to stick the C4 on the bottom. You can al charges on the upper portions of the cross sup Either way, the C4 needs to be as close to the surface as possible—use all five charges to ens demolition.

Once the charges are placed, retreat to a safe location and wait for an enemy vehicle to cross. When the vehicle reaches the spot where you placed the charges, detonate the explosives. Not only does this destroy enemy vehicles, but it also blasts a huge hole in the bridge.

FUSHE PASS

China's rich mining areas in the northeastern highlands have become contested by rapidly deploying US and Chinese forces. The narrow canyons carved into this region channel both forces into inevitable head-on confrontations as each seeks to secure the prized uranium mines with their advancing forces. In the context of this double assault, success will favor the bold, given the constrained nature of this rugged battlefield.

16-PLAYER

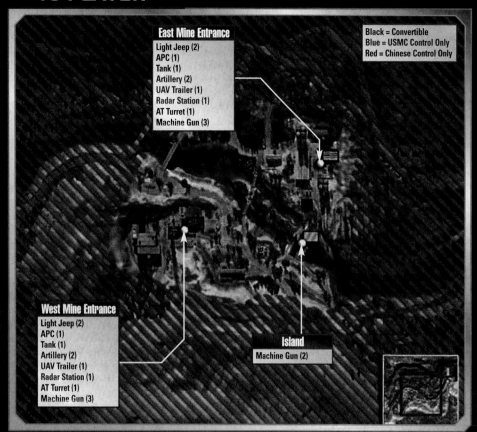

East Mine Entrance

Light Jeep (2)
APC (1)
Tank (1)
Artillery (2)
UAV Trailer (1)
Radar Station (1)
AT Turret (1)
Machine Gun (3)

Black = Convertible
Blue = USMC Control Only
Red = Chinese Control Only

West Mine Entrance

Light Jeep (2)
APC (1)
Tank (1)
Artillery (2)
UAV Trailer (1)
Radar Station (1)
AT Turret (1)
Machine Gun (3)

Island

Machine Gun (2)

Game Type:
Double Assault
Total Control Points: 3
Convertible Control Points: 3

This high ground south of the East Mine Entrance dominates both this control point and the Island.

US Strategy

There are three control points on this map. Because the US and Chinese each have one at the start, that leaves only one up for grabs. Whoever can take control of the Island will have an early advantage. Therefore, the US should send some troops in a light jeep racing out of the East Mine Entrance to get to the control point first. At the same time, send another group west, then across the double wooden bridges toward the Chinese base at the West Mine Entrance. While this spreads your force thin, it is a daring strategy to gain control of all three positions within the game's first few minutes. If you are successful, victory is yours. While going for the enemy base is daring and may not work, if you can at least get the important Island. Because the enemy must approach the flagpole on foot, have a sniper take up a position on the northeastern hills where the Mountain Lookout control point is in the 64-player game. While lying prone here, a sniper can cover the flagpole while keeping a location that is difficult for the enemy to spot and engage. Keep a few troops at your base, then go for the enemy base to win.

Chinese Strategy

The Chinese have a tougher time getting to the Island before the US. However, don't give up this control point without a fight. Send a couple of soldiers in a fast jeep to slow the US and keep it from taking control of the Island. Meanwhile, the rest of your team loads up in the tank and APC and heads across the double wooden bridges to the East Mine Entrance to take it from the US. With control of both bases, the Chinese will have access to the vehicles and the US will be stuck with a central control point and no vehicle spawns. Then it is just a matter of time until you can trap the US on the Island, hit it with artillery strikes, then take the Island to win the game.

32-PLAYER

Bridge Camp
Light Jeep (3)
APC (2)
Machine Gun (1)

East Mine Entrance
Light Jeep (3)
AA Turret (1)
AT Turret (1)
Machine Gun (3)

Black = Convertible
Blue = USMC Control Only
Red = Chinese Control Only

Upper Camp
Light Jeep (3)
APC (1)
AAV (1)
Tank (1)
Attack Helicopter (1)
RIB (2)
Artillery (2)
UAV Trailer (1)
Radar Station (1)
AA Turret (1)
AT Turret (1)
Machine Gun (3)

Powerplant
Light Jeep (4)
APC (1)
AAV (1)
Tank (1)
Attack Helicopter (1)
Artillery (2)
UAV Trailer (1)
Radar Station (1)
AA Turret (1)
AT Turret (1)
Machine Gun (3)

West Mine Entrance
Light Jeep (3)
AA Turret (1)
AT Turret (1)
Machine Gun (3)

Security HQ
Light Jeep (3)
APC Turret (2)
Machine Gun (1)

Game Type: Conquest Head-On
Total Control Points: 6
Convertible Control Points: 4

The attack helicopters in this mission make a difference when used effectively to engage enemy vehicles along the narrow roads and bridges.

US Strategy

This game is different from the 16-player game. Each side begins with a base which the enemy cannot capture. Between the two sides are four control points as well as several points for crossing the river canyon which divides the map in two. The team that captures over half of the control will cause the enemy's tickets to start counting down. Therefore, the Marines must begin by sending two teams in light jeeps to capture both the East and West Mine Entrances. A third smaller team can then go for the Security Headquarters. Because you can't capture the Upper Camp, you do not need access to it. However, you must limit the enemy from sending forces to attack you from this base. Therefore, a team with anti-tank soldiers and engineers should take the transport helicopter to the mine and cover the western dam south of the upper camp. Anti-tank soldiers positioned on the hills south of the eastern dam can take out enemies trying to cross the dam or the nearby bridge. Concentrate on boxing in the enemy around the Bridge Camp and make your assaults from the East Mine Camp's direction. Or you can hold the four control points and wait for the enemy's tickets to reach zero from taking losses while trying to break out of your gauntlet as well as from the countdown.

Chinese Strategy

The Chinese are at an initial disadvantage because their base is farther from the neutral control points than the US base is. While the Bridge Camp is easy and a must, the Chinese should also rush some troops to take control of the East Mine Entrance. Also make an effort for the West Mine Entrance to make the US pay for taking it. By capturing the control points north of the river, you can prevent the US from making your tickets count down. Cover or blow the bridges from the dam east along the river. Use the dam and the western bridge near the Upper Camp for crossing the river. The hill west of the West Mine Entrance offers a great location for you to fire down on the enemy at this control point, letting you clear the defenses before rushing in an assault force to take it. While holding the river crossings, the Chinese must advance east along the roads south of the river, pushing the enemy toward the Powerplant. Don't try to take the Powerplant, because it cannot be captured. However, a squad in the hills overlooking this can engage enemy units when they spawn, making life more difficult for the Marines.

64-PLAYER

Black = Convertible
Blue = USMC Control Only
Red = Chinese Control Only

Upper Camp
Light Jeep (2)
APC (2)
AAV (1)
Tank (1)
Transport Helicopter (1)
RIB (2)
Machine Gun (1)

Bridge Camp
Light Jeep (2)
APC (1)
AA Turret (1)
Machine Gun (1)

East Mine Entrance
Light Jeep (2)
AA Turret (1)
AT Turret (1)
Machine Gun (3)

US Airfield
Light Jeep (5)
Transport Helicopter (2)
Attack Helicopter (1)
Fighter (2)
RIB (2)
Artillery (3)
UAV Trailer (1)
Radar Station (1)
AA Turret (1)
AT Turret (2)

Chinese Airfield
Light Jeep (5)
Transport Helicopter (2)
Attack Helicopter (1)
Fighter (2)
RIB (2)
Artillery (3)
UAV Trailer (1)
Radar Station (1)
AA Turret (1)
AT Turret (2)

Mountain Lookout
Light Jeep (2)
APC (2)
AAV (1)
AT Turret (1)
Machine Gun (2)

Canyon Guard Post
Light Jeep (1)
APC (2)
AT Turret (1)
Machine Gun (2)

West Mine Entrance
Light Jeep (2)
AA Turret (1)
AT Turret (1)
Machine Gun (3)

Security HQ
Light Jeep (2)
APC (1)
AA Turret (1)
Machine Gun (1)

Powerplant
Light Jeep (3)
APC (2)
Tank (1)
Transport Helicopter (1)
Machine Gun (3)

Game Type:
Conquest Head-On

Total Control Points: 10

Convertible Control Points: 8

Airpower is important. Load the transport helicopters and fly your troops to take over the neutral control points before the enemy can get there.

US Strategy

This map begins as a race to see who can take the most control points in the game's first few minutes. Because of the geography and the US's starting location in the far northeast at the US Airfield, the US is at a disadvantage. To get to the closest control points, the US must travel along some steep winding roads. Therefore, if the Marines want to dominate at the start, forget the ground vehicles and use your aircraft. Get the fighters in the air to shoot down enemy aircraft and harass Chinese ground vehicles while your helicopters load. Drop individual soldiers by parachute at the Mountain Lookout, East Mine Entrance, Powerplant, and Security Headquarters to grab them for the US. Send squads to the Bridge Camp and the West Mine Entrance to capture these control points and form a front against the Chinese advance. These squads should include anti-tank troops as well as engineers for placing mines along the roads leading to these control points. If you are successful, the US will hold seven control points to the Chinese's three. From the Bridge Camp, advance on the Upper Camp to secure the river's northern side and blow the western bridge to make it easier to defend. Position your AAV to cover aircraft taking off from the Chinese Airfield and block their ground vehicles near the Canyon Guard Post as well as the road running along the river's south side. While holding the Chinese in place, attrition will do the rest and give you the victory.

Chinese Strategy

The Chinese base is in the better position at the start. The Chinese must use this advantage to grab as much territory as possible in the first few minutes. Send teams in light jeeps and other vehicles to capture the Upper Camp, Bridge Camp, Canyon Guard Post, and West Mine Entrance. Get your fighters in the air to not only shoot down US helicopters transporting troops to control points, but also to take out the eastern bridge near the US Airfield to prevent the US from sending ground vehicles across to the river's southern side at this point. That will allow you to send troops in your transport helicopters to take the Security Headquarters and Powerplant. This boxes in the US in the map's northeast corner. Taking the other two convertible control points is tough because the US will be concentrating there to get ready for assaulting your positions. However, you can easily cover the ford near the Island and the wooden bridges as well as the road leading east from the Bridge Camp. Because the US will have to attack to stop their tickets from counting down, assume a defensive strategy and hold them in place while pounding these control points with artillery and air attacks to cause casualties.

BASES AND CONTROL POINTS

Chinese Airfield

The Chinese Airfield is the main base for the Chinese in the 64-player game. It features two spawn points. The point by the Airfield contains the aircraft and helicopters as well as some light jeeps. The other spawn point is by the river where are RIB and light jeeps. Even though the US can't capture this base, leave a few soldiers here to guard against raids because airpower is an important asset; you don't want the enemy destroying it on the ground. The two AT Turrets are positioned to cover the roads along the river and from the Canyon Guard Post respectively, while the AA Turret is near the aircraft hangars.

Maps:
64-Player Only

Adjacent Bases/ Control Points:
- Canyon Guard Post
- Upper Camp

Chinese Airfield Assets

Chinese Control	16-Player	32-Player	64-Player
Paratrooper Jeep	—	—	5
Z-8	—	—	2
WZ-10	—	—	1
J-10	—	—	2
RIB	—	—	2
Artillery	—	—	3
UAV	—	—	1
Radar	—	—	1
AT Turret	—	—	2
AA Turret	—	—	1

Upper Camp

The Upper Camp is the Chinese base for the 32-player game, as well as an important control point in the 64-player game because it helps secure the map's northwestern corner. For this spot, cover the road leading along the river toward the Chinese Airfield. Also, a high road from the Upper Camp takes you to the Mountain Lookout as well as the East Mine Entrance. To defend this control point, watch the nearby dam, and have control of the Bridge Camp because this other control point is the eastern access to the Upper Camp. This control point offers a helipad in both the 32- and 64-player games where you can bring in helicopters for repair and to reload the ammo for attack helicopters.

Maps: 32- and 64-Player

Adjacent Bases/ Control Points:
- Bridge Camp
- Chinese Airfield

Upper Camp Assets

USMC Control	Chinese Control	16-Player	32-Player	64-Player
DPV	Paratrooper Jeep	—	3*	2
LAV-25	WZ 551	—	1*	2
M6 Bradley	Tunguska	—	1*	1*
M1A2	Type 98	—	1*	1
HH-60H	Z-8	—	—	1
AH-1Z	WZ-10	—	1*	—
RIB	RIB	—	2*	2
N/A	Artillery	—	2	
N/A	UAV	—	1	
N/A	Radar	—	1	
AT Turret	AT Turret	—	1	
AA Turret	AA Turret	—	1	
Machine Gun	Machine Gun	—	3	1

= Chinese Control Only

West Mine Entrance

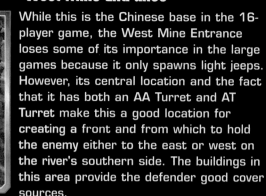

While this is the Chinese base in the 16-player game, the West Mine Entrance loses some of its importance in the large games because it only spawns light jeeps. However, its central location and the fact that it has both an AA Turret and AT Turret make this a good location for creating a front and from which to hold the enemy either to the east or west on the river's southern side. The buildings in this area provide the defender good cover sources.

Maps: All

Adjacent Bases/ Control Points:
- Bridge Camp
- Canyon Guard Post
- Island
- Security HQ

West Mine Entrance Assets

USMC Control	Chinese Control	16-Player	32-Player	64-Player
DPV	Paratrooper Jeep	2	3	2
LAV-25	WZ 551	1	—	—
M1A2	Type 98	1	—	—
N/A	Artillery	2	—	—
N/A	UAV	1	—	—
N/A	Radar	1	—	—
AT Turret	AT Turret	1	1	1
AA Turret	AA Turret	—	1	1
Machine Gun	Machine Gun	3	3	3

East Mine Entrance

This is the Marine's base in the 16-player game and serves the same purpose as the East Mine Entrance for the map's northern side. While it offers an AA Turret and an AT Turret, this control point is not as effective as a defensive position because it can be easily bypassed by the upper road. Furthermore, the Mountain Lookout dominates this position, allowing enemy troops at this higher control point to fire down on the East Mine Entrance and make this point untenable. Therefore, to hold the East Mine Entrance in the 64-player game, you must also hold the Mountain Lookout.

Maps: All

Adjacent Bases/ Control Points:
- Bridge Camp
- Island
- Mountain Lookout

East Mine Entrance Assets

USMC Control	Chinese Control	16-Player	32-Player	64-Player
DPV	Paratrooper Jeep	2	3	2
LAV-25	WZ 551	1	—	—
M1A2	Type 98	1	—	—
Artillery	N/A	2	—	—
UAV	N/A	1	—	—
Radar	N/A	1	—	—
AT Turret	AT Turret	1	1	1
AA Turret	AA Turret	—	1	1
Machine Gun	Machine Gun	3	3	3

Powerplant

The Powerplant is the US base for the 32-player game and provides the heavy firepower. You can also use its helipad in the 64-player game for taking care of helicopters, even though none spawn here during the larger game. This control point is the farthest east on the river's southern side. Unless there is an enemy held control point to the east, defend this position from the Security Headquarters west of it.

Maps: 32- and 64-Player

Adjacent Bases/Control Points:
- East Mine Entrance
- Security HQ
- US Airfield

Powerplant Assets

USMC Control	Chinese Control	16-Player	32-Player	64-Player
DPV	Paratrooper Jeep	—	4*	3
LAV-25	WZ 551	—	1*	2
M6 Bradley	Tunguska	—	1*	—
M1A2	Type 98	—	1*	1
HH-60H	Z-8	—	—	1
AH-1Z	N/A	—	1	—
Artillery	N/A	—	2	—
UAV	N/A	—	1	—
Radar	N/A	—	1	—
AT Turret	AT Turret	—	1	—
AA Turret	AA Turret	—	1	—
Machine Gun	Machine Gun	—	3	3

* = USMC Control Only

US Airfield

In the map's northeast corner, this is the US base for the 64-player game. Because there are no direct or easy road routes from this position to other control points, the air power here is more important than the ground vehicles here and the RIBs are worthless. Man the AA Turret near the helipads because you can expect attacks by enemy aircraft. The two AT Turrets guard the main road leading through the village to the Airfield. The US Airfield has three spawn points. One is by the helipads, the second is in the village, and the third is down by the boat dock on the river.

Maps: 64-Player Only

Adjacent Bases/Control Points:
- Mountain Lookout
- Powerplant

US Airfield Assets

USMC Control	16-Player	32-Player	64-Player
DPV	—	—	5
HH-60H	—	—	2
AH-1Z	—	—	1
F-18E/F	—	—	2
RIB	—	—	2
Artillery	—	—	3
UAV	—	—	1
Radar	—	—	1
AT Turret	—	—	2
AA Turret	—	—	1

Bridge Camp

While it may not spawn a lot of powerful vehicles, the Bridge Camp is the key to defending the Upper Camp. From this point, you can cover the nearby bridge and dam as well as the roads running north and south of the river. The Chinese must hold this control point to secure the two bases they need to hold in the west. The weakness to this control point is the upper road. Keep troops up there to prevent enemy forces from bypassing the Bridge Camp or from firing down on your troops there.

Maps: 32- and 64-Player

Adjacent Bases/ Control Points:
- East Mine Entrance
- Upper Camp
- West Mine Entrance

Bridge Camp Assets

USMC Control	Chinese Control	16-Player	32-Player	64-Player
DPV	Paratrooper Jeep	—	3	2
LAV-25	WZ 551	—	2	1
AA Turret	AA Turret	—	—	1
Machine Gun	Machine Gun	—	1	1

Canyon Guard Post

This control point defends the access to the southeastern Chinese Airfield. Its AT Turret is able to engage enemy vehicles headed from the West Mine Entrance. The Chinese should keep at least one soldier here to defend this control point. However, to hold against eastern US attacks, the West Mine Entrance is a better position. Use the APCs here to drive along the upper road leading to the Security Headquarters and the Powerplant.

Maps: 64-Player Only

Adjacent Bases/ Control Points:
- Chinese Airfield
- West Mine Entrance

Canyon Guard Post Assets

USMC Control	Chinese Control	16-Player	32-Player	64-Player
DPV	Paratrooper Jeep	—	—	1
LAV-25	WZ 551	—	—	2
AT Turret	AT Turret	—	—	1
Machine Gun	Machine Gun	—	—	2

Security Headquarters

As with some of the other control points, the Security Headquarters guards the access to another control point—this time the Powerplant. It is also a good spot for the US to use as a defensive position against attacks from the west because the roads from both the Canyon Guard Post and West Mine Entrance converge here. Use the AT Turret to take out enemy vehicles coming down the road before they get too close and try to take this control point from you.

Maps: 32- and 64-Player

Adjacent Bases/ Control Points:
- East Mine Entrance
- Powerplant
- West Mine Entrance

Security Headquarters Assets

USMC Control	Chinese Control	16-Player	32-Player	64-Player
DPV	Paratrooper Jeep	—	3	2
LAV-25	WZ 551	—	2	1
AA Turret	AA Turret	—	—	1
Machine Gun	Machine Gun	—	1	1

Island

This position is only a control point in the 16-player game. Unlike other control points, you must approach the flagpole here on foot because vehicles cannot drive up the stairs to the platform where it is. There are a couple of ladders leading from the ground level down to the river below. However, there is no real need to use them. Because it is low, the Island can be dominated by soldiers on the hills overlooking it.

Maps: 16-Player Only

Adjacent Bases/ Control Points:
- East Mine Entrance
- West Mine Entrance

Island Assets

USMC Control	Chinese Control	16-Player	32-Player	64-Player
Machine Gun	Machine Gun	2	—	—

Mountain Lookout

This is an important control point to whichever side wants to control the East Mine Entrance because the Mountain Lookout overlooks the lower control point. While it provides several vehicles, the US AAV is the most important. The Marines need to capture this control point so they can have access to this vehicle. They can use it to help protect the US Airfield from Chinese aircraft flying past this control point on the way to their targets. To help defend this position, use the AT Turret, which has a great field of fire down the road up the hill to the Mountain Lookout.

Maps: 64-Player Only

Adjacent Bases/ Control Points:
- East Mine Entrance
- US Airfield

Mountain Lookout Assets

USMC Control	Chinese Control	16-Player	32-Player	64-Player
DPV	Paratrooper Jeep	—	—	2
LAV-25	WZ 551	—	—	2
M6 Bradley	N/A	—	—	1
AT Turret	AT Turret	—	—	1
Machine Gun	Machine Gun	—	—	2

FUSHE PASS TACTICS

Air Supremacy

In the 64-player game, airpower plays a key role. Each side has fighters as well as helicopters that allow them to quickly get around and attack anywhere on the map. Therefore, if you can prevent the enemy from using its air units, or limit their use, you will gain an advantage over the enemy.

Fighters' speed and flares are their main defenses. Their main job is to shoot down enemy aircraft. However, they are useful for bombing bridges and creating bottlenecks at the dams which you can't destroy. While helicopters fly slower and are more vulnerable to enemy fire, they can use terrain masking to stay alive. The steep sides of the river canyon provide great cover for helicopters traveling across the map. Attack helicopters can hover down by the river, pop up to fire at targets using the gunner-controlled TV-guided missiles, then drop to the river for safety.

Use the AAVs as well as the AA Turrets for air defense. By dropping a supply crate by the AAV, you can ensure that it stays loaded with ammo. A nearby anti-tank soldier can provide cover for the AAV from enemy ground vehicles.

Road Race

In the larger games, there is a lot of territory to cover. Because the 32-player game only offers a single helicopter, this makes ground

Because each control point spawns vehicles—mainly light jeeps—you can use these new vehicles to go after other control points. In fact, most control

vehicles more important than in the 64-player game. Because these larger games are conquest head-on, you must capture more control points than your opponent as quickly as possible. Therefore, send teams of troops in light jeeps to get there first, then follow with APCs and tanks to help secure what you have captured.

points do not require you to get out of your vehicle. If you are alone in a light jeep, move to the top gunner position so you can engage enemies who might approach while you are waiting for your flag to rise.

Height Advantage

Many of the control points are next to one of the steep valley walls. This provides an excellent position from which a sniper or other enemy troops can fire on the base. In the larger games, players should have some type of patrol that watches for enemies above control points.

Because the control points are also spawn points for both troops and vehicles, the terrain of this map makes it a paradise for those players who like to camp. With the camouflage suit worn by snipers, these troops prone in the grass are impossible to spot visually from the ground. You can also use anti-tank troops for taking out vehicles when they spawn or become occupied. However, a sniper overlooking a base can be more useful as an observer, letting the team know what the enemy is doing and in which direction they are headed. Use observers to call in artillery strikes, as well.

SONGHUA STALEMATE

Newly formed Active Component brigades of the US Marines advance from the Russian plains into the territories of the People's Republic of China, where rapidly deployed Chinese forces mass to counter the assault. The stalemate situation along the Songhua River has deteriorated into reciprocal assaults by both sides, each seeking to capture this vital transportation artery. Stakes are high in this double assault that involves control of the main gateway to Southern Manchuria.

16-PLAYER

North Island
Light Jeep (1)
RIB (1)
Machine Gun (3)

Black = Convertible
Blue = USMC Control Only
Red = Chinese Control Only

West Perimeter
Light Jeep (1)
APC (1)
APC (1)
Transport Helicopter (1)
RIB (2)
Artillery (2)
UAV Trailer (1)
Radar Station (1)
AA Turret (1)
AT Turret (1)
Machine Gun (2)

Central Front
Light Jeep (1)
APC (1)
APC (1)
Transport Helicopter (1)
RIB (2)
Artillery (2)
UAV Trailer (1)
Radar Station (1)
AA Turret (1)
AT Turret (1)
Machine Gun (2)

Temple
Light Jeep (1)
RIB (1)
Machine Gun (4)

Game Type:
Double Assault
Total Control Points: 4
Convertible Control Points: 4

The one heavy tank serves as your heavy firepower. In the 16-player game, it is much more usable and closer to the fight than in the larger games, so be sure to make good use of it.

US Strategy

The key to this small map is speed, and the team that gets there first wins. The US base is located at the West Perimeter. Right at the start, send troops in an RIB toward the temple to secure it before the Chinese can. Take along some anti-tank troops to sink enemy RIBs and APCs that head your way. Meanwhile, send another group by light jeep to the North Island. You can drive across to the island along the ford in the river that's to the northwest of the base. By capturing these two control points, the Chinese tickets start ticking away. This forces the enemy to really try to take at least one of the control points away from you. Therefore, hold these two while you send a couple soldiers by helicopter to drop in on the Chinese base at the Central Front. Once you have all four points under your control, victory is yours.

Chinese Strategy

The Chinese strategy for this map mirrors the US strategy, since each side begins with the same situation. However, while the US is rushing to grab the two control points in the middle, the Chinese should load up their transport helicopter and fly in to take the US base at the West Perimeter. By controlling both bases, this limits the US to only light jeeps and RIBs once their initial vehicles have been destroyed. All that remains is to capture one of the two middle control points to start the USMC tickets counting down; afterward, mop up the enemy by taking the other central control point.

32-PLAYER

Chinese HQ
Light Jeep (3)
APC (1)
Tank (1)
Transport Helicopter (1)
Artillery (3)
UAV Trailer (1)
Radar Station (1)
Machine Gun (1)

North Island
Light Jeep (1)
APC (1)
RIB (1)
Machine Gun (3)

West Perimeter
Light Jeep (2)
APC (1)
APC (1)
Transport Helicopter (1)
RIB (2)
AA Turret (1)
AT Turret (1)
Machine Gun (2)

Black = Convertible
Blue = USMC Control Only
Red = Chinese Control Only

Central Front
Light Jeep (2)
APC (1)
APC (1)
Transport Helicopter (1)
RIB (2)
AA Turret (1)
AT Turret (1)
Machine Gun (2)

South Island
Light Jeep (1)
APC (1)
RIB (1)
Machine Gun (2)

Fish Factory
Light Jeep (3)
APC (1)
Tank (1)
Transport Helicopter (1)
Artillery (3)
UAV Trailer (1)
Radar Station (1)
Machine Gun (2)

Game Type:
Double Assault
Total Control Points: 6
Convertible Control Points: 6

APCs are more important in the larger maps, and their amphibious capability allows greater freedom of movement. They also pack more firepower than the light jeeps and RIBs which dominate this map. Keep an engineer aboard to quickly repair any damage you take.

US Strategy

This map is similar to the 16-player map except that each side now has a main base located farther away from the center of the map, and the Temple control point has been substituted with the South Island control point—the map has expanded farther south as well as east and west. As before, the middle control points are important to take at the beginning. With both the North and South Islands under US control, the Chinese start losing tickets. While defending the four control points in the middle and east, the US should then begin an assault on the Central Front control point. This effectively boxes the Chinese into the western corner of the map and denies them access to RIB, which can be used for fast raids along the river. Assaulting the Chinese HQ can be tough since it's up at the top of a hill and only accessible by ground units along a narrow road. However, the US has two transport helicopters it can use to drop troops down on the base, since the Chinese HQ does not have an AA turret to defend itself. Speed gives the US the victory.

Chinese Strategy

Since both sides of this map are evenly balanced, once again the Chinese can use the same strategy as the US. However, they can use another good tactic that can catch the enemy off guard—fill the two Chinese transport helicopters with troops, then fly them along either the northern or southern map edge and drop the troops off at the Fish Factory. This gives the Chinese the high ground overlooking the West Perimeter control point and at the same time deny the USMC a transport helicopter and access to a heavy tank. The result is that the Marines are usually forced into trying to retake the Fish Factory, leaving the North and South Islands open for the Chinese to move in and capture. Now the Chinese have the US surrounded at the West Perimeter—use tanks and APCs to overwhelm the US defenders with artillery strikes and a ground assault, and win.

64-PLAYER

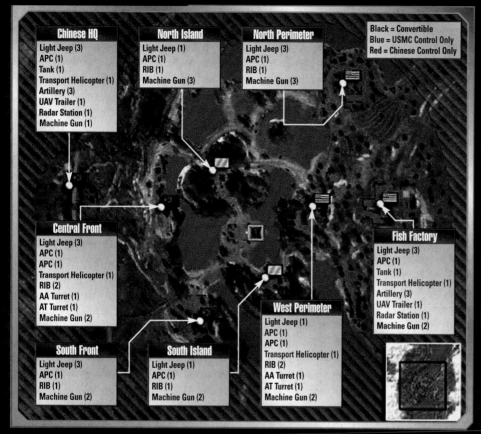

Chinese HQ
Light Jeep (3)
APC (1)
Tank (1)
Transport Helicopter (1)
Artillery (3)
UAV Trailer (1)
Radar Station (1)
Machine Gun (1)

North Island
Light Jeep (1)
APC (1)
RIB (1)
Machine Gun (3)

North Perimeter
Light Jeep (3)
APC (1)
RIB (1)
Machine Gun (3)

Black = Convertible
Blue = USMC Control Only
Red = Chinese Control Only

Central Front
Light Jeep (3)
APC (1)
APC (1)
Transport Helicopter (1)
RIB (2)
AA Turret (1)
AT Turret (1)
Machine Gun (2)

Fish Factory
Light Jeep (3)
APC (1)
Tank (1)
Transport Helicopter (1)
Artillery (3)
UAV Trailer (1)
Radar Station (1)
Machine Gun (2)

West Perimeter
Light Jeep (1)
APC (1)
APC (1)
Transport Helicopter (1)
RIB (2)
AA Turret (1)
AT Turret (1)
Machine Gun (2)

South Front
Light Jeep (3)
APC (1)
RIB (1)
Machine Gun (2)

South Island
Light Jeep (1)
APC (1)
RIB (1)
Machine Gun (2)

Game Type:
Head-On Conquest
Total Control Points: 8
Convertible Control Points: 8

Set up ambushes along the roads leading from your enemy's main base. A couple soldiers can easily prevent your opponent from bringing vehicles from these bases into battle against the rest of your team.

US Strategy

With the inclusion of two more control points—the North Perimeter and the South Front—the map expands more to the north and south than in the 32-player game. It also provides each side with an initial control point where they can spawn troops and gain access to more vehicles. Because of this arrangement, the US now has an advantage in the northern part of the map. As such, they should focus less on the central control points—the North and South Islands—and use their advantage to flank the Chinese positions to capture the main Chinese bases at the Central Front and the Chinese HQ. Send a squad containing several anti-tank troops from the North Perimeter in fast jeeps and the APC to move along the fords in the river and over to the road leading up to the Chinese HQ. When they get to the road, the anti-tank troops can dismount and engage any enemy tanks or other vehicles. After the road is clear, send the light jeeps up the hill to capture the control point.

Chinese Strategy

While the Marines are strong in the north, the Chinese are strong in the south. As such, the Chinese can hold in the south. Capturing the North Island and North Perimeter control points gives the Chinese strength in the north and prevent the US from attacking the Chinese northern flank. Once you have achieved this, the South Island is an easy target, so capture it; then all you have to worry about are the two US bases. By using helicopters to drop troops on the Fish Factory, along with ground vehicles assaulting from the north, you can attack the West Perimeter control point from all directions, eliminating enemy soldiers as they spawn. Move in to take control and win the game.

BASES AND CONTROL POINTS

Chinese HQ

Located at the top of a tall hill on the western edge of the map, the Chinese HQ is the main base for the Chinese in the 32- and 64-player games. While it spawns the only Chinese tank, the road leading down from this base is steep and winding; it will take a tank a while to get into the action. While the geography may limit the effectiveness of vehicles spawning here, this base is tough for the US to take by ground assault. Snipers and anti-tank troops—as well as engineer-placed mines—can easily deny the US access to the base. However, this control point is weak against enemy transport helicopters, since it has no AA turrets. In order to engage enemy helicopters, position your jeeps around the control point and use the mounted machine guns for air defense as well as for shooting at enemy soldiers dropping in by parachute. The Chinese must be careful not to lose this control point since it is very difficult to retake once it's in US hands.

Maps: 32- and 64-Player

Adjacent Bases/ Control Points:
- Central Front
- North Island

Chinese HQ Assets

USMC Control	Chinese Control	16-Player	32-Player	64-Player
DPV	Paratrooper Vehicle	—	3	3
LAV-25	WZ 551	—	1	1
N/A	Type 98	—	1	1
N/A	Z-8	—	1	1
N/A	Artillery	—	3	3
N/A	UAV	—	1	1
N/A	Radar	—	1	1
Machine Gun	Machine Gun	—	1	1

Central Front

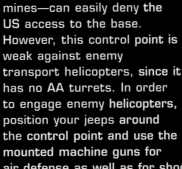

The Central Front is the Chinese base for the 16-player map and the most important control point for all games. In addition to ground vehicles, this base also provides RIBs for the Chinese team, allowing them a quick means of getting to the central control points and capturing them before the US does. This control point is also easier to defend than most since it offers both an AA turret as well as an AT turret. Be sure to keep the AT turret manned since it covers the river approaches and can deal with any APCs or RIBs coming at you. This is another control point that the Chinese cannot afford to lose, so no matter which size of map you are playing, always leave at least one defender behind to prevent the US from quickly taking this point. From here, the Chinese have a lot of options of where to attack next.

Maps: All

Adjacent Bases/ Control Points:
- Chinese HQ
- North Island
- South Front
- Temple

Central Front Assets

USMC Control	Chinese Control	16-Player	32-Player	64-Player
DPV	Paratrooper Vehicle	1	2	3
LAV-25	WZ 551	1 + 1*	1 + 1*	1 + 1*
N/A	Z-8	1	1	1
RIB	RIB	2	2	2
N/A	Artillery	2	—	—
N/A	UAV	1	—	—
N/A	Radar	1	—	—
AT Turret	AT Turret	1	1	1
AA Turret	AA Turret	1	1	1
Machine Gun	Machine Gun	2	2	2

= Chinese Control Only

South Front

The geography around the South Front is not as conducive for flanking attacks against the enemy as the North Perimeter. However, along with the Central Front, it provides a great staging area for prevent US attacks in the south as well as for launching Chinese attacks against the South Island and then the US bases. The main reason for defending this control point is to deny it to the enemy. If the Marines take it, they have a spawn point for their troops that makes attacking the Central Front much easier.

Maps: 64-Player Only

Adjacent Bases/ Control Points:
- Central Front
- South Island

South Front Assets

USMC Control	Chinese Control	16-Player	32-Player	64-Player
DPV	Paratrooper Vehicle	—	—	3
LAV-25	WZ 551	—	—	1
RIB	RIB	—	—	1
Machine Gun	Machine Gun	—	—	2

Fish Factory

The Fish Factory is the US main base for the 32- and 64-player games. Like the Chinese HQ, this base is set up on a hill which makes it somewhat difficult to assault by land. In fact, the only way a ground vehicle can get to this control point is via a steep road leading from the North Perimeter. Therefore, the best way to defend the Fish Factory is to hold the North Perimeter control point; if it falls, position troops and defenses on the north side of this base. A bigger threat is Chinese helicopter assaults, since there aren't any AA turrets. Use mounted machine guns on the vehicles to engage vehicles and infantry which drop in on you. It is vital that the US defend this base—if the Chinese take control, it's very difficult for the US to take it back.

Maps: 32- and 64-Player

Adjacent Bases/ Control Points:
- North Perimeter
- West Perimeter

Fish Factory Assets

USMC Control	Chinese Control	16-Player	32-Player	64-Player
DPV	Paratrooper Vehicle	—	3	3
LAV-25	WZ 551	—	1	1
M1A2	N/A	—	1	1
HH-60H	N/A	—	1	1
Artillery	N/A	—	3	3
UAV	N/A	—	1	1
Radar	N/A	—	1	1
Machine Gun	Machine Gun	—	2	2

West Perimeter

This is one of the most important control points for the US and must be held at all cost. For the 16-player game, this is the main base. However, this base provides access to all of the central control points, making it the springboard for all US attacks in the middle and south. The AA turret and AT turret located here provide some heavy firepower for the Marines. While the AT turret's field of fire is somewhat limited and only covers the northwestern river approach, the AA turret is positioned on top of the building near the flagpole, making any enemy attempt to fly in and drop off troops risky.

Maps: All

Adjacent Bases/ Control Points:
- Fish Factory
- North Perimeter
- North Island
- South Island
- Temple

West Perimeter Assets

USMC Control	Chinese Control	16-Player	32-Player	64-Player
DPV	Paratrooper Vehicle	1	2	1
LAV-25	WZ 551	1* + 1	1* + 1	1* + 1
HH-60H	N/A	1	1	1
RIB	RIB	2	2	2
Artillery	N/A	2	—	—
UAV	N/A	1	—	—
Radar	N/A	1	—	—
AT Turret	AT Turret	1	1	1
AA Turret	AA Turret	1	1	1
Machine Gun	Machine Gun	2	2	2

* = USMC Control Only

North Perimeter

For the 64-player map, this is the US's northern control point and protects access to the Fish Factory. While it lacks any AA or AT turrets, the North Perimeter does have machine guns positioned to engage any attacks from the west. Because of the haze and its limitations on long range fire, defenders manning these machine guns do not have to worry as much about snipers as in clearer maps.

The two machine guns along the westernmost wall can put up a withering amount of fire that make fast attacks by light jeeps suicidal for the enemy. However, a carefully placed artillery strike on this position right before an assault usually clears the way, so the defender must be sure to spread out the defenses.

Maps: 64-Player Only

Adjacent Bases/ Control Points:
- Fish Factory
- North Island
- West Perimeter

North Perimeter Assets

USMC Control	Chinese Control	16-Player	32-Player	64-Player
DPV	Paratrooper Vehicle	—	—	3
LAV-25	WZ 551	—	—	1
RIB	RIB	—	—	1
Machine Gun	Machine Gun	—	—	3

North Island

Because of its location near the center of the map and directly between the US and Chinese bases, the North Island often becomes a point of intense conflict. Whichever side controls the North Island not only is one control point closer to victory, they also have a spawn point closer to the enemy and a forward defensive position against attacks aimed at their bases. While there are three machine guns for defending this position, they are all facing different directions. However, because they are positioned in bunkers, soldiers manning these weapons have fairly good protection. It is a good idea, especially in the large games, to have each of these machine guns manned and some anti-tank troops handy to deal with APCs and other vehicles.

Maps: All

Adjacent Bases/ Control Points:
- Chinese HQ
- Chinese Central Front
- North Perimeter
- Temple
- West Perimeter

North Island Assets

USMC Control	Chinese Control	16-Player	32-Player	64-Player
DPV	Paratrooper Vehicle	1	1	1
LAV-25	WZ 551	—	1	1
RIB	RIB	1	1	1
Machine Gun	Machine Gun	3	3	3

South Island

The South Island doesn't have a lot to offer. However, if you can get there before the enemy, it isn't too tough to defend. This is because a steep ridge wraps around this control point on three sides, making it only accessible by ground from the north. The two machine guns have a limited usefulness because of obstructions to their fields of fire. However, a clever engineer can place mines in the ford leading to this area and destroy any vehicles trying to rush in and take control.

Maps: 32- and 64-Player

Adjacent Bases/ Control Points:
- South Front
- West Perimeter

South Island Assets

USMC Control	Chinese Control	16-Player	32-Player	64-Player
DPV	Paratrooper Vehicle	—	1	1
LAV-25	WZ 551	—	1	1
RIB	RIB	—	1	1
Machine Gun	Machine Gun	—	2	2

Temple

Located on a small island between the North and South Islands, the Temple is only a control point in the 16-player game. However, once taken, it offers four machine guns to help defend it. Since each team only has a maximum of eight players, it is unlikely that either side could leave more than one or two soldiers to defend it. Therefore, the attacking player just needs to locate where the defenders are located, and attack from a different direction or drop an artillery strike down on the temple to clear out the enemy troops.

Maps: 16-Player Only

Adjacent Bases/ Control Points:
- Central Front
- North Island
- West Perimeter

Temple Assets

USMC Control	Chinese Control	16-Player	32-Player	64-Player
DPV	Paratrooper Vehicle	1	—	—
RIB	RIB	1	—	—
Machine Gun	Machine Gun	4	—	—

SONGHUA STALEMATE TACTICS

River Fords

While this map contains several small islands broken up by water and narrow rivers, you can still get from one control point to another in any ground vehicle by using the fords.

it is also a good idea for APCs to also use them since they can travel at their ground speed—which is a lot faster than their swimming speed.

These shallow areas in the water allow ground vehicles to cross the water as if it were dry land. Not only can the light jeeps and tanks use these, it is also a good idea for APCs to also use them since they can travel at their ground

Getting Around Quickly

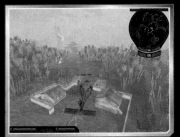

Though ground vehicles can move through the water at fords, the RIBs are one of the quickest modes of transportation. They can travel quickly down the river and go over fords without having to slow down. Furthermore, the rivers in the south allow a quick way to move from one side of the map to the other while avoiding machine gun positions and other defenses.

The transport helicopters available to each side also provide a fast way to get from one point to another. With only two AA turrets total on the maps, there is a low risk in using the helicopters as long as you don't hover right over the enemy and provide an easy target.

Helicopters are especially useful for assaulting the two main bases, which are difficult to reach by land.

Artillery

Since both sides don't have a lot of heavy firepower, artillery plays an even more important role on this map—especially for attack enemy defenses. Fords and other chokepoints also make good targets.

If squad leaders are not calling in artillery strikes to help them with their assaults, the commander should be ordering bombardment of the enemy's bases. In fact, artillery should be one of the commander's main jobs. Using the extreme zoomed-in view from the commander's screen, you can target individual vehicles and spawn points. Not only will you take out the vehicles, you will usually hit enemy troops moving to get in them.

GULF OF OMAN

A USMC Marine Expeditionary Unit (MEU) has landed on this Persian Gulf beach during the night in the hopes of quickly seizing the nearby MEC airbase.

The stakes are high for both sides. The Marines face possibly being driven into the sea and destroyed. The MEC forces could lose a key airbase and open the door for US forces to take strategic oilfields. Both sides have been using the morning to prepare for the final assault.

16-PLAYER

Construction Site
Heavy Jeep (2)
Tank (1)
Artillery (1)
UAV Trailer (1)
Radar Station (1)

Black = Convertible
Blue = USMC Control Only
Red = MEC Control Only

City
Machine Gun (1)

Village
Machine Gun (1)

Beach
Heavy Jeep (2)
Tank (1)
Artillery (1)
UAV Trailer (1)
Radar Station (1)
Machine Gun (1)

Game Type:
Conquest
Total Control Points: 4
Convertible Control Points: 4

The railroad tracks serve as a boundary dividing the map in half with the MEC to the north and the Marines to the south.

US Strategy

This map is fairly small and allows for some quick, intense battles—even with only 16 players in the game. The US begins in control of the Beach control point. This is where all of the US vehicles spawn, and it contains the Marine artillery and support structures. As such, it is usually a good idea to leave a soldier behind to guard this important base.

Right from the start, the US team should send a jeep with a couple soldiers toward the Village and take this control point. Send the rest of the team in the tank and the other jeep to the City control point. The MEC will definitely be headed in that direction as well. Drop an artillery strike on the City control point, then move in to take control when the rounds stop falling. Watch for enemies on the rooftops overlooking this control point. Call in artillery strikes in the buildings if you start taking fire from them. If you can take the two middle control points, the MEC tickets begin to count down. This forces the MEC to assault the control points, so be ready to hold. Use mines and other defenses to keep them away. Their rush to take a control point may leave the MEC base at the Construction Site vulnerable, so try to sneak a couple soldiers in to capture it if possible— this prevents the MEC from spawning and gives you a quick victory if you can pull it off.

MEC Strategy

THE MEC strategy is similar to the Marines'—however, the MEC has some important advantages. Because the MEC base is the Construction Site control point, you have a number of high structures on which you can position snipers and anti-tank soldiers. These include several of the buildings in the town as well as the crane. From these positions, you can engage the Marines as they head toward the City.

Right at the start, send a couple troops up high and the rest of your team toward the City control point. It is tough to hold the City from the point itself. Instead, pull back a bit, using the buildings for cover and take out the enemies as they approach it. Be sure to leave behind some mines or other surprises to deal with any Marines that get too close to your flag.

Aim for taking the Village next. You can use the train to provide cover as you approach. However, if you can get some Special Forces troops to the Beach, they can really put the hurt on the US. Approach along the eastern edge of the map and blow up the artillery to prevent the enemy from dropping it on you. Then proceed to make this control point your own. Once you take it, the US will have trouble putting up much of a fight with only the Village, since it spawns no vehicles. Then it's just a matter of assaulting this last control point from both the north and south to bring the battle to a close.

BATTLEFIELD

PRIMA OFFICIAL GAME GUIDE

32-PLAYER

Black = Convertible
Blue = USMC Control Only
Red = MEC Control Only

Construction Site
Light Jeep (1)
APC (1)

River Fort
Light Jeep (1)
APC (1)
Tank (1)
RIB (1)
AA Turret (1)

USS Essex
Attack Helicopter (1)
Transport Helicopter (1)
Fighter (2)
RIB (2)
Artillery (2)
UAV Trailer (1)
Radar Station (1)

Olive Hill Fort
Light Jeep (1)
APC (1)
AA Turret (1)

Rock Fort
Light Jeep (1)
Light Jeep (1)
APC (1)
Tank (1)
AA Turret (1)
Machine Gun (1)

Hotel
APC (1)
Tank (1)
AA Turret (1)
Machine Gun (2)

Airfield Base
Light Jeep (1)
Tank (1)
Attack Helicopter (1)
Fighter (1)
Fighter Bomber (1)
Artillery (2)
UAV Trailer (1)
Radar Station (1)
AA Turret (1)
Machine Gun (1)

Game Type:
Conquest
Total Control Points: 7
Convertible Control Points: 5

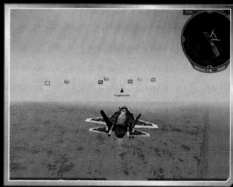

With the inclusion of the US Carrier and Airfield Base, each side now has both planes and helicopters to add a third dimension to the conflict.

US Strategy

In the 32-player game, all control points are assigned to either one side or the other at the beginning of the game. There isn't the rush to grab neutral points. You'll be better off getting organized before heading into enemy territory. First, ensure that the three forts are defended. Man each of the AA turrets and be ready for early enemy air strikes. Meanwhile, have the Marine airpower head toward the MEC airfield to shoot down enemy aircraft or destroy it while still on the ground.

There are only two MEC control points on this map that you can capture—the Hotel and the Construction Site. The best strategy is to make sure your troops can hold in the west, then send your tanks, APCs, and attack helicopters toward the Hotel. Soften the area up with an artillery strike, then have the UAV hover over everything so you can see the location of all enemies. Helicopters can clear off the rooftop of the Hotel and even drop troops to secure this area. These troops can then fire down on the defenders below as the rest of your assault force moves in. Capturing the Hotel not only starts the MEC tickets counting down, but it also give your team an elevated position from which to engage the enemy. Snipers and anti-tank troopers can make a counterattack by the enemy costly. The next step is to go after the Construction Site. Remember to hold your forts as you attack the central control point from the west, south, and east. As before, use helicopters to clear off the rooftops and clear the way. A daring tactic is to fly a transport helicopter over the Construction Site and either drop troops by parachute or land just to the north of the flagpole so the troops can dismount and rush in to take control. Now all that remains is to defend these positions. Since you know where the enemy must spawn, keep up constant artillery and air strikes against the Airfield Base until the battle is won.

MEC Strategy

The MEC starts off with the best defensive positions. Use the rooftops for your troops to defend against US attacks. However, the MEC must leave their defenses and attack if they want to win. The best place to start is either at the River Fort or the Rock Fort. The Rock Fort is close to the Hotel and easier to get an assault for at the beginning. However, the River Fort offers an RIB which you can use to attack other control points; control of this fort gives the MEC superiority in the western half of the map. The River Fort also allows the MEC to attack the other forts from the water and to make raids against the US artillery. The key to deciding which way to attack is to do some recon and see where most of the enemy force is located—then attack where the defenses are weakest. Once you have one fort, use it to begin an attack against the next in the line.

While the MEC has some good air assets, the US has a lot of AA turrets so pilots need to be ready to drop flares if they don't want to end up as a big fireball. The MEC should use its jets to try and shoot down US aircraft as well as to attack US vehicles and troops moving into your territory. Another important tactic is to take out the US artillery since it can really cause some damage to your defenses.

64-PLAYER

River Fort
Light Jeep (1)
APC (1)
Tank (1)
AA Turret (1)
RIB (1)
Machine Gun (1)

Village
Light Jeep (1)
APC (1)
AA Turret (1)
Machine Gun (1)

Construction Site
Light Jeep (1)
APC (1)

Black = Convertible
Blue = USMC Control Only
Red = MEC Control Only

Airfield Base
APC (2)
Tank (1)
Attack Helicopter (1)
Transport Helicopter (1)
Fighter (1)
Fighter Bomber (1)
Artillery (3)
UAV Trailer (1)
Radar Station (1)
AA Turret (2)
Machine Gun (3)

Olive Hill Fort
Light Jeep (1)
APC (1)
AA Turret (1)

USS Essex
Attack Helicopter (1)
Transport Helicopter (2)
Fighter (2)
RIB (2)
Artillery (3)
UAV Trailer (1)
Radar Station (1)

Hotel
APC (1)
Tank (1)
AA Turret (1)
Machine Gun (2)

Rock Fort
Light Jeep (1)
Tank (1)
AA Turret (1)
Machine Gun (1)

Village Fort
Light Jeep (1)
APC (1)
AA Turret (1)

Game Type:
Conquest
Total Control Points: 9
Convertible Control Points: 7

Speed can be almost as important as firepower in the larger games—it forces your enemy to spread out to defend all of their control points.

US Strategy

The main difference between the 32- and 64-player games is that the 64-player game adds two more control points—effectively expanding the battlefield to both the east and west. The US strategy stays mainly the same. The Hotel has to be captured first. This time it is even more important since the Hotel towers over the Village Fort—from the protection of their tall building, the MEC can engage US troops on the US base. After the Hotel, take the Village in the west next. Doing so forces the MEC to stay in the middle and thus protects the US flanks. The decision to attack the Construction Site depends on the MEC's strategy. The US can win without taking this central control point—instead, just use artillery and air power to pummel the defenders and force their tickets to count down even quicker. If an assault on the Hotel is made, be sure to clear the rooftops and attack from several different directions.

The opening up of the western part of the map allows the US to use some raid tactics. Load up a light jeep or two with troops, then race north along the western road to the MEC Airfield Base. While driving along the landing strip, you can attack MEC aircraft and even drop off special forces troops to destroy the MEC artillery and support structures. This forces the enemy to keep more troops back on this base to defend against raids and less troops at other points on the map.

MEC Strategy

This map gives the MEC some more possibilities for raiding and using the river. However, it also confines them to using one main strategy. While you could begin attacking the US forts either in the east or west, the fact that the Hotel overlooks the Village Fort makes attacking this fort early less desirable, since you will then lose the advantage over an enemy spawn point. Control of the River Fort is vital to secure the MEC's western flank and to prevent the Marines from using the western road as a highway to your Airfield Base.

Once you control the river, you can attack any fort you want by coming at them from both the sea to the south as well as by land from the north. Each fort you take also gives you an AA turret which you can then use to engage enemy aircraft coming in from the US Carrier—thus limiting the Marines' use of airpower. Once you have captured all of the forts, you have cut off the Marines from all of their ground vehicle spawn points and should have enough anti-aircraft firepower to shoot down anything that gets close to the shore. Keep your own aircraft back to engage enemy planes and helicopters and drop artillery on the rear of the US Carrier where all of the aircraft spawn.

BASES AND CONTROL POINTS

USS *Essex*

The US Carrier is the Marine's main source of firepower for the 32- and 64-player games. Not only does it have the aircraft which can attack the enemy as well as deliver troops all over the map, the carrier is also the US base where the support structures are located. While the artillery is a part of this control point, it is actually located on the shore rather on the carrier itself. Because of its location at sea, the US Carrier is difficult for the MEC to attack due to its anti-air defenses. These consist of two batteries of dual turrets. Each battery contains a Phalanx auto cannon as well as a Sea Sparrow missile launcher that can fire eight missiles before it must reload. If properly manned, it is extremely difficult for the MEC to get near the US Carrier and hope to cause any damage to the aircraft onboard.

Because the US Carrier offers some important firepower, it is vital that the Marines have at least one soldier manning the anti-aircraft batteries. This control point actually has two spawn points. One puts you on the deck of the carrier while the other is located in the rear well, where you can find some RIBs. Unless the US has lost the land control points, they rarely need the RIBs. However, this well can offer an access point for MEC raiders who want to sneak in under the anti-aircraft defenses using an RIB of their own.

Maps: 32- and 64-Player

Adjacent Bases/Control Points:
- River Fort
- Olive Hill Fort
- Rock Fort

USS *Essex* Assets

USMC Control	16-Player	32-Player	64-Player
HH-60H	—	1	2
AH-1Z	—	1	1
JSF	—	2	2
RIB	—	2	2
Artillery	—	2	3
UAV	—	1	1
Radar	—	1	1

Airfield Base

Airfield Base Assets

MEC Control	16-Player	32-Player	64-Player
FAV	—	1	—
BTR-90	—	—	2
T-90	—	1	1
Mi-17	—	—	1
Mi-28	—	1	1
Mig-29	—	1	1
Su-34	—	1	1
Artillery	—	2	3
UAV	—	1	1
Radar	—	1	1
AA Turret	—	1	2
Machine Gun	—	1	3

For the larger two games, this is the MEC base. While the enemy cannot capture it, this control point is the most important for the MEC since it offers all of the airpower as well as some ground vehicles, plus artillery and support structures. Since the Airfield Base is a constant target for enemy air strikes, be sure to keep the AA turrets manned. These soldiers can also protect the base against raids as well. In the 64-player version, there are actually two different spawn points. The eastern spawn point is located near the two jets as well as the flagpole while the western point is near the helipad.

Maps: 32- and 64-Player

Adjacent Bases/Control Points:
- Construction Site
- Hotel
- Village (64)

Beach

The Beach is the US base for the 16-player game. As such, it is important to leave at least one person behind to defend it. However, the key to holding this control point is to maintain control of the Village, since it covers the road leading to the Beach. Avoid focusing all your attention on enemies approaching from the northeast. Instead, watch out for enemies trying to sneak in from the sides or even from the ocean to the rear. The MEC should definitely try to take this control point since its loss seriously hurts the US team.

Maps:
16-Player Only

Adjacent Bases/ Control Points:
• Village (16)

Beach Assets

USMC Control	MEC Control	16-Player	32-Player	64-Player
HMMWV	GAZ 39371	2	—	—
M1A2	T-90	1	—	—
Artillery	N/A	1	—	—
UAV	N/A	1	—	—
Radar	N/A	1	—	—
Machine Gun	Machine Gun	1	—	—

Village (16)

While this control point only offers a single machine gun position, it helps the Marines secure the Beach. The flagpole is located on the lower half of the area, near the machine gun. However, it is better to defend this position from the higher ground to the east—there you have a better field of fire over the battlefield, and you can engage any enemies approaching the flagpole. You can also put troops in the train to the north of this location, using it for cover as well as for ambushing enemy vehicles from the rear as they drive to the Village.

Maps:
16-Player Only

Adjacent Bases/ Control Points:
• Beach
• City

Village (16) Assets

USMC Control	MEC Control	16-Player	32-Player	64-Player
Machine Gun	Machine Gun	1	—	—

River Fort

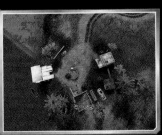 

This is the westernmost US defense along the shore. Along with the US Carrier, this is the only other location where an RIB spawns. As such, the US can use this control point as a staging area for raids up the river. On the other hand, if the MEC can take control, they can use the RIB for sea-based attacks against other forts along the coast or even against the US Carrier. The US should be ready to defend this fort from attacks to the north. Be sure to watch out for an MEC APC coming down the river where you might not expect it. Because this fort is close to the US artillery, the Marines should keep some troops here to defend against any MEC raids coming down the river or along the open ground to the east.

Maps: 32- and 64-Player

Adjacent Bases/ Control Points:
• Olive Hill Fort
• Village (64)
• US Carrier

River Fort Assets

USMC Control	MEC Control	16-Player	32-Player	64-Player
DPV	FAV	—	1	1
N/A	BTR-90	—	1	1
M1A2	N/A	—	1	1
RIB	RIB	—	1	1
AA Turret	AA Turret	—	1	1
Machine Gun	Machine Gun	—	—	1

Olive Hill Fort

This is one of the middle forts in the 32-player game and offers some fast vehicles for attacking the enemy. Unless one of the forts to either side has been captured by the MEC, the US only really needs to worry about attacks from the north. While this fort has some walls surrounding it, the walls facing the sea have several holes through which MEC troops can fire in at the Marine defenders.

Maps: 32- and 64-Player

Adjacent Bases/Control Points:
- Construction Site
  - River Fort
  - Rock Fort
  - US Carrier

Olive Hill Fort Assets

USMC Control	MEC Control	16-Player	32-Player	64-Player
DPV	FAV	—	1	1
LAV-25	BTR-90	—	1	1
AA Turret	AA Turret	—	1	1

Rock Fort

The Rock Fort is a middle fort in the 64-player game and the eastern end of the line in the 32-player game. As an end fort, you must be prepared to defend the Rock Fort from both the north as well as the east. Because it spawns a tank, this control point is an important asset for the US. While it does not give the MEC a tank, denying the heavy armor to the US makes this a worthy target. This is also one of the smaller, more confined forts, making this a good target for MEC artillery strikes.

Maps: 32- and 64-Player

Adjacent Bases/Control Points:
- Hotel
- Olive Hill Fort
- US Carrier
- Village Fort

Rock Fort Assets

USMC Control	MEC Control	16-Player	32-Player	64-Player
DPV	FAV	—	1 + 1*	1
N/A	BTR-90	—	1	1
M1A2	N/A	—	1	1
AA Turret	AA Turret	—	1	1
Machine Gun	Machine Gun	—	1	1

* = MEC Control Only

Village Fort

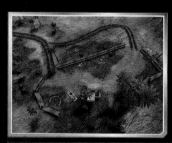

This fort takes on the role of end of the line in the 64-player game for the US defenses. Its main threat comes directly from the north where the Hotel is located. Due to its close proximity to the Hotel, enemy soldiers on the rooftop of the Hotel can fire down on US troops at this control point. Therefore, be careful about static defenses. The US might even want to assign a sniper to this location to take out MEC soldiers on the rooftop.

Maps: 64-Player Only

Adjacent Bases/Control Points:
- Hotel
- Rock Fort

Village Fort Assets

USMC Control	MEC Control	16-Player	32-Player	64-Player
DPV	FAV	—	—	1
LAV-25	BTR-90	—	—	1
AA Turret	AA Turret	—	—	1

City

This control point can be tough for the US to take if the MEC already has it—the buildings located to the north of it offer a great position for enemy soldiers to fire down on the City. Advance on it from the east since the MEC usually expects a frontal assault from the southwest. Whichever side controls this point should place mines or other explosives to discourage anyone who gets too close to the flagpole, and prevent them from taking control away.

Maps:
16-Player Only

Adjacent Bases/ Control Points:
• Construction Site
• Village

City Assets

USMC Control	MEC Control	16-Player	32-Player	64-Player
Machine Gun	Machine Gun	1	—	—

Hotel

The Hotel serves as the eastern flank of the MEC front. Dominated by the tall hotel building, this control point features two machine gun positions as well as an AA turret, allowing a few troops to defend this point against US raids or fast attacks. Troops on top of the building have a commanding view of the surrounding area and can engage enemy troops at the Village Fort and at the approaches to the Construction Site.

Maps: 32- and 64-Player

Adjacent Bases/ Control Points:
• Construction Site
• Rock Fort
• Village Fort

Hotel Assets

USMC Control	MEC Control	16-Player	32-Player	64-Player
LAV-25	BTR-90	—	1	1
M1A2	T-90	—	1	1
AA Turret	AA Turret	—	1	1
Machine Gun	Machine Gun	—	2	2

When the US attacks the Hotel, it is important to move in fast. Use aircraft to drop troops on top of the hotel building, and from there they can clear out enemy troops below. Then jump off the roof and parachute down to the flagpole and take control of the point before the enemy reinforces it or sends troops to counterattack.

Construction Site

The Construction Site is the only control point found in all three maps. In the 16-player game, this is the MEC base. However, in all games this point is important to the MEC, even though not much spawns here in the 32- and 64-player games. It serves as the center of the battlefield. As long as the MEC controls this point, it is difficult for the Marines to advance and capture other control points.

Maps: All

Adjacent Bases/ Control Points:
- Airfield
- Hotel
- Olive Hill Fort
- Village (16)
- Village (64)

The tall buildings and crane are what make this control point so important to the MEC. From the tops of these, MEC soldiers can snipe or even fire anti-tank rockets at US forces as they advance toward MEC positions. This makes the Construction Site a regular target for US artillery strikes. The flagpole is located near the crane and must be approached on foot since obstacles make it difficult to get close while in a vehicle. Furthermore, since the flagpole is surrounded by tall structures, the US must clear the crane and buildings before attempting to seize control of the Construction Site.

Construction Site Assets

USMC Control	MEC Control	16-Player	32-Player	64-Player
DPV	FAV	—	1	1
HMMWV	GAZ 39371	2	—	—
LAV-25	BTR-90	—	1	1
M1A2	T-90	1	—	—
N/A	Artillery	1	—	—
N/A	UAV	1	—	—
N/A	Radar	1	—	—

Village (64)

This control point guards the western approaches to MEC territory and also provides a point from which to defend against Marine advances along the river. With the APC spawned here, the MEC can choose to move down the river to attack the Marine forts from the water or use this as a point for raids against the enemy—hitting the US in the flank from here. When the MEC defends this control point, an engineer should place mines on the nearby bridge to destroy Marine vehicles that try to race across— or just blow up the bridge to prevent crossings altogether.

Maps: 64-Player Only

Adjacent Bases/ Control Points:
- Airfield Base
- Construction Site
- River Fort

Village (64) Assets

USMC Control	MEC Control	16-Player	32-Player	64-Player
DPV	FAV	—	—	1
LAV-25	BTR-90	—	—	1
AA Turret	AA Turret	—	—	1
Machine Gun	Machine Gun	—	—	1

GULF OF OMAN TACTICS

Using Elevation to Dominate the Battlefield

The tall buildings provide spots for both snipers and anti-tank soldiers. From these vantages, you can see over a lot of the terrain and can engage the enemy at long range—making it harder for them to shoot back at you. In addition, there are several control points which can be covered from a nearby tall structure including the Hotel and the Construction Site.

Request a supply drop on the rooftop where you are located, then you can replenish your ammo as well as your health, as needed. If you are a sniper, place a claymore near the top of the ladder to discourage any enemies from trying to sneak up on you.

Attack Helicopters

The attack helicopters can be a real asset in this game if you use them correctly. Since the US often has to deal with MEC units on the rooftops, attack helicopters provide a way of attacking these elevated enemies. Try to move in from the side or rear where the enemies are less likely to be looking for you to claim the element of surprise.

There are a lot of AA turrets on this map. Keep a finger poised over the button which releases flares or you'll have trouble. The MEC will find tempting targets on the US Carrier; a few strafing runs can leave the US airpower in ruins. If the Marines man the anti-aircraft batteries on the carrier, though, your pilots will end up making good use of their parachutes. However, if the MEC drops special forces troops on an enemy airbase, they can plant explosives on the aircraft and blow them up for the same effect.

Raid on the US Artillery

The US artillery is located on a small finger of land near the shore. Since there is not much defending it, the MEC should consider a raid against this artillery which usually gets dropped on your rooftop troops. The best way to get to the artillery is by water. Either take an APC down the river or steal an RIB at the River Fort.

Send at least two special forces troops to plant explosives on the artillery pieces, then take them out. If you bring along a sniper as well, you can plant some claymores near the wrecked guns to kill any engineers who rush up to fix them without looking for booby traps.

KUBRA DAM

Active Component brigades of the US Marines are deploying toward a key dam site in the Saudi desert, intent upon control of this strategic location. To counter the threat, MEC forces are advancing their own mobile brigades to blunt the US spearhead. This rough desert terrain contains a mix of terrain types, requiring the utmost tactical flexibility by both US and MEC soldiers. The ultimate objective of both sides in this battle is to gain control of the entire Kubra Dam sector.

16-PLAYER

Lower Dam
Heavy Jeep (1)
APC (1)
Transport Helicopter (1)
AA Turret (1)
AT Turret (1)

Black = Convertible
Blue = USMC Control Only
Red = MEC Control Only

Power Station
Heavy Jeep (2)
Tank (1)
Artillery (2)
UAV Trailer (1)
Radar Station (1)
AA Turret (1)

Upper Dam

Construction Site
Heavy Jeep (2)
Tank (1)
Artillery (2)
UAV Trailer (1)
Radar Station (1)
AA Turret (1)
AT Turret (1)

Game Type:
Conquest Double Assault
Total Control Points: 4
Convertible Control Points: 4

The tower near the Upper Dam flag is a great defensive position whether covering the road to the east or west.

US Strategy

As soon as the battle begins, the race is on for the two central control points at the dam's center. Starting at the Construction Site, the Marines need to use their DPVs to reach the Upper Dam control point first. This attacking force should consist of special forces and at least one anti-tank soldier. Once they reach the control point, instead of worrying about converting the flag, they need to stop the MEC advance from the west. Anti-tank troops can suppress incoming vehicles while special forces blow the improvised road span to the west. The machine guns on the DPV are also effective at halting infantry. While one squad secures the Upper Dam, a second squad should follow closely behind and base jump down to the Lower Dam control point. Parachuting from the upper deck is much faster and safer than descending the series of ladders and staircases. At the Lower Dam, the Marines gain access to a Seahawk transport helicopter, which can be used to stage raids on the Power Station. But simply holding the three easternmost control points is enough to cause an MEC ticket drain. Consider digging in at each control point to outlast the enemy.

MEC Strategy

Since the Construction Site is extremely difficult to capture, the MEC's best chance of success is by capturing the two dam control points while holding the Power Station. Like the Marines, the MEC troops need to rush to the center of the dam with their FAVs. While one squad secures the Upper Dam, another squad should parachute down to the Lower Dam. The eastern span of the road crossing the top of the dam can be blown in two separate spots, but a total of six C4 charges are need to do this. The greater the damage done to the eastern span, the longer it takes Marine engineers to repair the bridge, which buys the Upper Dam's defenders more time to pick off the attackers. Even if the Upper and Lower Dam control points are held, defenders still need to watch the Power Station. Marines can circumvent the dam control points altogether and climb up the western wall of the Power Station using either the staircase or ladder. Getting surrounded by Marine attackers from the Construction Site and Power Station is an ugly situation and should be avoided at all costs.

32-PLAYER

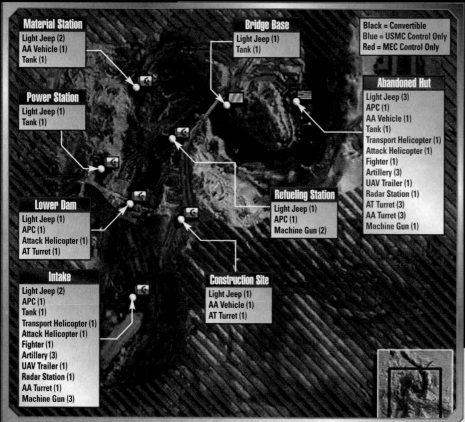

Material Station
Light Jeep (2)
AA Vehicle (1)
Tank (1)

Power Station
Light Jeep (1)
Tank (1)

Lower Dam
Light Jeep (1)
APC (1)
Attack Helicopter (1)
AT Turret (1)

Intake
Light Jeep (2)
APC (1)
Tank (1)
Transport Helicopter (1)
Attack Helicopter (1)
Fighter (1)
Artillery (3)
UAV Trailer (1)
Radar Station (1)
AA Turret (1)
Machine Gun (3)

Bridge Base
Light Jeep (1)
Tank (1)

Construction Site
Light Jeep (1)
AA Vehicle (1)
AT Turret (1)

Refueling Station
Light Jeep (1)
APC (1)
Machine Gun (2)

Abandoned Hut
Light Jeep (3)
APC (1)
AA Vehicle (1)
Tank (1)
Transport Helicopter (1)
Attack Helicopter (1)
Fighter (1)
Artillery (3)
UAV Trailer (1)
Radar Station (1)
AT Turret (3)
AA Turret (3)
Machine Gun (1)

Black = Convertible
Blue = USMC Control Only
Red = MEC Control Only

Game Type:
Conquest Assault
Total Control Points: 8
Convertible Control Points: 7

Make use of the perimeter roads as much as possible to avoid crossing the deadly no-man's land of the northern valley.

MEC Strategy

As the defenders, the MEC's first priority is to secure the Intake from an early capture. The AA turret and Mig-29 are essential to keeping the southern portion of the map safe from air assault, and should be manned at all times. A couple of troops positioned around the flag can fight off any Marines that parachute into the area. Once the southern portion of the map is secure, the second most important asset is the dam. At least one squad should be placed at each of three control points. The Material and Refueling Stations in the northern valley are more expendable but should be held as long as possible to prevent the Marines from stopping their ticket drain. But as soon as either control point is captured by the enemy, retreat back to the dam and carefully fortify the Power Station, Lower Dam, and Construction Site control points. Allowing the Marines to get a foothold in the northern valley can actually work to the MEC's favor. Snipers and anti-tank troops positioned along the top of the dam can fire down into the northern valley and rack up tons of kills. The Mi-28s are also very effective, especially if they hover behind the dam and pop up occasionally to fire guided missiles at approaching tanks and other vehicles. Think of the dam as a giant castle wall and focus all your efforts on keeping the Marines isolated on its northern side. Consolidating defensive efforts at the dam gives MEC forces their best chance of repelling the Marine attack, all while inflicting heavy losses.

US Strategy

On this assault map, the US forces are the attackers and must quickly pick up a control point in the northern valley to stop their ticket drain. Two separate assault teams should be organized early, each consisting of a couple of squads. One team should drive west from the Abandoned Hut and quickly capture the neutral Bridge Base control point before MEC troops can reach it. Meanwhile, the second assault team should pass the Bridge Base and attack the Refueling Station in an effort to halt the ticket drain. The Refueling Station also provides a solid foothold in the northern valley, acting as a staging area for future attacks on the Construction Site and Lower Dam. But before striking the dam control points, it's important to wipe out resistance on the western flank at the Material Station. This control point is best attacked from the north, utilizing the road that running along the valley's perimeter—it can be accessed from the Bridge Base. Artillery and air strikes can help soften up the defenders before ground troops move in for the capture. Once the northern valley is under US control, begin the push on the dam control points. Take the high ground first, capturing the Construction Site and Power Station, then squeeze in on the Lower Dam from the north, east, and west. With the northern valley and dam under Marine control, all that's left is the Intake. Isolate the MEC forces to the south using the F-18 and M6 Bradleys to shoot down their aircraft. The western turbine tunnel at the base of the dam should also be mined to prevent rush vehicle attacks on the northern valley. Hold strong at the dam's three control points and take advantage of the high elevation to fire down on the MEC troops spawning to the south. Wait until the MEC tickets dwindle away before moving in to capture the Intake.

TIP Although the Supervisor Base control point is not available on this map, the same site can still be accessed. A Marine squad leader positioned here can spawn squad members which can be used to attack the Material Station.

64-PLAYER

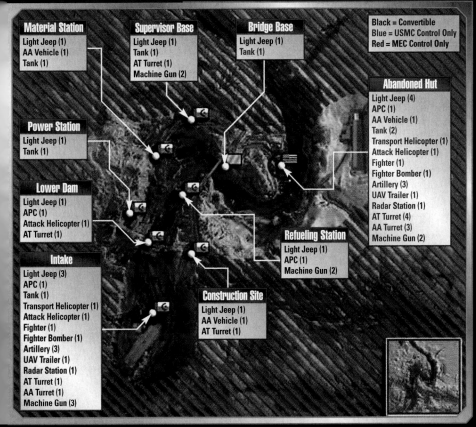

Material Station
Light Jeep (1)
AA Vehicle (1)
Tank (1)

Supervisor Base
Light Jeep (1)
Tank (1)
AT Turret (1)
Machine Gun (2)

Bridge Base
Light Jeep (1)
Tank (1)

Power Station
Light Jeep (1)
Tank (1)

Lower Dam
Light Jeep (1)
APC (1)
Attack Helicopter (1)
AT Turret (1)

Intake
Light Jeep (3)
APC (1)
Tank (1)
Transport Helicopter (1)
Attack Helicopter (1)
Fighter (1)
Fighter Bomber (1)
Artillery (3)
UAV Trailer (1)
Radar Station (1)
AT Turret (1)
AA Turret (1)
Machine Gun (3)

Construction Site
Light Jeep (1)
AA Vehicle (1)
AT Turret (1)

Refueling Station
Light Jeep (1)
APC (1)
Machine Gun (2)

Abandoned Hut
Light Jeep (4)
APC (1)
AA Vehicle (1)
Tank (2)
Transport Helicopter (1)
Attack Helicopter (1)
Fighter (1)
Fighter Bomber (1)
Artillery (3)
UAV Trailer (1)
Radar Station (1)
AT Turret (4)
AA Turret (3)
Machine Gun (2)

Black = Convertible
Blue = USMC Control Only
Red = MEC Control Only

Game Type:
Conquest Assault
Total Control Points: 9
Convertible Control Points: 8

The MEC Mi-28s can peek over the dam when attacking Marine units to the north, then drop back down to avoid incoming AA fire—but the US jets are still a serious threat.

US Strategy

The addition of the Supervisor Base control point in the northern valley is the main difference between this map and the 32 player version. But the increase in available manpower also allows for more aggressive tactics on both ends of the battlefield. Establishing control of the northern valley is still the first primary objective, but expect heavier resistance especially at the Refueling Station and Supervisor Base. Artillery strikes can help soften up these control points before the attackers arrive. Taking control of the Material Base and Construction Site are also important, since these control points spawn the MEC's only Tunguskas. Denying the enemy access to these devastating AA vehicles allows for much greater aerial flexibility, making it safer to insert troops with the Seahawk. As on the 32 player map, it's best to work from north to south while carefully guarding your flanks. But watch for opportunities to capture the Intake too. Eliminating the MEC's primary source of aircraft is a sure way to tilt the odds in your favor.

MEC Strategy

Once again, the Intake and dam are the main concerns of the MEC defenders and should be held at all costs. But with more players to spread around, it's now possible to put up stiffer resistance in the northern valley. Focus the bulk of your troops at the Refueling Station and Supervisor Base as these are the front line positions in the opening moments of the land battle. Use mines, anti-tank troops, and the two Mi-28s to help reinforce these sites. If possible, harass the Marine advance at the Bridge Base too. Blowing the bridge here with C4 or bombs is a great delaying action, cutting off direct access to the Refueling Station. Remember, the longer you can delay the Marines from capturing any control points other than the Bridge Base, the more tickets they'll lose. For this reason, don't just defend the northern valley, but launch immediate counterattacks if one of the control points fall. Still, the commander must watch these events closely and order a retreat to the dam if Marine gains in the valley appear to be irreversible. At the dam, make sure all access points to the Construction Site and Power Station are well defended. Anti-tank troops and snipers are the heroes here, capable of eliminating US targets in the valley from the various levels of the dam. Hold at the dam as long as possible, then slowly recapture the valley control points as the Marine assault loses steam.

BASES AND CONTROL POINTS

Abandoned Hut

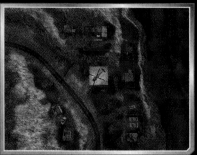

This small village and nearby airfield are the staging areas for the Marine assault on the dam. Two separate spawn points are provided here, allowing US troops easy access to each distinct area. The eastern spawn point drops troops at the airfield where they can hop in a jet or attack helicopter. This is also the site of the Marine commander's tools, like the artillery. Therefore it's important that these assets are protected from air strikes or theft—especially in 64 player games. If manned, the AA turret between the two runways can deter most air attacks. The spawn point to the west gives US troops quick access to the village where the bulk of their ground vehicles appear. Like the airfield, the high concentration of US vehicles makes this area a tempting target for MEC pilots and thieves. Fortunately there are plenty of defensive features scattered around the village, including two rooftop AA turrets. There are two main paths leading out of the village, the most obvious being the paved road running to the west. This is the quickest way for US troops to reach the Bridge Base control point and should be used early in the battle. Its also possible to move vehicles along the shallow river bed to the east. This path is a good way to circumvent any MEC defenses at the Bridge Base. It's also a good way to sneak up on the Refueling Station or enter the valley floor on the eastern side of the dam. Before spawning at either Abandoned Hut spawn points, watch the map and make sure your desired vehicle is available. Otherwise you'll have a long run ahead of you if you have to hike between the airfield and village to hitch a ride into combat.

Maps: 32- and 64-Player

Adjacent Bases/ Control Points:
• Bridge Base

Abandoned Hut Assets

USMC Control	16-Player	32-Player	64-Player
DPV	—	3	4
LAV-25	—	1	1
M6 Bradley	—	1	1
M1A2	—	1	2
HH-60H	—	1	1
AH-1Z	—	1	1
F-18 E/F	—	1	1
F-15E	—	—	1
Artillery	—	3	3
UAV Trailer	—	1	1
Radar Station	—	1	1
AT Turret	—	3	4
AA Turret	—	3	3
Machine Gun	—	1	2

Bridge Base

Its close proximity to the Abandoned Hut makes this neutral control point relatively easy to capture for the Marines at the start of each battle. But it's important to note that capturing the Bridge Base does not stop the US ticket count from dwindling—one of the other control points must be captured to stop the ticket drain. In addition to providing the Marines with one more M1A2, the Bridge Base serves as a good staging area for attacks on the Refueling Station or Supervisor Base. Both adjacent control points can be accessed via separate branches of the nearby paved road. It's in the Marines' best interest to keep the nearby bridge open and repaired. But MEC troops may want to sabotage the bridge to hinder the Marine advance. The bridge can be blown at three separate points using either C4 charges or ordnance from aircraft. Destroying this bridge is the best way for MEC troops to defend the Refueling Station.

Maps: 32- and 64-Player

Adjacent Bases/ Control Points:
• Abandoned Hut
• Refueling Station
• Supervisor Base

Bridge Base Assets

USMC Control	MEC Control	16-Player	32-Player	64-Player
DPV	FAV	—	1	1
M1A2	N/A	—	1	1

TIP The Bridge Base control point can be converted/contested from within the vertical ladder shaft next to the flagpole. If you can't find the attacker or defender, check this shaft.

Refueling Station

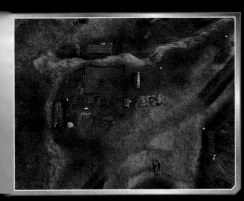

Sitting on the western rim of the dam site, the Refueling Station is a key control point for both the US and MEC forces. The Marines should capture this control point early to halt their ticket drain and get a foothold within the northern valley. Using this spawn point they can branch out to numerous surrounding control points, including the Construction Site and Lower Dam. For this very reason, MEC forces need to prevent the Marines from capturing this control point. With only two machine guns covering the sloped road to the north, the defenders need to use mines and vehicles from other control points to prevent the Refueling Station from being overrun. An Mi-28 can rack up a ton of kills just by hovering nearby and staying low, picking off one Marine attack after another with cannon fire, rockets, and guided missiles.

Maps: 32- and 64-Player

Adjacent Bases/ Control Points:

- Bridge Base
- Construction Site
- Lower Dam

Refueling Station Assets

USMC Control	MEC Control	16-Player	32-Player	64-Player
DPV	FAV	—	1	1
LAV-25	BTR-90	—	1	1
Machine Gun	Machine Gun	—	2	2

Supervisor Base

This somewhat distant control point is located on a hill at the far north end of the valley, just opposite of the dam. Like the Refueling Station, the Supervisor Base is another front-line position for the MEC defenders and should be fortified early. The Marines can easily attack this control point from the Bridge Base using the narrow winding road to the east. To prevent such attacks, the defenders should block the road with mines and the T-90. When positioning the T-90, park it at the base of the hill to the east so attacking units won't see it till it's too late. The shallow canyon walls flanking the road can also help protect the tank from air strikes. For added protection, the AT turret can cover the eastern road as well as the western road leading to the Material Station. Due to the heavy defensive assets, the Marines should always call in an artillery strike on this control point before attacking. Even then, the MEC infantry have plenty of hiding spots, including two guard posts on the eastern and western flanks, each equipped with a machine gun.

Maps: 64-Player Only

Adjacent Bases/ Control Points:

- Bridge Base
- Material Station

Supervisor Base Assets

USMC Control	MEC Control	16-Player	32-Player	64-Player
DPV	FAV	—	—	1
N/A	T-90	—	—	1
AT Turret	AT Turret	—	—	1
Machine Gun	Machine Gun	—	—	2

Material Station

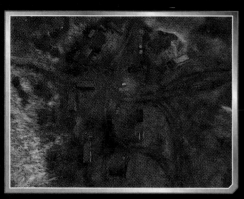

Of all the control points in the northern valley, the Material Station is the most valuable in terms of vehicle spawn points. For the MEC defenders its Tunguska is critical for keeping US aircraft away from the surrounding control points. To protect the Tunguska from counterattacks, park it along the road to the south in between the two mounds of earth. It can also be camouflaged by parking it on the hill to the west, among the trees. Either way, the Tunguska should remain nearby to suppress US air strikes in the northern valley. Because the Material Station lacks any stationary weapons, it's best defended by the tank and a few infantry. Some engineers and anti-tank troops should be able to hold back most enemy vehicle attacks. The Material Station is also a crossroads of sorts too, with approaches to three surrounding control points. This flexibility makes it an ideal staging area for the Marine attackers. The road to the north leads to the Supervisor Base and the road to the south leads to the Lower Dam. A less noticeable dirt road winds up the steep cliff to the west and eventually ends near the Power Station. By continuing past the Power Station, units can access the top of the dam and even continue on to the Construction Site.

Maps: 32- and 64-Player

Adjacent Bases/ Control Points:
- Supervisor Base
- Power Station
- Lower Dam

Material Station Assets

USMC Control	MEC Control	16-Player	32-Player	64 Player
DPV	FAV	—	2	1
M6 Bradley	Tunguska	—	1	1
M1A2	T-90	—	1	1

Power Station

The Power Station control point sits on the dam's western flank and overlooks the northern valley. It's also one of two control points that allows easy vehicle access to the top of the dam. This is most useful during 16 player battles when this control point serves as the MEC's starting point. But in 32 and 64 player games, the Power Station's role is a bit more subtle. If necessary, MEC special forces should use this spawn point to access the top of the dam and demolish the road. This is a good idea if the enemy holds the Construction Site on the other side of the dam. But remember, the Power Station can also be assaulted from the dirt road to the west, especially if the enemy spawns troops at the Material Station. Infantry attacks are also possible from the east via a ladder and staircase. Lone or outnumbered defenders should take cover in the small flat-roofed building just east of the flagpole. This protects them from most vehicle and artillery

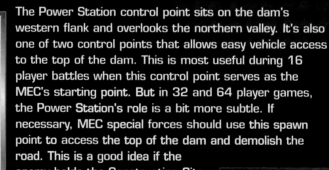

Maps: All

Adjacent Bases/ Control Points:
- Material Station
- Upper Dam
- Construction Site
- Intake

Power Station Assets

USMC Control	MEC Control	16-Player	32-Player	64 Player
DPV	FAV	—	1	1
HMMWV	GAZ 39371	2	—	—
M1A2	T-90	1*	1	1
N/A	Artillery	2	—	—
N/A	UAV Trailer	1	—	—
N/A	Radar Station	1	—	—
AA Turret	AA Turret	1	—	—

* = MEC Control Only

attacks, but it can also protect attackers attempting to convert the control point. Mines are effective if placed near the base of the ramp leading down from the main road—rushing attackers will have a hard time spotting them here.

Upper Dam

Available only on the 16 player map, the Upper Dam has no assets, but that doesn't keep it from being one of the most hotly contested control points during these small-scale games. Since it's sandwiched between the MEC forces to the west and the US forces to the east, both sides have a good chance of taking control of this area, but speed is the key to win the race. Whoever makes it to the center of the dam must prevent the other side from counterattacking. At the moment the road crossing the top of the dam uses large metal planks to span a couple of gaps in the concrete structure. These large flat pieces of metal can be destroyed with C4 planted by special forces. Only one huge hole can be blasted in the short western span, using three charges. But the two large gaps can be created in the longer eastern span. Blowing these makeshift bridges may keep vehicles from crossing, but infantry can still make their way across by carefully jumping the narrowest gaps or navigating the girders running beneath each bridge. Infantry defenders can use the central tower near the flagpole as a good platform for firing on attackers. Defenders should also watch the ladder to the southeast, leading up from the Lower Dam. Deploying a claymore at the top of the ladder should surprise any attackers attempting to sneak up on this position from below. Attackers using the Upper Dam as a staging area for Lower Dam assaults should avoid using the ladders and stairways altogether. Instead, simply leap off the northern side of the dam and parachute down to the Lower Dam.

Maps:
16-Player Only

Adjacent Bases/ Control Points:
- Power Station
- Lower Dam
- Construction Site

Lower Dam

This control point is actually located inside the base of the dam, and depending on the map size, it produces a wide variety of vehicles. On the 16 player map, the Lower Dam generates a transport helicopter which either side can use to assault the remaining control points. But on the 32 and 64 player maps, an attack helicopter is spawned on the helipad positioned on the south side of the dam. This helipad can be reached by sets of stairs and ladders on the northern and southern sides of the dam. Near the helipad is a huge crane. Although it's not the only crane on the map, it is by far the tallest one. Snipers positioned on this crane can engage enemy troops in all directions as well as cover the flag poles at the Refueling Station, Material Station, Construction Site, and Intake. Therefore, the MEC defenders should place a good sniper here early to help defend the surrounding control points. Down at the dam's base, defenders should use mines and the spawned APC to prevent the control point from being captured. Since attacks can come from just about every direction (including from above) all defensive efforts should be closely focused around the flagpole.

Maps: All

Adjacent Bases/ Control Points:
- Refueling Station
- Upper Dam
- Material Station
- Intake

Lower Dam Assets

USMC Control	MEC Control	16-Player	32-Player	64-Player
DPV	FAV	—	1	1
HMMWV	GAZ 39371	1	—	—
LAV-25	BTR-90	1	1	1
HH-60H	Mi-17	1	—	—
AH-1Z	Mi-28	—	1	1
AT Turret	AT Turret	1	1	1
AA Turret	AA Turret	1	—	—

Construction Site

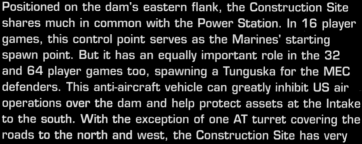

Positioned on the dam's eastern flank, the Construction Site shares much in common with the Power Station. In 16 player games, this control point serves as the Marines' starting spawn point. But it has an equally important role in the 32 and 64 player games too, spawning a Tunguska for the MEC defenders. This anti-aircraft vehicle can greatly inhibit US air operations over the dam and help protect assets at the Intake to the south. With the exception of one AT turret covering the roads to the north and west, the Construction Site has very little defensive firepower. Fortunately, its flagpole is positioned on the roof of the partially constructed building, making it difficult to convert. The roof can be reached through an interior staircase or by ladders on the scaffolds surrounding the structure. A good transport helicopter pilot can make the capture even easier by dropping troops directly onto the roof.

Maps: All

Adjacent Bases/Control Points:
- Refueling Station
- Upper Dam
- Lower Dam
- Intake

Construction Site Assets

USMC Control	MEC Control	16-Player	32-Player	64-Player
DPV	FAV	—	1	1
HMMWV	GAZ 39371	2	—	—
M6 Bradley	Tunguska	—	1	1
M1A2	N/A	1	—	—
Artillery	N/A	2	—	—
UAV Trailer	N/A	1	—	—
Radar Station	N/A	1	—	—
AT Turret	AT Turret	1	1	1
AA Turret	AA Turret	1	—	—

Intake

The Intake serves as the MEC's main base and primary source of aircraft. However, this being an assault map, the control point can be converted by the Marines. As a result, the defenders should expect frequent and persistent attacks on the Intake. Since it's difficult to move vehicles here, most attacks will come by air. For instance, if a Seahawk filled with Marines manages to slip through the MEC defenses, they can convert the control point within a few seconds. The first line of defense for such air attacks in the Mig-29. Instead of bombing ground targets, it should prowl the skies for US helicopters and jets. The AA turret at the end of the runways should also be manned at all times. But even shooting down helicopters and planes may not be enough to keep US troops from parachuting down to this control point. The control point's BTR-90 is the best defensive option to fight off infantry and should stay nearby when possible to repel such attacks. Infantry positioned in the building next to the flagpole can also put up a good fight by firing through the windows.

Maps: 32- and 64-Player

Adjacent Bases/Control Points:
- Power Station
- Lower Dam
- Construction Site

Intake Assets

USMC Control	MEC Control	16-Player	32-Player	64-Player
DPV	FAV	—	2	3
LAV-25	BTR-90	—	1	1
N/A	T-90	—	1	1
HH-60H	Mi-17	—	1	1
N/A	Mi-28	—	1	1
N/A	Mig-29	—	1	1
N/A	SU-34	—	—	1
N/A	Artillery	—	3	3
N/A	UAV Trailer	—	1	1
N/A	Radar Station	—	1	1
AT Turret	AT Turret	—	—	1
AA Turret	AA Turret	—	1	1
Machine Gun	Machine Gun	—	3	3

KUBRA DAM TACTICS

Behind Enemy Lines

The Seahawk (spawned at the Abandoned Hut) can transport up to six Marines almost anywhere on the map. To avoid the predictable grinding ground combat at the front-line control points, use this transport helicopter to insert squads in remote areas of the map.

Once in position, a squad can launch an attack on a control point from an unexpected direction. Focus on control points far removed from the action first, as they're less likely to be heavily defended—the Power Station is a good candidate. During attacks, the squad leader should hold back in a safe position and simply serve as a spawn point. MEC forces can utilize similar tactics with their Mi-17 when counterattacking key control points.

Control the Skies

For either side, establishing and maintaining air superiority is one of the best ways to give your team an advantage. This should be the primary concern of the fighter pilots. Remember, it's easier to strafe enemy aircraft while they're still on the ground. Even jets protected by hangars aren't safe from strafing runs.

The Tunguskas and M6 Bradleys also play a pivotal role in eliminating enemy jets and helicopters. Park them in spots where they're hard to see and target. Still, firing missiles leaves behind a smoke trail that can be traced back to your position, so move frequently to keep your location a mystery.

Dam Defense

   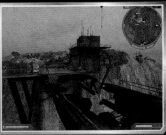

For the MEC forces, the dam is like a giant castle wall and should be used as such to prevent the Marines from breaking through and attacking the Intake to the south. The towering crane at the center can be accessed near the Lower Dam's helipad. Snipers positioned here can cover most of the northern valley as well as the Intake, but it takes immense skill to gain kills from this height and distance.

While snipers are handy for repelling infantry, anti-tank troops are the best way to deal with incoming vehicles. Half a dozen anti-tank troops positioned at different locations along the dam can target all incoming vehicles from the northern valley control points. But they'll need plenty of ammo, so make sure a support soldier or supply crate is nearby.

The western turbine tunnel is the only ground-level breach point in the dam and should be mined by engineers. Parking a T-90 in this tunnel can also be a good deterrent.

If the Power Station or Construction Site is captured by the Marines, use C4 charges or bombs to blow holes in the two temporary bridge spans at the top of the dam. This halts all east-west vehicle movement across the top of the bridge—at least until their engineers repair the spans.

Base Jumping

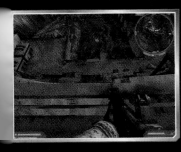

Although there are various staircases and ladders available, the quickest way to reach the Lower Dam from the top is by jumping off the ledge and parachuting down. For best results, jump off the northern side at the center of the dam. Make sure you're centered before making the leap.

While free-falling, tap ⑨ repeatedly until the parachute opens. Look straight down to avoid drifting too far off course. You should land at the large opening in the center of the dam. One more jump may be needed to reach the Lower Dam control point. Base jumping is also a quick way to get down from other high elevations like cranes.

MASHTUUR CITY

Leading elements of the US ground force must capture Mashtuur City, a primary Middle East axis of advance. In response, MEC units are rushing forward to hold the city at all costs. In this double assault upon a key urban asset, all elements of modern warfare are likely to be deployed, attempting to secure vital CPs that dot the city. Victory will go to the side that controls the majority of Mashtuur when hostilities cease.

16-PLAYER

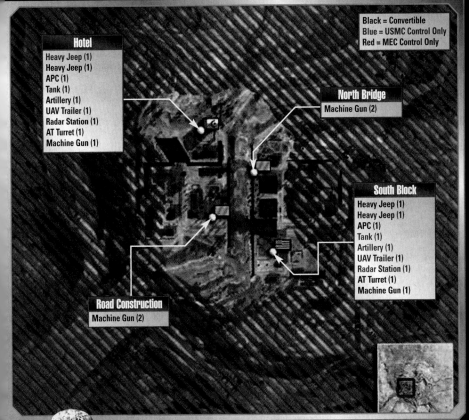

Black = Convertible
Blue = USMC Control Only
Red = MEC Control Only

Hotel
Heavy Jeep (1)
Heavy Jeep (1)
APC (1)
Tank (1)
Artillery (1)
UAV Trailer (1)
Radar Station (1)
AT Turret (1)
Machine Gun (1)

North Bridge
Machine Gun (2)

South Block
Heavy Jeep (1)
Heavy Jeep (1)
APC (1)
Tank (1)
Artillery (1)
UAV Trailer (1)
Radar Station (1)
AT Turret (1)
Machine Gun (1)

Road Construction
Machine Gun (2)

Game Type:
Double Assault
Total Control Points: 4
Convertible Control Points: 4

The few tanks on this map give you some long range firepower to destroy enemy APCs and jeeps. If you don't want to blow up a bridge, use a tank to keep the enemy away.

US Strategy

The 16-player map is small and consists of only four control points. A dry river divides the map into east and west sections with bridges crossing it at the north and south points. The USMC starting base is at the South Block control point. From here the Marines must expand quickly both to the north and to the west. Send a few soldiers in the heavy jeep to the North Bridge to capture it and, if possible, blow the bridge to make it more difficult for the MEC to get to this control point. The tank and the rest of your troops should then move towards the Construction Site to secure it. Artillery strikes against the MEC base at the Hotel will help keep the enemy from massing against you and might also take out some of their vehicles as well. Mines are also useful in the narrow streets to keep enemy tanks and other vehicles from approaching your position. While you can just hold with the three control points and engage the enemy as they come at you, taking the Hotel gives you a quicker victory.

MEC Strategy

The MEC strategy is similar to the USMC's. Right at the start, you need to get your troops moving towards the North Bridge and the Construction Site. Since the North Bridge is across the river from your base at the Hotel, don't blow this bridge. Instead, place some mines around it, then cover it from the roof of the hotel with snipers and anti-tank troops. The Construction site is a bit tougher to get to first; send your tank and APC to cover your troops as they secure the control point and blow the bridge. While you cannot blow this large bridge completely—a jeep can still drive across—it does prevent tanks from crossing the river here. You can then use mines to keep the jeeps on the other side. Afterward, secure this control point with a couple of soldiers while the rest of your force gathers near the North Bridge and slowly advances towards the South Block. Clear out defenders on the rooftops with sniper fire, then move in to take the position for a win.

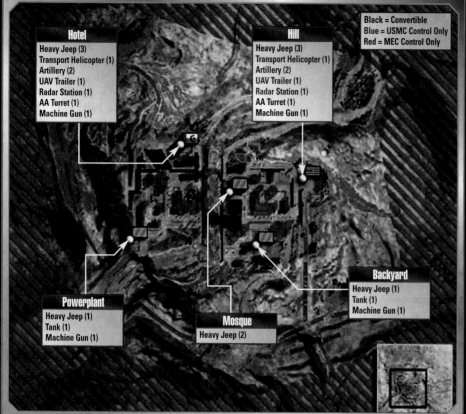

Hotel
Heavy Jeep (3)
Transport Helicopter (1)
Artillery (2)
UAV Trailer (1)
Radar Station (1)
AA Turret (1)
Machine Gun (1)

Hill
Heavy Jeep (3)
Transport Helicopter (1)
Artillery (2)
UAV Trailer (1)
Radar Station (1)
AA Turret (1)
Machine Gun (1)

Black = Convertible
Blue = USMC Control Only
Red = MEC Control Only

Backyard
Heavy Jeep (1)
Tank (1)
Machine Gun (1)

Powerplant
Heavy Jeep (1)
Tank (1)
Machine Gun (1)

Mosque
Heavy Jeep (2)

Game Type:
Double Assault
Total Control Points: 5
Convertible Control Points: 5

Thinking in three dimensions is the key to winning this map. Don't limit your tactics to just the ground. Climb up ladders and onto rooftops or into the upper rooms of tall buildings. In the same vein, watch for enemies above as you advance.

US Strategy

On this map, the US begins with a single control point at the Hill as well as another spawn point by the South Gas Station (which is not a control point in the 32-player game). The first thing the Marines should do is to send troops in the jeeps to secure the Mosque and the Backyard control points while sending a third team to blow the northern bridge. This helps prevent the MEC from making raids into the northeastern part of the map. Your next objective is the Powerplant. Once you've secured this, you'll have the MEC boxed up in the northwestern corner of the map. Send in some special forces troops via helicopter to raid the North Gas Station, blowing up the MEC artillery and support structures. Then use the hills north of the Hotel as a firing position to cover the main assault against the Hotel.

MEC Strategy

The MEC begins with only one control point nearby their base at the Hotel on their side of the river—the Powerplant. Secure it quickly, then blow the bridge to the south of it to prevent the US from making a quick run at it. Blow the central bridge near the mosque as well as the high bridge overlooking the Powerplant. This prevents the US from making ground raids against you in the south. Leave the northern bridge standing and be sure to prevent the US from blowing it up. This bridge serves as your highway into the US territory. Since the US usually begins by expanding south to grab the control points on their side of the river, this is the MEC's opportunity to grab the Marine base. Send a large force across the northern bridge to take the Hill control point. Additional troops can drop in by parachute from the transport helicopter. Without this important control point, the US will have a tough time putting up resistance, allowing the MEC to take over the remaining two control points to win the game.

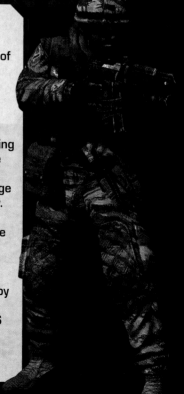

64-PLAYER

Black = Convertible
Blue = USMC Control Only
Red = MEC Control Only

North Gas Station
Heavy Jeep (1)
Transport Helicopter (1)
AA Turret (1)

Mosque
Heavy Jeep (2)

Hill
Heavy Jeep (2)
Artillery (2)
UAV Trailer (1)
Radar Station (1)
Machine Gun (1)

Hotel
Heavy Jeep (2)
Artillery (2)
UAV Trailer (1)
Radar Station (1)
Machine Gun (1)

South Gas Station
Heavy Jeep (1)
Transport Helicopter (1)
AA Turret (1)

Powerplant
Heavy Jeep (1)
Tank (1)
Machine Gun (1)

Backyard
Heavy Jeep (1)
Tank (1)
Machine Gun (1)

Game Type:
Head-On Conquest
Total Control Points: 7
Convertible Control Points: 5

A road runs along the tops or the hills by the southern and western map edges. This provides a way to get from one side of the map to the other—and hit the enemy in the flank where they're probably not expecting you.

US Strategy

This map is almost exactly like the 32-player game except that each side has a permanent control point at their respective Gas Stations. As in the 32-player game, the US must quickly secure the Mosque and Backyard control points. Since you cannot capture all of the control points for a quick win, there is no need to rush across the river to take control of the Powerplant or the Hotel. In fact, taking and holding the hotel can be difficult with the North Gas Station (which the MEC controls and uses as a spawn point) overlooking the Hotel. Instead, blow all of the bridges and hold, forcing the enemy to come to you. In order to win the game, the US should defend from positions of strength, such as cover, rooftops overlooking the bridges, and access routes to the eastern side of the map—while at the same time making raids into the western side of the map. You can drop in troops by helicopter or send snipers and other troops to fire down on MEC spawn points from surrounding hills and other locations. Even a small squad with an anti-tank soldier and a supply drop can cause some real damage to the enemy, hitting them right at their bases.

MEC Strategy

The MEC should take a more aggressive strategy than the US. Since the Marine base at the Hill is not so close to the South Gas Station, the Hill becomes a viable target for capture right at the start of the game. Send most of your team to capture this control point while the rest secure the Powerplant and blow the central and southern bridges and hold there. Once the MEC has the Hill, a quick push south secures the remaining two control points which can be captured. Now the US only has their South Gas Station up on the Hill which seriously limits the Marines' access to vehicles and makes a breakout very difficult. Hold the control points you capture while firing artillery strikes against the South Gas Station until you have achieved victory.

BASES AND CONTROL POINTS

North Gas Station

While this is also a spawn point in the 32-player game, it is considered part of the Hotel control point. Only in the 64-player game is this an actual control point; it can't be captured by the enemy. Because of its location up in the hills of the northwest, it can only be reached by roads running up from the south or by air. However, despite its immunity to capture, you must still defend it—for both the 32- and 64-player games, the support structures located here and artillery nearby will be targets for Marine raids. Since this is the only location where the MEC helicopter spawns, be sure to keep some troops here to ensure you can make air assaults against the enemy. The North Gas Station's position overlooking the Hotel below makes this a great position for troops to cover the Hotel against enemy attacks while remaining at a distance.

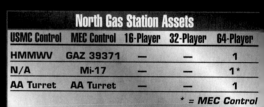

Maps:
64-Player Only

Adjacent Bases/ Control Points:
- Hotel

North Gas Station Assets

USMC Control	MEC Control	16-Player	32-Player	64-Player
HMMWV	GAZ 39371	—	—	1
N/A	Mi-17	—	—	1*
AA Turret	AA Turret	—	—	1

* = MEC Control

South Gas Station

This functions in the same way for the US as the North Gas Station does for the MEC. Unfortunately, its location does not allow it to cover the Marine base at the Hill to the same degree that the North Gas Station covers the Hotel. Therefore, use it to ensure that the Backyard does not fall. The roads running to the west of this control point takes your troops to the Powerplant if they follow the lower route, or all the way to the North Gas Station (if they take the upper route across the high bridge in the southwest corner of the map). Plus, this is where the US transport helicopter spawns, making this location great for staging raids against the MEC—which can be an important part of the Marine strategy.

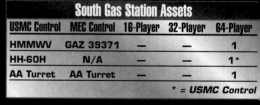

Maps:
64-Player Only

Adjacent Bases/ Control Points:
- Hill
- Backyard

South Gas Station Assets

USMC Control	MEC Control	16-Player	32-Player	64-Player
HMMWV	GAZ 39371	—	—	1
HH-60H	N/A	—	—	1*
AA Turret	AA Turret	—	—	1

* = USMC Control

Hotel

The Hotel is the MEC base for all three games, and is important no matter how many players are in the game. The building to the south of the flagpole provides a rooftop with a machine gun position that covers the northern bridge as well as the area to the south. Depending on the game, you may also find either an AA or AT turret to help defend this position. Because the Hotel sits up above the surrounding area to the south, enemies approaching must come up one of two ramps to the east and west of the control point. These can be easily covered and mined if necessary. Control of the North Gas Station is also important to the defense of the Hotel, since an enemy positioned there can fire down on the area surrounding the flagpole and engage the vehicles which spawn there.

Maps: All

Adjacent Bases/ Control Points:
- North Gas Station
- Powerplant
- Hill
- North Bridge
- Road Construction

Hotel Assets

USMC Control	MEC Control	16-Player	32-Player	64-Player
HMMWV	GAZ 39371	1*+1	3	2
LAV-25	BTR-90	1	—	—
N/A	T-90	1	—	—
N/A	Mi-17	—	1	—
N/A	Artillery	1	2	2
N/A	UAV	1	1	1
N/A	Radar	1	1	1
AT Turret	AT Turret	1	—	—
AA Turret	AA Turret	—	1	—
Machine Gun	Machine Gun	1	1	1

* = USMC Control

North Bridge

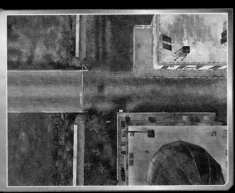

Even though it is only a control point in the 16-player game, the North Bridge is an important part to all games. It is the only connection between the east and west in the northern part of the map. Depending on which side you are playing, and your strategy, you either want to blow this bridge to deny its use to the enemy or defend it to prevent the enemy from destroying it. Machine gun positions can be found here during the 16-player game. However, it's better for the US to blow the bridge rather than try to defend it against an MEC assault across it.

Maps: 16-Player Only

Adjacent Bases/ Control Points:
- Hotel
- South Block

North Bridge Assets

USMC Control	MEC Control	16-Player	32-Player	64-Player
Machine Gun	Machine Gun	2	—	—

Hill

The Hill serves as the USMC base for the 32- and 64-player games. It is positioned higher than the area to the south and west and can only be accessed by a single ramp. As a result, this is a tough control point to capture by ground assault. While there is an AA turret here during the 32-player game, it is not there for the 64-player game, making this control point ripe for an airborne assault. Dropping enemy troops onto the rooftops overlooking the flagpole can provide cover for other troops as they secure the control point—most of the defenders will be facing in the opposite direction.

Maps: 32- and 64-Player

Adjacent Bases/ Control Points:
- Hotel
- Mosque
- Backyard
- South Gas Station

Hill Assets

USMC Control	MEC Control	16-Player	32-Player	64-Player
HMMWV	GAZ 39371	—	3	2
HH-60H	N/A	—	1	—
Artillery	N/A	—	2	2
UAV	N/A	—	1	—
Radar	N/A	—	1	—
AA Turret	AA Turret	—	1	—
Machine Gun	Machine Gun	—	1	1

Powerplant

The Powerplant is located in the southwest corner of the map and is near the lower of the two southern bridges. While a machine gun provides some defense against enemies attacking form the east, this is a difficult control point to defend from the inside. The high bridge and upper road to the west look down on the Powerplant, allowing snipers and anti-tank troops to fire down on either the defenders or enemies moving in to take control of it. To help protect this control point, the lower and high bridge should both be blown to prevent the Marines from driving right up to it or taking up a position overlooking it.

Maps: 32- and 64-Player

Adjacent Bases/ Control Points:
- Hotel
- Mosque

Powerplant Assets

USMC Control	MEC Control	16-Player	32-Player	64-Player
HMMWV	GAZ 39371	—	1	1
N/A	T-90	—	1	1
Machine Gun	Machine Gun	—	1	1

Road Construction

This control point is located on the western side of the central bridge with the flagpole on the side of the road. An occupied vehicle can drive up right next to the flagpole and gain control without the troops inside having to dismount. In addition to the access by the road, the MEC can also approach this control point through the pipes in the ditch. These pipes not only

Maps:
16-Player Only

Adjacent Bases/Control Points:
- Hotel
- South Block

Road Construction Assets

USMC Control	MEC Control	16-Player	32-Player	64-Player
Machine Gun	Machine Gun	2	—	—

run north to south, but there is also an intersection which leads out to the riverbed. Two machine guns cover the central bridge and the ditch, respectively. Stairs in a nearby building lead up to the roof, allowing troops on the rooftop to cover to the north and west.

Mosque

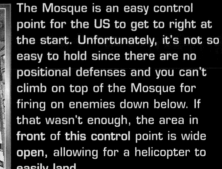

The Mosque is an easy control point for the US to get to right at the start. Unfortunately, it's not so easy to hold since there are no positional defenses and you can't climb on top of the Mosque for firing on enemies down below. If that wasn't enough, the area in front of this control point is wide open, allowing for a helicopter to easily land and drop off troops. Protect this control point

Maps: 32- and 64-Player

Adjacent Bases/Control Points:
- Backyard
- Hill
- Powerplant

Mosque Assets

USMC Control	MEC Control	16-Player	32-Player	64-Player
HMMWV	GAZ 39371	—	2	2

by defending at the north and central bridges since they are the main access points the MEC will take to get to the Mosque.

South Block

This is the USMC base for the 16-player game. The arrangement of the buildings protect the vehicles which spawn here and force the enemy to come right into the control point to access the flagpole or get the vehicles. The tall buildings to the north of the flagpole provide great rooftops from which snipers and other troops can cover the central bridge and Mosque area. Also be sure to use the AT turret to deal with any enemy vehicles which get in close.

Maps:
16-Player Only

Adjacent Bases/ Control Points:
- North Bridge
- Road Construction

South Block Assets

USMC Control	MEC Control	16-Player	32-Player	64-Player
HMMWV	GAZ 39371	1* + 1	—	—
LAV-25	BTR-90	1	—	—
M1A2	N/A	1	—	—
Artillery	N/A	1	—	—
UAV	N/A	1	—	—
Radar	N/A	1	—	—
AT Turret	AT Turret	1	—	—
Machine Gun	Machine Gun	1	—	—

* = MEC Control

Backyard

Though the Backyard isn't much of a control point—it consists of a flagpole surrounded by fence—it's important for the US to maintain control of it. If the MEC captures it, not only do they get a spawn point on the eastern side of the river, this control point will generate a tank while under MEC control. Therefore, it's more useful for the Marines to deny it to the enemy than actually use it for their own vehicular needs. If the northern and central bridges have been destroyed, then

Maps: 32- and 64-Player

Adjacent Bases/ Control Points:
- Hill
- Mosque
- South Gas Station

Backyard Assets

USMC Control	MEC Control	16-Player	32-Player	64-Player
HMMWV	GAZ 39371	—	1	1
M1A2	N/A	—	1	1
Machine Gun	Machine Gun	—	1	1

the Backyard is in the path of the MEC advance into the southern part of US territory.

MASHTUUR TACTICS

Blowing the Bridges

Bridges connect the eastern and western sides of the map, providing access across the dry riverbed. Control or denial of these bridges represents an important part of the strategy for each side.

Since some bridges need to be blown before the enemy can use them, you need a quick tactic at the start of the game for taking out a bridge. Send a heavy jeep with a special forces soldier sitting in the back position. As they drive over a bridge, the special forces soldier drops explosives, then detonates them as the jeep drives away.

The central bridge is very wide and no matter how many explosives you detonate on it, there will always be a strip down the middle you can drive a jeep along. However, a few mines should stop anyone from driving across.

Transport Helicopter Assaults

Helicopters play a major role in the 32- and 64-player games. With only two AA turrets on these maps, so as long as you stay away from them, you can fly around fairly safely. Furthermore, though the dust in the air decreases visibility, it can also help hide helicopters in flight.

To avoid being spotted by the enemy, fly at high altitude and use your map to navigate since you can't see landmarks below. Then you can either land straight down or on your target, or drop your troops down on it by parachute. Since the enemy can't see the helicopter, they won't expect troops falling from the sky until the troops are almost to the ground.

Defending Control Points

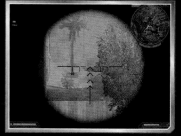

Since most of the fighting in this mission is urban, with lots of buildings to provide cover and concealment, the defender has the advantage. Also, several machine gun positions allow you to dominate access to the control points. Be careful, though: while these machine guns can lay down a lot of lead, continuously manning them makes you a prime target for snipers.

Rooftops can also be dangerous. When possible, try to take up positions inside the buildings and fire out through the windows. These are great spots for snipers and if you come under fire, just drop prone, then move to another window and fire from there. If you keep firing from one spot, the enemy will get wise and wait for your head to pop up so they can take it off.

CLEAN SWEEP

This vital entrance to the Persian Gulf is held by local MEC forces who have established a strong defensive presence on the scattered islands of the waterway. For the US Rapid Deployment force to clear the waterway they must first deploy air assets to disable a key MEC power station, after which the US force must enter the channel and capture the islands defended by these determined MEC fighters.

16-PLAYER

US Airfield
APC (1)
Transport Helicopter (1)
Fighter Bomber (1)
RIB (2)
Artillery (3)
UAV Trailer (1)
Radar Station (1)
AA Turret (1)
Machine Gun (1)

Black = Convertible
Blue = USMC Control Only
Red = MEC Control Only

Control Center
Light Jeep (4)
APC (1)
Tank (1)
RIB (1)
AA Turret (1)
AT Turret (2)
Machine Gun (3)

Small Airstrip
Light Jeep (2)
APC (1)
AAV (1)
Tank (1)
Fighter Bomber (1)
RIB (2)
Artillery (3)
UAV Trailer (1)
Radar Station (1)
AA Turret (1)
AT Turret (1)
Machine Gun (2)

Refueling Station
Light Jeep (2)
APC (1)
AA Turret (1)
Machine Gun (4)

Game Type:
Assault
Total Control Points: 4
Convertible Control Points: 3

This map requires coordination, even in the Bootcamp game. Take command and focus on one control point at a time.

US Strategy

Since the US only has a single control point at the start of the game, you begin losing tickets right away. Therefore, you need to take control of at least one of the MEC control points as quickly as possible. While the Control Center is the closest, it is almost always the most heavily defended. Your best chance to get a foothold on the MEC landmass is at the Refueling Station. In fact, send a couple soldiers there, at least one of them anti-tank, in the F-15E right at the start of the mission. Bail out and parachute down to the control point, letting the jet crash. Since the plane will respawn shortly, you won't be without air support for too long. If the enemy has not already occupied the APC here, send one soldier to pick it up while the other heads for the flagpole. For those times when the enemy decides to defend here, your anti-tank soldier can take care of the APC.

You now have the enemy boxed in. They must defend from two different directions. Take out the long bridge between the Control Center and the Small Airstrip using bombs dropped by the F-15E. This prevents the MEC from moving tanks from one location to the other. You can then attack wherever the MEC has less defenses. The Small Airstrip is usually the best choice since while you are there, you can destroy the enemy artillery and other support structures. You can either keep them bottled up on the Control Center island and bombard them until their tickets are reduced to zero or assault the small, final control point for a quicker win. Remember to use your artillery and air power to pummel the MEC before you attack.

MEC Strategy

The MEC begins with the advantage. However, since the US Airfield can't be captured, you are forced onto the defensive right from the start. The US sends their main attack against the Control Center, so position most of your force here. Use the AT and AA positions as well as the tank to fight off enemies before they can land. Be sure to get your Su-34 up in the air to not only engage enemy aircraft but also to attack the US as they send troops in RIB and APCs toward your control points. In addition to covering the Control Center, have one soldier at the Refueling Station. By manning the AA position, you can take attack any enemy aircraft that approach. Then use the APC to take care of any Marines that try to parachute down to take this control point. Don't worry about attacking the US Airfield. Since you don't have a lot of troops, you are better off defending and inflicting as many casualties on the enemy as possible.

32-PLAYER

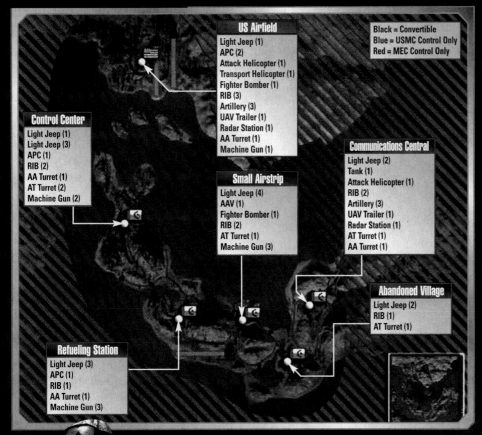

US Airfield
Light Jeep (1)
APC (2)
Attack Helicopter (1)
Transport Helicopter (1)
Fighter Bomber (1)
RIB (3)
Artillery (3)
UAV Trailer (1)
Radar Station (1)
AA Turret (1)
Machine Gun (1)

Black = Convertible
Blue = USMC Control Only
Red = MEC Control Only

Control Center
Light Jeep (1)
Light Jeep (3)
APC (1)
RIB (2)
AA Turret (1)
AT Turret (2)
Machine Gun (2)

Small Airstrip
Light Jeep (4)
AAV (1)
Fighter Bomber (1)
RIB (2)
AT Turret (1)
Machine Gun (3)

Communications Central
Light Jeep (2)
Tank (1)
Attack Helicopter (1)
RIB (2)
Artillery (3)
UAV Trailer (1)
Radar Station (1)
AT Turret (1)
AA Turret (1)

Abandoned Village
Light Jeep (2)
RIB (1)
AT Turret (1)

Refueling Station
Light Jeep (3)
APC (1)
RIB (1)
AA Turret (1)
Machine Gun (3)

Game Type:
Assault
Total Control Points: 6
Convertible Control Points: 5

Airpower is an important aspect of this map. Use fighter/bombers and attack helicopters to hit the enemy hard and fast.

US Strategy

The US must move quickly and take a control point in order to stop their tickets from counting down. However, unlike in the 16-player map, the enemy is forced to defend more locations and their vehicles are more spread out. This time the Control Center is easier to take. In addition, it also provides the US with lots of vehicles which can then be used to capture other control points. The next target is the Small Airfield. While capturing it does not provide another fighter/bomber spawn point for you, it does deny this type of vehicle to the enemy. Continue on to the Refueling Station. After that, defend your control points and continue to put pressure on the enemy, taking the remaining control points as possible.

It is important for the US to defend the control points they capture. Keep some troops back at the Control Center since it serves as the forward headquarters for your force as they advance on MEC positions. It is usually a good idea to keep at least one soldier back at the Airfield as well to guard against raids by the enemy.

MEC Strategy

For the MEC, this map is defensive at the start. The Control Center can be tough to hold. However, at least half of your force should begin there, manning the positional defenses and engaging the enemy while they are still crossing the waterway. Anti-tank and support troops are the most useful here. It is also important that you maintain the Small Airstrip as well as the Communications Center since these provide important vehicles such as the Su-34 and Mi-28 as well as tanks, artillery, and your support structures. As the US captures control points, be sure to send small raids against these as well as against the US Airfield. The goal of these raids is to force the enemy to use troops to defend them and in the case of the Airfield, to destroy the US artillery and support structures.

64-PLAYER

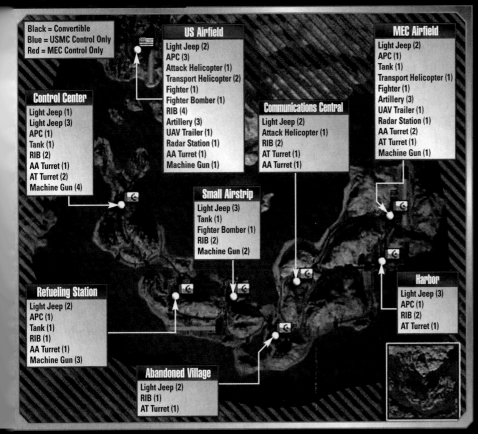

Black = Convertible
Blue = USMC Control Only
Red = MEC Control Only

US Airfield
Light Jeep (2)
APC (3)
Attack Helicopter (1)
Transport Helicopter (2)
Fighter (1)
Fighter Bomber (1)
RIB (4)
Artillery (3)
UAV Trailer (1)
Radar Station (1)
AA Turret (1)
Machine Gun (1)

MEC Airfield
Light Jeep (2)
APC (1)
Tank (1)
Transport Helicopter (1)
Fighter (1)
Artillery (3)
UAV Trailer (1)
Radar Station (1)
AA Turret (2)
AT Turret (1)
Machine Gun (1)

Control Center
Light Jeep (1)
Light Jeep (3)
APC (1)
Tank (1)
RIB (2)
AA Turret (1)
AT Turret (2)
Machine Gun (4)

Communications Central
Light Jeep (2)
Attack Helicopter (1)
RIB (2)
AT Turret (1)
AA Turret (1)

Small Airstrip
Light Jeep (3)
Tank (1)
Fighter Bomber (1)
RIB (2)
Machine Gun (2)

Harbor
Light Jeep (3)
APC (1)
RIB (2)
AT Turret (1)

Refueling Station
Light Jeep (2)
APC (1)
Tank (1)
RIB (1)
AA Turret (1)
Machine Gun (3)

Abandoned Village
Light Jeep (2)
RIB (1)
AT Turret (1)

Game Type:
Assault
Total Control Points: 8
Convertible Control Points: 7

The US must get their troops onto the shore and capture a control point as quickly as possible.

US Strategy

The 64-player version of this map provides a lot of opportunity for the US. There are now 7 different control points which are capable of being captured. While the Control Center is an obvious choice for starting, an ambitious US team can move quickly to capture the MEC Airfield (at the opposite end of the map from the US Airfield). Speed is of essence. Since the MEC must divide their forces to cover several different spots, the Marines have the advantage in that they can focus on a specific control point and gain numerical superiority. With several planes and helicopters, send a large squad or two to capture the MEC Airfield. Not only does this give you a new spawn point, but it also forces the MEC to worry about attacks from two different directions. It's important to destroy the MEC artillery and support structures or they'll definitely be used against you.

Now begin taking other control points. The key is to hit the enemy where they are weak. Try to pick up undefended or lightly defended control points first so you can stop your tickets from counting down. The Abandoned Village and Communication Central are usually good spots to start. However, in your quest to conquer, it is important to defend the control points you have captured. You want to avoid the need to recapture them. With two airfields under your control, you have air superiority—even though new planes and helicopters don't spawn at the captured control points. Use it along with artillery to bombard MEC positions and cause as much damage as possible in support of your ground troops.

MEC Strategy

The MEC has it tough at the start. It must defend seven different control points and can't ever capture the US's headquarters point. You should have enough troops to have at least one soldier at each control point just so the enemy can't take any for free. However, there are some control points that you cannot allow the enemy to capture. Position a squad each at the Control Center, MEC Airfield, and then either the Refueling Station or the Communication Central. This positions your troops at both ends of your line as well as in the middle. Because of the Control Center's somewhat isolated location, it can be tough to bring in support. In fact, you can actually lose this control point and still be fine—just make the enemy pay dearly for it. Once the US has the Control Center, blow up the bridge to prevent them from using the vehicles that spawn there to capture the rest of your control points.

While you can't capture the US Airfield, its ability to provide all of the Marines' airpower still makes this an important target. Send in a small team of Special Forces and Support troops to destroy aircraft as they spawn and blow up the artillery and support structures. These raids force the US team to defend this base, thus allowing for less soldiers attacking you. Most of the control points spawn boats. Use them to get around and to recapture control points taken by the US. Often the Marines are not expecting you to hit them from the sea. Finally, try to recapture any lost control points, with the exception of the Control Center. The longer you can maintain more control points than your enemy, the more tickets they lose.

BASES AND CONTROL POINTS

US Airfield

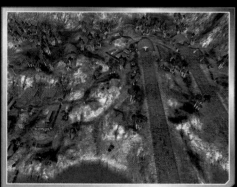

This is the US's only base at the beginning of all games. Furthermore, the enemy cannot capture it. However, its supply of aircraft and the location of the US artillery make it a juicy target for raids by the MEC. It's separated from the rest of the control points by water and can only be accessed by air or by taking an RIB or APC across to it. While the jets spawn in protective hangars, the helicopters are all out in the open and vulnerable to bombing raids.

The Airfield consists of several different areas. RIBs are located in the western part of the area near the docks, as are most of the ground vehicles. Helicopters and planes can be found to the east. In addition to a single machine gun position, an anti-aircraft position is located by the docks and can be used to engage enemy aircraft as they approach. It is usually a good idea for the US player to leave at least one soldier back to guard the base, especially during 32- and 64-player games, since an enemy could really wreak havoc here.

Maps: All

Adjacent Bases/Control Points:
- Control Center

US Airfield Assets

USMC Control	16-Player	32-Player	64-Player
DPV	—	1	2
LAV-25	1	2	3
HH-60H	1	1	2
AH-1Z	—	1	1
F-18E/F	—	—	1
F-15E	1	1	1
RIB	2	3	4
Artillery	3	3	3
UAV	1	1	1
Radar	1	1	1
AA Turret	1	1	1
Machine Gun	1	1	1

Control Center

The Control Center represents an important part in the MEC defensive strategy. The closest control point to the enemy base, it offers a lot of vehicles and weapons which can be used to repel a US invasion. For most games, this is where at least one squad should spawn at the beginning and take up defensive positions. The two AT positions located on the small islands to the north allow the MEC to engage US RIB and APCs as they make their way across the water. In fact, control of these two weapons positions can allow the MEC to deny the US amphibious capabilities.

For the US, the Control Center is an important objective since it allows the Marines to get a foothold on MEC territory. Using the light vehicles found here, the US can quickly begin advancing on other control points. However, the importance of this control point can be diminished by the destruction of the long bridge which connects it to the rest of MEC territory. If the bridge is down, the light vehicles and tanks which spawn there can't get to the rest of the map. Therefore, the US might consider taking out the bridge if they're concentrating on the rest of the control points first and want to prevent reinforcements from leaving the Control Center. The MEC should also destroy the bridge once the US takes the Control Center to keep the Marines boxed in on another island.

Maps: All

Adjacent Bases/Control Points:
- US Airfield
- Refueling Station

Control Center Assets

USMC Control	MEC Control	16-Player	32-Player	64-Player
DPV	FAV	4	1* + 3	1* + 3
LAV-25	BTR-90	1	1*	1*
M1A2	T-90	1	—	1*
RIB	RIB	1	2	2
AT Turret	AT Turret	2	2	2
AA Turret	AA Turret	1	1	1
Machine Gun	Machine Gun	3	2	4

* = USMC Control Only

Refueling Station

This is another important control point—especially in the 16- and 32-player games, since it's roughly in the center of the map. It covers access between the Control Center and the Small Airstrip.

Though it offers several machine gun positions which can be useful in defending against infantry and light vehicles, it's a tough spot to defend. If you control the Refueling Station and the enemy has the Control Center, blow the long bridge—your defense gets a lot easier.

In the smaller games, where fewer control points make each one more important, you are more likely to fight it out for the Refueling Station. Position your troops in the several bunkers and use the buildings for cover. Ordering a UAV to fly overhead during a battle allows you to locate enemies who might be hiding and waiting to ambush your team. When attacking, fire anti-tank rockets or grenades into the bunkers to clear them out quickly and prevent the enemy from using the machine guns inside.

Maps: All

Adjacent Bases/ Control Points:
- Control Center
- Small Airstrip

Refueling Station Assets

USMC Control	MEC Control	16-Player	32-Player	64-Player
DPV	FAV	2	3	2
LAV-25	BTR-90	1	1	1
M1A2	T-90	—	—	1
RIB	RIB	—	1	1
AA Turret	AA Turret	1	1	1
Machine Gun	Machine Gun	4	3	3

Small Airstrip

The Small Airstrip is another vital control point for the MEC. For the 16- and 32-player maps, this is the only location where a fixed wing aircraft spawns. The MEC needs this plane for not only attack against the US but also for air defense. Furthermore, a Tunguska also spawns here which is also useful for putting a major crimp in the US invasion plans. Even though a plane won't spawn here after the Small Airstrip is captured by the US, the fact that it prevents the MEC from getting a plane makes it a very desirable objective.

This control point is actually spread out. In fact, there are two different spawn locations—one by the flagpole and the other by the airplane hangar. All of the weapons positions, with the exception on one machine gun, are located around the flagpole. In fact, the machine gun bunkers and AT turret cover the roads leading to this control point. For the 16-player map, the Small Airstrip is also the headquarters location where the artillery and support structures are located.

Maps: All

Adjacent Bases/ Control Points:
- Refueling Station
- Communications Central

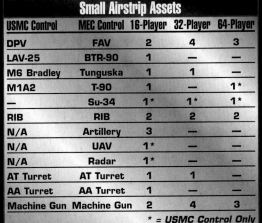

Small Airstrip Assets

USMC Control	MEC Control	16-Player	32-Player	64-Player
DPV	FAV	2	4	3
LAV-25	BTR-90	1	—	—
M6 Bradley	Tunguska	1	1	—
M1A2	T-90	1	—	1*
—	Su-34	1*	1*	1*
RIB	RIB	2	2	2
N/A	Artillery	3	—	—
N/A	UAV	1*	—	—
N/A	Radar	1*	—	—
AT Turret	AT Turret	1	1	—
AA Turret	AA Turret	1	—	—
Machine Gun	Machine Gun	2	4	3

* = USMC Control Only

Communications Central

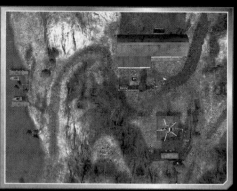

This is the MEC headquarters for the 32-player game. It is also the location where the MEC attack helicopter spawns. These factors make this an important control point during 32-player games. However, the helicopter is the only thing that makes this spot worth defending during the 64-player game. While there are no machine guns here, the single AT turret can cover ground advances from the Harbor, the MEC Airfield, and the Abandoned Village, forcing attackers to use caution when advancing—a single enemy soldier can cause some serious damage.

Maps: 32- and 64-Player

Adjacent Bases/ Control Points:

- Small Airstrip
- Abandoned Village

Communications Central Assets

USMC Control	MEC Control	16-Player	32-Player	64-Player
DPV	FAV	—	2	2
M1A2	T-90	—	1	—
N/A	Mi-28	—	1*	1*
RIB	RIB	—	2	2
N/A	Artillery	—	3*	—
N/A	UAV	—	1*	—
N/A	Radar	—	1*	—
AT Turret	AT Turret	—	1	1
AA Turret	AA Turret	—	1	1

* = MEC Control Only

Abandoned Village

This is probably the least important control point in the game. While it does provide a few vehicles, those can be found at any of the other control points. The only redeeming factor here is an AT turret, which a single soldier can man and prevent this point from being an easy capture or a drive-thru on the way to other control points. For the US, this can be a good spot to grab at the beginning of the game just to stop the tickets from counting down. Usually a soldier or two can get there quickly by air, take control, and provide a spawn point for other soldiers to join them.

Maps: 32- and 64-Player

Adjacent Bases/ Control Points:

- Communications Central
- Harbor
- MEC Airfield

Abandoned Village Assets

USMC Control	MEC Control	16-Player	32-Player	64-Player
DPV	FAV	—	2	2
RIB	RIB	—	1	1
AT Turret	AT Turret	—	1	1

Harbor

This is another control point that is not very important by itself. It does offer several vehicles, but nothing special. In addition, the AT turret can cover the roads leading from both the north and west, making this point easier to defend with a smaller force. For the US, this point can be good to capture prior to an assault on the MEC Airfield to the north. It provides a close spawn point as well as light vehicles for a fast attack.

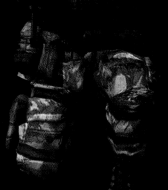

Maps:
64-Player Only

Adjacent Bases/ Control Points:
- Abandoned Village
- MEC Airfield

Harbor Assets

USMC Control	MEC Control	16-Player	32-Player	64-Player
DPV	FAV	—	—	3
LAV-25	BTR-90	—	—	1
RIB	RIB	—	—	2
AT Turret	AT Turret	—	—	1

MEC Airfield

In the 64-player game, this becomes the most important control point for the MEC. Not only is it the headquarters with artillery and support structures, it also spawns both a fighter as well as a transport helicopter, giving the MEC fast mobility and defense against US air power. For that same reason the US will want to take control of this point as soon as possible.

Since it is located at the far end of the map from the US Airfield, the MEC can expect mainly air attacks at the beginning of the game. However, the two AA turrets located here make such as attack dangerous. The AT turret gives a great coverage of the runway, but doesn't offer a great field of fire for taking out distant enemies approaching along the roads to the south and west.

Maps:
64-Player Only

Adjacent Bases/ Control Points:
- Abandoned Village
- Harbor

MEC Airfield Assets

USMC Control	MEC Control	16-Player	32-Player	64-Player
DPV	FAV	—	—	2
LAV-25	BTR-90	—	—	1
M1A2	T-90	—	—	1
HH-60H	N/A	—	—	1*
F-15E/F	Mig-29	—	—	1*
Artillery	N/A	—	—	3*
UAV	N/A	—	—	1*
Radar	N/A	—	—	1*
AT Turret	AT Turret	—	—	1
AA Turret	AA Turret	—	—	2
Machine Gun	Machine Gun	—	—	1

= MEC Control Only

CLEAN SWEEP TACTICS

Airpower and Anti-Air Tips

Airpower plays a major role on this map. The US team must use it not only to attack the MEC, but also to transport troops quickly across the sea to enemy-held control points. Therefore, it's vital that the MEC establish an anti-air defense strategy. Use the Tunguska as well as the AA turrets scattered about the map to take down the US aircraft.

US pilots should act as bomb couriers—making deliveries onto targets such as the bridges to slow down enemy movement as well as enemy troops and vehicles themselves. Fly a circuit where you drop your bombs on a target, return to your base, then make a low pass over the runway and hangar to reload bombs and repair any damage you may have taken. Afterward, go out to drop another load of bombs and repeat this cycle.

Naval Defense

Since the US troops must cross the sea to get to the MEC control points, the MEC should send soldiers north from the Control Center to man the two AT turrets on the small islands facing the US Airfield. With these turrets, you can destroy the Marine APCs and RIBs as they head your way. Also use vehicles to help defend your shores. The Tunguska's cannons will shred an RIB while your tanks and APCs will deal heavy damage to the US APCs.

In addition to firing on the AT turrets from the RIBs and APCs, the US team can also deploy snipers along the docks to take out the MEC soldiers manning the turrets.

APC or RIB

While the US can use aircraft to get troops to the enemy control points, this team is also provided with APCs and RIBs. Each has its own advantage and disadvantage. The APC is armored, allowing it to take more damage. Furthermore, it also packs more firepower with an auto cannon as well as missiles. If you want to have a better chance of getting your APCs to shore, send two of them close together with an engineer in each. This allows the APCs to repair one another while on the move and under fire. Also, this doubles the amount of firepower that can target enemies on the shore.

What the RIB lacks in armor and firepower it makes up for with speed. The longer you are on the water, the more shots the enemy can take at you. Therefore, the RIB lets you get in quick. A good tactic is to jink back and forth to throw off the aim of enemy troops firing at you from the shore.

SHARQI PENINSULA

This vital position on the Persian Gulf possesses a TV station with a powerful transmitter, allowing it to aid propaganda support for the ongoing MEC campaign. US Rapid Deployment forces have captured this coastal position and now face a determined counter-attack by converging MEC forces. This lazy seaside resort of villas, markets, and beach houses is about to become a modern battlefield as US forces attempt to hold onto their newly-captured communications prize.

BATTLEFIELD 2

16-PLAYER

Office Buildings
Heavy Jeep (1)
AT Turret (1)
Machine Gun (1)

Construction Site
Heavy Jeep (1)
Machine Gun (1)

Black = Convertible
Blue = USMC Control Only
Red = MEC Control Only

Hotel
Heavy Jeep (2)
Tank (1)
Artillery (2)
UAV Trailer (1)
Radar Station (1)
AT Turret (1)
Machine Gun (1)

TV Station
Heavy Jeep (1)
Tank (1)
Artillery (2)
UAV Trailer (1)
Radar Station (1)
AT Turret (1)
Machine Gun (1)

Game Type:
Conquest Assault
Total Control Points: 4
Convertible Control Points: 3

Marine snipers and support troops positioned on the Construction Site's tall crane can fire down on the MEC spawn points at the southern Hotel.

US Strategy

As the defenders, the Marines need to hold tight and prevent the MEC forces from taking control of the TV Station. Because the enemy spawns at the Hotel, most early fighting takes place around the Construction Site. Engineers should mine the eastern and western streets to prevent enemy vehicles from slipping past and rushing the Office Buildings or TV Station. The Marines should also use the height advantage of the Construction Site's buildings and crane to fire down on approaching MEC troops. The M1A2 should hold back, covering the eastern road leading into the TV Station facility. The M1A2's main objective is to prevent vehicle rush attacks, but its machine guns are also effective against infantry. Pinning the enemy troops at the Hotel keeps them from breaking out and capturing control points—and the longer they go without capturing a control point, the more tickets they'll lose. At least one sniper (and maybe an anti-tank soldier) should defend the TV Station. Using the building's balcony or roof, it's possible to spot any attackers moving in from the west. Defenders at the TV Station should also watch the Office Buildings to the north. In a worse-case scenario, the Marines should fall back to the TV Station and stiffen defenses around the balcony and stairwell. Assault troops, special forces, and engineers are best suited for such close-quarter combat.

MEC Strategy

The MEC attackers begin the battle at a huge disadvantage. Not only are their tickets draining away, but they're likely to be harassed by Marine defenders firing down on them from the Construction Site north of the Hotel. Achieving a victory hinges on either taking the Construction Site or circumventing it. Using Vodniks as troop transports, it is possible to sneak up along the western road and flank the Construction Site from the north—there's a small hole in the northern fence. But any infantry assaults on the Construction Site should be initiated with an artillery strike targeting the northeast building with the flag. If the Construction Site can be captured quickly, MEC forces should dig in and prepare for a counterattack. If Marine attacks persist, hold at the Construction Site and wait for the Marine forces to weaken before moving east to capture the Office Buildings and TV Station. The other option is to rush past the Construction Site and attack the TV Station. Capturing the TV Station would be devastating to the Marine defense, denying them access to their only tank and artillery. Attacking from the Hotel and TV Station is ideal, allowing MEC troops to squeeze the Marines in the center.

32-PLAYER

Club House
Heavy Jeep (3)
APC (1)
AT Turret (1)
AA Turret (1)
Machine Gun (1)

Surveillance Post
AT Turret (1)
AA Turret (1)
Machine Gun (1)

Black = Convertible
Blue = USMC Control Only
Red = MEC Control Only

Construction Site
Heavy Jeep (1)
Machine Gun (1)

City Entrance
AT Turret (2)
Machine Gun (3)

TV Station
Heavy Jeep (1)
Tank (1)
Attack Helicopter (1)
Artillery (2)
UAV Trailer (1)
Radar Station (1)
AT Turret (1)
AA Turret (1)
Machine Gun (1)

Outskirts
Heavy Jeep (2)
Tank (1)
Artillery (2)
UAV Trailer (1)
Radar Station (1)
AT Turret (1)
Machine Gun (1)

Hotel
Heavy Jeep (2)
AT Turret (1)
AA Turret (1)
Machine Gun (1)

Beach House
Heavy Jeep (2)
RIB (2)
Attack Helicopter (1)
AA Turret (1)
Machine Gun (1)

Game Type:
Conquest Assault
Total Control Points: 8
Convertible Control Points: 5

The attack helicopters give both sides some badly needed firepower. Use rockets and missiles to destroy the enemy's vehicles, but steer clear of the city's various AA Turrets.

US Strategy

On the expanded 32-player map, MEC forces attack from three directions. The most likely points of contention are at the City Entrance to the far west and the Hotel to the south. Expect heavy enemy vehicle activity to the west, approaching from the Club House and Outskirts. The AH-1Z and M1A2 (spawned at the TV Station) will help push back the attackers moving against the City Entrance. Attacks against the Hotel will come from the south via RIBs. Infantry (including some anti-tank troops) positioned south of the Hotel can engage the incoming boats before they land. Vehicle attacks from the west are also a possibility. The MEC Mi-28 poses the largest threat, and not just because of its awesome offensive capability. In addition to blasting US vehicles, it can be used to drop troops at rear positions like the Construction Site or TV Station. To prevent such attacks, make sure all AA Turrets are manned. They are at the Hotel, TV Station, and Surveillance Post. But even if the Mi-28 is shot down, crew members may escape by parachuting. Therefore, at least one player should defend each control point—especially the TV Station.

MEC Strategy

Capturing the TV Station early is the key to a quick MEC victory. However this vital control point is the also the most difficult to reach given the layout of the map. This is where the Mi-28 comes in handy. While the bulk of the MEC troops grind against the Marine positions at the Hotel and City Entrance, at least one squad leader should board the Mi-28 at the Beach House and fly northeast. To avoid anti-aircraft fire, fly low and approach the TV Station from the eastern cliffs—the AA Turret is in the western front courtyard. After the squad leader is on the ground near the TV Station, squad members can use him as a spawn point. By assaulting from the rear of the TV Station, a full squad (comprised of assault troops and special forces) can convert the control point and destroy the Marine artillery. The squad leader should stay behind and remain alive as long as possible to provide the squad members with a spawn point until the TV Station falls. Capturing the TV Station gives the MEC forces another tank, tilting the odds in their favor. Before branching out, make sure a few troops stay behind and guard the TV Station. Secure the City Entrance and Surveillance Post next, then work on the Construction Site. Leave the Hotel for last, as it forces the Marines south at one of the most indefensible control points.

Surveillance Post
AT Turret (1)
AA Turret (1)
Machine Gun (1)

Alleyway
Heavy Jeep (1)
Machine Gun (1)

Club House
Heavy Jeep (3)
APC (1)
AT Turret (1)
AA Turret (1)
Machine Gun (1)

Construction Site
Heavy Jeep (1)
Machine Gun (1)

City Entrance
AT Turret (2)
Machine Gun (3)

TV Station
Heavy Jeep (1)
Tank (1)
Attack Helicopter (1)
Artillery (2)
UAV Trailer (1)
Radar Station (1)
AT Turret (1)
AA Turret (1)
Machine Gun (1)

Outskirts
Heavy Jeep (2)
Tank (2)
Artillery (2)
UAV Trailer (1)
Radar Station (1)
AT Turret (1)
Machine Gun (1)

Hotel
Heavy Jeep (2)
AT Turret (1)
AA Turret (1)
Machine Gun (1)

Beach House
Heavy Jeep (2)
Boat (1)
Attack Helicopter (1)
AA Turret (1)
Machine Gun (1)

Black = Convertible
Blue = USMC Control Only
Red = MEC Control Only

Game Type:
Conquest Assault
Total Control Points
Convertible Control Po

*When attacking a control poin
leaders should hold back and
suppressive fire. In urban comba
leader needs to stay alive so squa
can use his spawn point to stay
action. This is the best way to
offensive pressure.*

US Strategy

The addition of the Alleyway control point is the only major difference between this map and the 32-player version. But the increase in manpower allows the Marines to better guard each control point without the fear of spreading their defenses too thin. The City Entrance and Hotel are the first likely sites of heavy fighting. However, the Alleyway may also come under attack either by parachuting troops or amphibious assault from the northern coast. As usual, it's important to keep several troops around the TV Station too. In fact, defending the TV Station should be the full-time job of one squad. This squad should be prepared for assaults from any direction, including the rooftop. Meanwhile, use the TV Station's assets, like the M1A2, AH-1Z, to battle MEC forces elsewhere in the city. The Marines must hold out at all control points as long as possible to prolong the drain on enemy tickets.

MEC Strategy

A higher concentration of Marine defenders makes it difficult for the MEC forces to gain a foothold within the city. Still, distracting them at the Hotel and City Entrance is the best way to draw their defenders away from other control points they view as less vital. The TV Station is still the key focus, but don't expect it to be as easy to assault now that the Marines have more troops guarding it. Instead, set your sights on the northern Alleyway. Using RIBs, it's possible to land on the northern coast and move troops up the trail along the steep cliff. A low profile attack is the best way to approach the Alleyway. Once captured, use the Alleyway to spawn more troops and stage attacks on the City Entrance, Surveillance Post, and the Construction Site. While harassing the western Marines, continual efforts to capture the TV Station should proceed. Like on the 32-player map, force the Marines south, toward the Hotel. Prevent them from using the TV Station as their last control point. Its assets and fortress-like features can lead to heavy losses for the MEC attackers, especially if the full Marine contingent is defending it.

BASES AND CONTROL POINTS

Beach House

The Beach House's diverse vehicle spawns allow MEC forces to conduct air, sea, and land raids on the city from the south. The Mi-28 is useful for softening Marine defenses around the city's perimeter. Use it to conduct small-scale rooftop raids on the TV Station. The RIBs are the quickest way to move troops to the north for assaults on the Hotel. These boats can also be used to circle around the eastern peninsula and open a new front on the city's northern edge—the eastern cliffs are too steep for infantry to scale. Troops can also be transported in the Vodniks, but they'll have to take one of the two roads to the west before they can move into the city. The Beach House's distance from the battle is one of its best defensive features. With the exception of the Marine AH-1Z, the MEC defenders have little to worry about. Even then, American helicopter raids can be deterred with the AA Turret. Although the Beach House can't be captured, in rare cases, American special forces may attempt raids to knock out the artillery or to steal the Mi-28. For this reason, it's a good idea to keep at least one engineer around to mine the nearby roads and conduct repairs on damaged gear.

Maps:
32- and 64-Player

Adjacent Bases/ Control Points:
- Outskirts
- Hotel

Beach House Assets

MEC Control	16-Player	32-Player	64-Player
GAZ 39371	—	2	2
RIB	—	2	2
Mi-28	—	1	1
AA Turret	—	1	1
Machine Gun	—	1	1

Outskirts

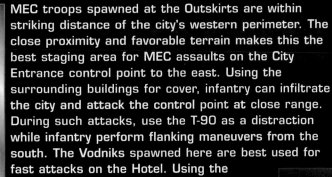

MEC troops spawned at the Outskirts are within striking distance of the city's western perimeter. The close proximity and favorable terrain makes this the best staging area for MEC assaults on the City Entrance control point to the east. Using the surrounding buildings for cover, infantry can infiltrate the city and attack the control point at close range. During such attacks, use the T-90 as a distraction while infantry perform flanking maneuvers from the south. The Vodniks spawned here are best used for fast attacks on the Hotel. Using the winding road to the southeast, the Vodniks can access the street running along front of the Hotel. However, if transporting troops, it's best to unload them before getting too close to the Hotel's AT Turret. US ground assaults on the Outskirts control point are unlikely, but the lack of air-defense makes the T-90 (and other vehicles) vulnerable to attacks by the Super Cobra. In a pinch, defenders can turn the AT Turret on the attack chopper, but scoring a hit is difficult unless it's moving slowly.

Maps:
32- and 64-Player

Adjacent Bases/ Control Points:
- Beach House
- Hotel
- City Entrance

Outskirts Assets

MEC Control	16-Player	32-Player	64-Player
GAZ 39371	—	2	2
T-90	—	1	1
Artillery	—	2	2
UAV Trailer	—	1	1
Radar Station	—	1	1
AT Turret	—	1	1
Machine Gun	—	1	1

Club House

The open terrain between the Club House and City Entrance makes MEC attacks from this direction risky. Marine defenders at the City Entrance can fire machine guns and anti-tank missiles at any units approaching from the Club House. For this reason, MEC forces should consider using this spawn point lightly until the City Entrance is captured. Unlike the Outskirts, the Club House does have an AA Turret. Use this to counter the Marine Super Cobra, especially if it's harassing advances from the Outskirts. After you capture the City Entrance, MEC troops can put the Club House's Vodniks and BTR-90 to work on securing more Marine-held control points. The BTR-90 is useful for rushing enemy control points, allowing troops to unload and assault at close range.

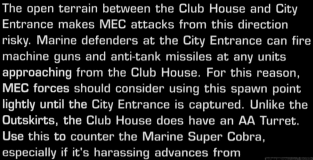

Maps: 32- and 64-Player

Adjacent Bases/ Control Points:

- Outskirts
- City Entrance

Club House Assets

MEC Control	16-Player	32-Player	64-Player
GAZ 39371	—	3	3
BTR-90	—	1	1
AT Turret	—	1	1
AA Turret	—	1	1
Machine Gun	—	1	1

City Entrance

With the MEC-controlled Club House and Outskirts sitting to the west, the Marine defenders at the City Entrance face a tough fight. Fortunately, there are three separate spawn points connected to this control point, making it easier for US forces to prepare for the impending assault. The spawn point to the southwest is best suited for handling attacks originating from the Outskirts. The AT Turret and machine gun can cover the barricaded road, but you need mines and claymores on the northern adjacent road. Troops positioned here should also watch for infantry flank attacks from the south. Defenders and the northwest spawn point are most likely to face MEC troops attacking from the Club House. The guard post's machine gun and nearby AT Turret have a good view of the nearby bridge as well as the open terrain beyond. Special forces troops can delay both infantry and vehicle attacks from this direction by blowing the bridge with C4. The spawn point near the flagpole sits on higher terrain than the areas to the west. Anti-tank troops positioned along the low wall on the building's western side can use this height advantage to fire down on approaching vehicles from both the Outskirts and Club House.

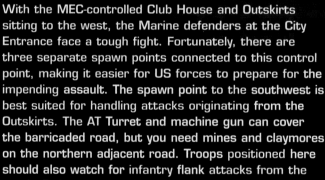

Maps: 32- and 64-Player

Adjacent Bases/ Control Points:

- Outskirts
- Club House
- Surveillance Post
- Alleyway

City Entrance Assets

USMC Control	MEC Control	16-Player	32-Player	64-Player
AT Turret	AT Turret	—	2	2
Machine Gun	Machine Gun	—	3	3

Surveillance Post

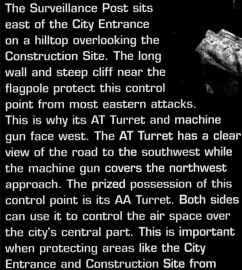

The Surveillance Post sits east of the City Entrance on a hilltop overlooking the Construction Site. The long wall and steep cliff near the flagpole protect this control point from most eastern attacks. This is why its AT Turret and machine gun face west. The AT Turret has a clear view of the road to the southwest while the machine gun covers the northwest approach. The prized possession of this control point is its AA Turret. Both sides can use it to control the air space over the city's central part. This is important when protecting areas like the City Entrance and Construction Site from enemy chopper attacks.

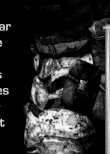

Maps:
32- and 64-Player

Adjacent Bases/ Control Points:
- City Entrance
- Alleyway
- Construction Site

Surveillance Post Assets

USMC Control	MEC Control	16-Player	32-Player	64-Player
AT Turret	AT Turret	—	1	1
AA Turret	AA Turret	—	1	1
Machine Gun	Machine Gun	—	1	1

Alleyway

This control post is only available on the 64-player map, offering another spawn point within the tight cluster of buildings comprising the city's north-western part. The Marines will find this position useful for launching counterattacks on the City Entrance or Surveillance Post. But if left unguarded, MEC troops may stage an amphibious attack with RIBs, landing on the northern coast. If MEC units can establish a foothold here early, it will be easier for them to take control of the surrounding control points. To prevent such sneak attacks, defenders should be placed on the rooftop east of the flagpole. If resources allow, park the Humvee on the open street to the north and man its machine gun. Any troops approaching from the coast have to cross this street. The mounted machine gun next to the flagpole can cover the next street to the south, capable of gunning down enemy troops assaulting from the City Entrance.

Maps:
64-Player Only

Adjacent Bases/ Control Points:
- City Entrance
- Surveillance Post
- Construction Site

Alleyway Assets

USMC Control	MEC Control	16-Player	32-Player	64-Player
HMMWV	GAZ 39371	—	—	1
Machine Gun	Machine Gun	—	—	1

Hotel

On the 16-player map, the Hotel serves as the MEC base, and US troops cannot capture it. As such, there's little reason to attack or defend it. But this changes in the 32- and 64-player maps, as the Hotel makes up the Marine southern flank and is likely to come under attack by MEC troops moving in from the Beach House and Outskirts. Its AT and AA Turrets are useful in dealing with approaching vehicles, but you need more firepower to handle incoming infantry. The control point's only machine gun faces west, making it useless against amphibious attacks from the south. Anti-tank troops should be deployed south of the Hotel and target incoming MEC RIBs. Support troops are also effective at cutting down enemy infantry before they can make it too far out of the water. Snipers can help out too by picking off enemies at long distances or by placing claymores at the tops of the staircases leading up to the main street near the Hotel. The Hotel's rooftop is inaccessible from the ground, but attack helicopters can be used to ferry troops to the top. Snipers and anti-tank troops are effective from the roof, but they'll need ammo. A support soldier or supply crate can give them all the ammo they'll need. At closer ranges, use the apartment across the western street for concealment and cover when engaging attackers gathered around the flagpole.

Maps: All

Adjacent Bases/ Control Points:
- Beach House
- Construction Site

Hotel Assets

USMC Control	MEC Control	16-Player*	32-Player	64-Player
HMMWV	GAZ 39371	2	2	2
M1A2	T-90	1	—	—
N/A	Artillery	2	—	—
N/A	UAV Trailer	1	—	—
N/A	Radar Station	1	—	—
AT Turret	AT Turret	1	1	1
AA Turret	AA Turret	—	1	1
Machine Gun	Machine Gun	1	1	1

* = MEC Control Only

NOTE Whether attacking or defending, you cannot jump the low wall surrounding the flagpole at the Hotel.

Construction Site

Three buildings are under construction at this fenced off work site, and the flag is on the northeastern structure's roof. The rooftop flagpole makes the Construction Site the most difficult control point to capture. In most cases, enemy troops have to run up a series of stairs in order to reach the roof. Then they have to wait around while the flag is first neutralized, then converted. The flag can also be converted by a hovering helicopter, but chances are it won't survive long enough the complete the job. You can reach the flag from the roofs of the surrounding buildings too. A running start and a lucky leap is all it takes to jump from the western building. Those wanting to test their balance while under fire can use the steel beam to cross from the southern building's rooftop.

Because you can reach the flag from multiple directions, defenders are best hanging back and covering the area around the flag from a distance. The huge crane to the southwest offers multiple platforms serving as ideal sniper perches—the crane is also useful for covering the area around the Hotel. More snipers can cover the rooftop from the western Surveillance Post. You can locate one of the best defensive sniping positions to the north, from the roof of the four story building. Several palm trees grow on this building's south side, providing great concealment and enough space to peak through the fronds and pick off enemies gathered around the Construction Site's flagpole. Use the same roof to cover the flag at the Alleyway. Place mines and claymores around the Construction Site to slow attackers.

Maps: All

Adjacent Bases/ Control Points:
- Hotel
- Surveillance Post
- Alleyway
- Office Buildings

Construction Site Assets

USMC Control	MEC Control	16-Player	32-Player	64-Player
HMMWV	GAZ 39371	1	1	1
Machine Gun	Machine Gun	1	1	1

Office Buildings

This control point only appears on the 16-player map, and serves as a buffer between the Construction Site and TV Station. US troops spawning here should reinforce the northern approach to the TV Station by placing mines and using the elevated AT Turret to prevent vehicle rush attacks. Snipers can also be positioned on the building's roof. This is helpful for picking off enemies crossing the exposed southern terrain as they attempt to move from the Construction Site to the TV Station.

Maps:
16-Player Only

**Adjacent Bases/
Control Points:**
• Construction Site
• TV Station

Office Buildings Assets

USMC Control	MEC Control	16-Player	32-Player	64-Player
HMMWV	GAZ 39371	1	—	—
AT Turret	AT Turret	1	—	—
Machine Gun	Machine Gun	1	—	—

TV Station

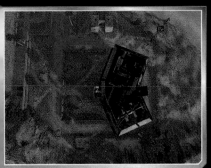

On every map, the TV Station should be the centerpiece of the Marine defensive effort. For the Marines, their only AH-1Z Super Cobra is essential for stopping MEC vehicle advances from the south and west. This control point also produces the Marine's only tank and serves as home to their artillery and other key assets. There are two spawn points connected to this structure. The eastern spawn point drops troops on the TV Station's rooftop while the western one deploys them on the ground outside the structure. The TV Station's flagpole sits on a second-story balcony on the structure's western side. You can access this balcony via the building's central stairwell or an exterior ladder on the southern side. Either way, attackers must reach this balcony (or hover nearby) to convert the control point. Use the building's stairwell to access the rooftop, where an attack helicopter spawns on the 32- and 64-player maps. Snipers positioned on the rooftop (or balcony) can cover the approach from the Construction Site—watch for enemy troops pouring through the hole in the fence to the west. On the ground below, the AA Turret is vital for turning back enemy chopper attacks. Don't be surprised if the enemy tries to drop troops on the rooftop. Position troops or claymores inside the building to prevent such sneak attacks from succeeding. If MEC forces capture the TV Station, the balance of the whole battle will shift, allowing them to pound the remaining Marine positions with their monopoly of tanks and attack helicopters.

Maps: All

**Adjacent Bases/
Control Points:**
• Office Buildings
• Construction Site

TV Station Assets

USMC Control	MEC Control	16-Player	32-Player	64-Player
HMMWV	GAZ 39371	1	1	1
M1A2	T-90	1	1	1
AH-1Z	N/A	—	1	1
Artillery	N/A	2	2	2
UAV Trailer	N/A	1	1	1
Radar Station	N/A	1	1	1
AT Turret	AT Turret	1	1	1
AA Turret	AA Turret	—	1	1
Machine Gun	Machine Gun	1	1	1

TIP You can convert the TV Station flag from within the building by standing in the lobby east of the balcony. Take cover inside if artillery begins to fall, and watch the stairwell door for counterattacks.

SHARQI PENINSULA TACTICS

Sniper City

Like most urban combat zones, this city offers plenty of great sniping spots. One of the best (and most obvious) is the crane at the Construction Site. Snipers positioned on any of the various levels can engage enemy infantry at the Hotel, Surveillance Post, and Alleyway.

The roof of the four-story building north of the Construction Site is also a good spot with many uses. The palm trees growing on the building's south side provide excellent concealment when covering the flagpole at the Construction Site. This roof can also be used to target the Alleyway to the west or the Office Buildings to the east.

As the second-tallest accessible point on the map, the TV Station's rooftop is another fine sniping post. Marine defenders can use this spot to pick off any MEC troops charging through the gate (or hole in the fence) to the west.

The large western water tank is another obvious sniping post, but its remote location gives the sniper the benefit of distance. Snipers positioned here can engage enemies at the Hotel, Surveillance Post, or on the crane at the Construction Site.

Construction Site Assault

On each map, the Construction Site is one of the toughest control points for MEC troops to capture. But with artillery support and careful timing, it's possible to storm the control point and convert it. Get as close to the Construction Site as possible without exposing yourself to enemy fire—this southwest staircase works well.

Before moving in on the position, request artillery support on the flagpole at the northeastern building. Hold until you can hear the incoming shells.

During the confusion of the artillery strike, lead your squad toward the northeast building. By the time you reach the building, the artillery strike will be over.

Clear floor by floor of the building till you make it to the rooftop. Watch for enemy snipers and other defenders on the adjacent rooftops while converting the flag. The more squad members that make it to the roof, the quicker the conversion process.

Urban Survival

Engineers and anti-tank troops are the best way to prevent the control points from being overrun by enemy vehicles. But they'll need a constant supply of ammo to replenish their stocks of mines and anti-tank missiles. Drop supply crates at critical front-line control points like the City Entrance and Construction Site so defenders can retrieve ammo as needed.

The life span of a tank in the tight confines of the city is short unless an engineer is nearby to provide repairs. You can use a Humvee or Vodnik (driven by an engineer) as a repair vehicle. Drive next to the damaged tank to automatically conduct repairs.

Stopping the flow of MEC vehicles before they move into the city can slow the enemy advance. Use the Super Cobra in a standoff role by hovering north of the City Entrance. From this position, it can easily engage all enemy vehicles approaching from the Club House.

Helicopter Obstacle Course

Think you're a good pilot? This map has a couple features you can use to test your skills. First, fly beneath the steel beam spanning the two buildings at the Construction Site. This is easiest when approached from the east. You have to fly low enough so the helicopter blades clear the beam, but high enough to avoid clipping the perimeter fence.

TV Station Raid

As the Marine's only source of armor and air support, the TV Station is the map's biggest prize. Although it's only a two-seater, the Mi-28 is the quickest way to move infantry to this position. Approach from the east to avoid anti-air missile attacks and begin the assault by strafing the TV Station's rooftop with cannon and rocket fire.

Land on the roof and exit the Mi-28. The stairwell can be accessed through a door on the northern side of the roof—watch for traps!

Rush down the stairwell and take up a position near the balcony to convert the flag. To avoid the risk of encountering ambushes or claymores in the dark stairwell, base jump off the building's west side and parachute onto the balcony. Once near the flagpole, keep an eye on the balcony's ladder as well as stairwell doorway.

Fly south of the Outskirts and slalom these trans-mission towers while staying beneath the power lines. Don't worry, clipping the power lines does no damage—but smashing into a transmission tower does!

BATTLEFIELD 2

STRIKE AT KARKAND

Control of the industrial facility and harbor at Karkand motivates this assault by US forces, where they find MEC forces marshalling to defend the industrial city and determined to meet the attack with stiff resistance. The terrain surrounding Karkand is sufficiently open to allow for sweeping fields of fire, but the open ground increases the danger posed by anti-vehicle missiles and sniping. It is vital for both sides to secure firebases in Karkand's sheltered city center.

16-PLAYER

Black = Convertible
Blue = USMC Control Only
Red = MEC Control Only

Market
Heavy Jeep (1)
Tank (1)
Artillery (2)
UAV Trailer (1)
Radar Station (1)
AT Turret (1)
Machine Gun (1)

Square
AT Turret (1)
Machine Gun (1)

Hotel
Machine Gun (1)

Gas Station
Heavy Jeep (1)
APC (1)
Tank (1)
Artillery (2)
UAV Trailer (1)
Radar Station (1)
AT Turret (1)
Machine Gun (3)

Game Type:
Conquest Assault
Total Control Points: 4
Convertible Control Points: 3

Rushing the Market with a Humvee is a risky move for the Marines, but the payoff is well worth it—if the attack succeeds.

US Strategy

The Marines must quickly capture one of the control points inside the city to stop the ticket drain. The Hotel is the most obvious choice for the first assault, but the MEC forces are probably expecting this move and will reinforce the southern edge of the city with most of their troops. Therefore, consider staging a fast assault on the Market. Capturing the Market deprives the enemy of all their vehicles, making the Hotel and Square much easier to assault. However, a diversion is needed to slip past the front lines. Move the bulk of your forces (six troops) in an aggressive attack against the Hotel using the M1A2, the LAV-25, and plenty of artillery. This will keep the MEC forces occupied, allowing one or two special forces troops to take the Humvee along the eastern perimeter of the city for a rush attack on the Market. Once the Market is captured, the artillery guns to the east should be destroyed. Now it's possible to squeeze the Square and Hotel from the north and south, using tanks spawned at the Gas Station and Market.

MEC Strategy

As noted in the US strategy, maintaining control of the Market is vital to an MEC victory. But it's also important to delay the US troops from gaining a foothold within the city limits. The longer the Marines can be held back, the more tickets they'll lose. Blocking enemy vehicles at the Hotel is the best way to prevent the Marines from making it deep inside the city. Start by moving all vehicles from the Market toward the Hotel. The main streets to the east and west of the Hotel also need to be mined to prevent rush attacks on the rear control points. The concrete obstacles and cars near the Hotel provide great cover for infantry. Support and anti-tank troops are most effective at holding back the attackers. The T-90's job is to destroy the M1A2. Park it behind the concrete barriers near the Hotel so it can engage any Marine units rushing down the road to the south. Position at least one sniper on the rooftop next to the Square. From this place, they can spot and engage any troops trying to sneak up on the Square or Market. If the US troops are intent on making runs at the northern control points, consider shifting a couple of troops from the Hotel back to the Market. If the Hotel falls, stage an immediate counter-attack while beefing up defenses at the Square. Preventing the Marines from holding a single control point is the quickest way to ensure a victory.

32-PLAYER

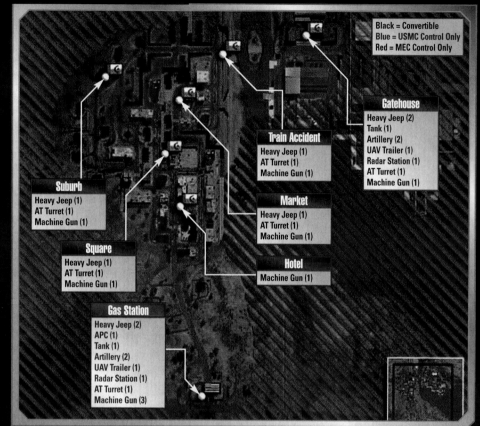

Black = Convertible
Blue = USMC Control Only
Red = MEC Control Only

Gatehouse
Heavy Jeep (2)
Tank (1)
Artillery (2)
UAV Trailer (1)
Radar Station (1)
AT Turret (1)
Machine Gun (1)

Train Accident
Heavy Jeep (1)
AT Turret (1)
Machine Gun (1)

Market
Heavy Jeep (1)
AT Turret (1)
Machine Gun (1)

Suburb
Heavy Jeep (1)
AT Turret (1)
Machine Gun (1)

Square
Heavy Jeep (1)
AT Turret (1)
Machine Gun (1)

Hotel
Machine Gun (1)

Gas Station
Heavy Jeep (2)
APC (1)
Tank (1)
Artillery (2)
UAV Trailer (1)
Radar Station (1)
AT Turret (1)
Machine Gun (3)

Game Type:
Conquest Assault
Total Control Points: 7
Convertible Control Points: 6

Special forces can blow the stone bridge near the Train Accident with a couple of charges each. The damage looks impressive, but the bridges can still b repaired by engineers.

US Strategy

As on the 16-player map, the Marines must make it into the city quickly. Vehicle spawns at the Gas Station give them a slight advantage, but they'll need to move fast—the only MEC tank starts at the distant Gatehouse. Get the M1A2 to the Hotel as quickly as possible and use it to thin out the ranks of the defenders. Follow closely behind with the LAV-25 and rush troops in to capture the Hotel. Secure the Hotel with mines and other defensive features to hold back the inevitable counter-attacks. Meanwhile, use a Humvee to rush a few troops along the western side of the city and attack the Suburb. The Suburb is less likely to be defended than the other more central control points, and capturing it allows the Marines to open a new front on the MEC's right flank. By spawning troops at the Hotel and Suburb, it's much easier to capture the Square and Market. Keep pushing east until friendly troops hold the Train Accident. If everything went as planned, the MEC forces should only be left with the Gatehouse. Sometimes it's easier and less costly to simply hold them at the river, covering the bridges and river ford while pounding their spawn point with artillery. Whatever the situation, once the MEC units are isolated to the eastern side of the city, don't let them break out.

MEC Strategy

Keeping the Marines out of the city can be a challenge, especially if they rush the Hotel with their vehicles early on. Still, a couple of squads comprised of engineers, anti-tank, and support troops can hold back even the most aggressive assaults. Use the engineers to litter the streets with mines while the anti-tank and support troops take up defensive positions. Infantry must hold back the Marine vehicles until the T-90 can make it to the front lines near the Hotel. A stalemate at the Hotel greatly benefits the MEC forces, but it may cause the enemy to alter their strategy. At least one defender should be placed at each of the control points to the north and used to call out enemy breakthroughs. Like before, use the rooftop of the tall building next to the Square as a reconnaissance post. If the Marines gain ground on the western side of the city, consider falling back to the Gatehouse. Destroying the bridges near the Train Accident leaves only the river ford to the south as a potential crossing. If the Marines take the bait, the MEC can rack up tons of kills by simply focusing vehicle and artillery fire on this narrow choke point.

64-PLAYER

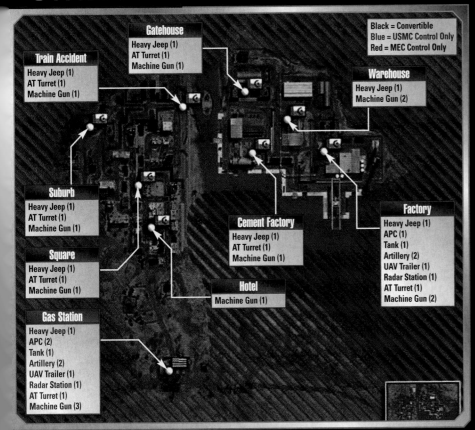

Black = Convertible
Blue = USMC Control Only
Red = MEC Control Only

Gatehouse
Heavy Jeep (1)
AT Turret (1)
Machine Gun (1)

Train Accident
Heavy Jeep (1)
AT Turret (1)
Machine Gun (1)

Warehouse
Heavy Jeep (1)
Machine Gun (2)

Suburb
Heavy Jeep (1)
AT Turret (1)
Machine Gun (1)

Square
Heavy Jeep (1)
AT Turret (1)
Machine Gun (1)

Cement Factory
Heavy Jeep (1)
AT Turret (1)
Machine Gun (1)

Hotel
Machine Gun (1)

Factory
Heavy Jeep (1)
APC (1)
Tank (1)
Artillery (2)
UAV Trailer (1)
Radar Station (1)
AT Turret (1)
Machine Gun (2)

Gas Station
Heavy Jeep (1)
APC (2)
Tank (1)
Artillery (2)
UAV Trailer (1)
Radar Station (1)
AT Turret (1)
Machine Gun (3)

Game Type:
Conquest Assault
Total Control Points: 9
Convertible Control Points: 8

Whether attacking or defending, team work is essential to achieving a victory on this bloody map. Medics and support troops should accompany every squad, keeping them at full health and stocked on ammo.

US Strategy

An even greater MEC vehicle shortage on the western side of the city allows the US troops to make some impressive progress in the opening moments of this battle. An early artillery strike on the Hotel can make its capture much faster and less costly as the M1A2 and LAV-25s cruise north. Before branching out to the nearby control points, consider staging a sneak attack on key MEC assets to the east. The LAV-25s can move along the eastern streets and access the bay at the river ford, just south of the Train Accident. Once in the water, the APCs can hook around from the south to assault either the Factory or Cement Factory. A successful surprise attack on the Factory can be totally devastating to the MEC forces, depriving them of their T-90 as well as their only APCs and artillery guns. An early attack on the Factory is also the best chance the US has of attaining a solid foothold on the eastern side of the city. With a presence in the east and west, the Marines can then squeeze the MEC troops in the middle, using their superior vehicles to take one control point at a time.

MEC Strategy

The amount of manpower available in a 64-player game makes it easier for the MEC to defend the southern edge of the city. But a near solid line of defense is needed to prevent any breakthroughs. This means placing and maintaining minefields in the streets as well as covering the alleys. In addition to covering the streets near the Hotel, the eastern and western flanks of the city must also be monitored for Marine squads attempting to sneak past the main defensive line. A pair of sniper teams at the Square and Suburb can keep the Commander informed of enemy activity in the northern and central parts of the city. While most of the team holds near the Hotel, preparations should be made near the Gatehouse to defend the eastern control points. As usual, the bridges near the Train Accident should be demolished, but the river ford should remain open to facilitate the movement of friendly vehicles into the western side of the city. The river ford should still be monitored, preferably by anti-tank troops positioned near the Cement Factory. These troops are also necessary to watch for potential amphibious APC assaults approaching from the south. Like the 32-player map, MEC forces should hold out as long as possible at the Hotel and other western control points before retreating east and making a stand at the river.

BASES AND CONTROL POINTS

Gas Station

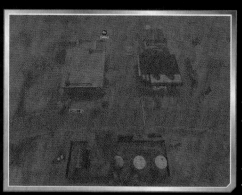

The Gas Station is located to the far south and serves as the staging area for the Marine assault on Karkand. As such, it cannot be captured by MEC forces. However, its artillery guns and UAV trailer may draw sabotage attempts by MEC special forces. There are three separate spawn points connected to the Gas Station. Players looking to grab a vehicle should spawn at the southern point. Infantry preparing to infiltrate the city by foot can spawn at one of two spawn points to the north. These two spawn points flank the main road leading into Karkand and may come under fire by enemy troops positioned near the city limits. US troops entering the battle here should be mindful of MEC spawn campers located to the north or even on the western or eastern flanks. The open terrain just south of the city offers little cover for the attackers—a detail that won't be overlooked by savvy MEC troops intent on keeping the Marines out of the city.

Maps: All

Adjacent Bases/ Control Points:
- Hotel

Gas Station Assets

USMC Control	16-Player	32-Player	64-Player
HMMWV	1	2	1
LAV-25	1	1	2
M1A2	1	1	1
Artillery	2	2	2
UAV Trailer	1	1	1
Radar Station	1	1	1
AT Turret	1	1	1
Machine Gun	3	3	3

Hotel

Located on the southern edge of the city, the Hotel acts as the MEC's first line of defense, making this the site of some extremely intense firefights. Although it spawns no vehicles, the strategic significance of the Hotel is obvious to both sides. If the MEC troops can hold the Hotel and surrounding territory, they have a good chance of preventing the Marines from making further progress into Karkand. For the Marines, the Hotel provides a foothold within the urban terrain, making deeper incursions much easier. The flagpole is positioned on an elevated slab, accessible by steps from the west or by ladders in the alleys to the north and south. The control point can also be converted from the street level by moving near the telephone stand just below the flagpole, but this isn't advisable—standing still in the street is a quick way to get killed. Defenders should cover all approaches to the flagpole with claymores. Mining the street to the west will prevent vehicles from getting close too. Attackers should avoid the main streets altogether and stick to the narrow alleys. Before rushing in for the capture, infantry should toss grenades up around the flagpole's base to neutralize any concealed defenders.

Maps: All

Adjacent Bases/ Control Points:
- Gas Station
- Square

Hotel Assets

USMC Control	MEC Control	16-Player	32-Player	64-Player
Machine Gun	Machine Gun	1	1	1

Square

The control point configuration of the Square varies based on the different maps. On the 16-player map, the flagpole is located directly in the middle of the Square with the machine gun placed at its base and the AT turret nearby to the west. The lack of cover on this setup makes the control point extremely difficult to convert, especially if it's well defended. A mix of mines and claymores deployed near the flag will prevent any troops or vehicles from getting within conversion range.

On the 32- and 64-player maps, the flagpole is a bit more protected, placed in a fenced area on the opposite side of the building to the Square's west. The machine gun and AT turret also shift near this enclosed area, each capable of covering the street to the south. In any configuration, the nearby buildings make this control point relatively easy to defend. The roof of the tall building next to the Square can be accessed from a ladder on its western side. Another building sits to the southeast, overlooking the Square. The interior of this building can be accessed from a nearby alley, allowing snipers to watch the Square and nearby streets from its upper floor windows.

Maps: All

Adjacent Bases/ Control Points:
- Hotel
- Market
- Suburb

Square Assets

USMC Control	MEC Control	16-Player	32-Player	64-Player
HMMWV	GAZ 39371	—	1	1
AT Turret	AT Turret	1	1	1
Machine Gun	Machine Gun	1	1	1

Market

The street-side Market in central Karkand only serves as a control point on the 16- and 32-player maps. This area of the city sits lower than the southern and western portions, sometimes making the downhill drive toward the control point a perilous one for attackers. Defenders should mine the main roads, particularly the downhill slope near the Square. The nearby AT turret should also be used to target incoming vehicles from the south. Infantry creeping though the alleys can be eliminated with claymores or by snipers positioned on the surrounding rooftops. On the 16-player map, the Market is the MEC's most valuable control point, producing their only T-90. It's also home to their artillery. These assets alone make the Market's defense the highest priority.

Maps: 16- and 32-Player

Adjacent Bases/ Control Points:
- Square
- Suburb
- Train Accident

Market Assets

USMC Control	MEC Control	16-Player	32-Player	64-Player
HMMWV	GAZ 39371	1	1	—
M1A2	T-90	1	—	—
N/A	Artillery	2	—	—
N/A	UAV Trailer	1	—	—
N/A	Radar Station	1	—	—
AT Turret	AT Turret	1	1	—
Machine Gun	Machine Gun	1	1	—

Suburb

This control point is located to the northwest, overlooking the city from the nearby hills. Although its assets are modest, the Suburb should not be ignored. Early in the battle, US troops can put this spawn point to use as a second staging area for assaults on the city's interior. Such a move could put the MEC forces at a major disadvantage. Even though the control point is often far removed from the action, steps should be taken by the defenders to secure the surrounding approaches. The two main roads leading to the Suburb (to the south and east) can both be covered by troops positioned on the roof of the house next to the flagpole—the machine gun on the roof is ideal for covering the road to the south. Vehicle rush attacks can be discouraged by mining these roads as well.

Maps: 32- and 64-Player

Adjacent Bases/ Control Points:
- Market
- Square
- Train Accident

Suburb Assets

USMC Control	MEC Control	16-Player	32-Player	64-Player
HMMWV	GAZ 39371	—	1	1
AT Turret	AT Turret	—	1	1
Machine Gun	Machine Gun	—	1	1

Train Accident

At some point, a train derailed at this crossing, foreshadowing the carnage that will surround this hotly contested control point. The two stone bridges next to the Train Accident link the western and eastern sides of the city. For the MEC, maintaining control of this choke point is vital to safeguarding the eastern control points. The flagpole itself is located on the western bank, and can be converted from the interior of the nearby boxcar. Not far from the flagpole are the control point's assets. The machine gun and AT Turret have a perfect view of the street to the south, capable of halting almost every attack from this direction. Early in the battle, the two bridges should be demolished with C4—two charges per bridge are sufficient. Once the bridges are blown, the river ford to the south is the only usable crossing.

Maps: 32- and 64-Player

Adjacent Bases/ Control Points:
- Gatehouse
- Market
- Suburb

Train Accident Assets

USMC Control	MEC Control	16-Player	32-Player	64-Player
HMMWV	GAZ 39371	—	1	1
AT Turret	AT Turret	—	1	1
Machine Gun	Machine Gun	—	1	1

TIP Use gunfire to destroy the crossing guard arms at the railroad tracks. Crashing into them will cause damage to your vehicle.

Gatehouse

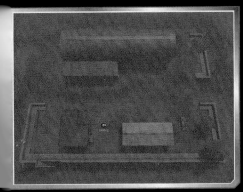

The Gatehouse facility sits on a hill and is surrounded by a large wall with vehicle access points to the west and east. Infantry can access the control point by climbing the staircase along the retaining wall to the south. The control point's most useful defensive feature is its AT turret, positioned in the street to the south, capable of covering the bridges near the Train Accident. On the 32-player map, the Gatehouse is the only control point on eastern side of the city. It also serves as a mini-base for the MEC, home to their artillery, radar station, and UAV trailer—it also produces the MEC's only T-90. On the 64-player map the Gatehouse plays a lesser role in terms of assets, but should still be defended by MEC forces to prevent Marine advances into the eastern control points. Anti-tank and other troops can cover the nearby bridges from the facility's western wall, firing down on any attackers. Even if the bridges are destroyed, they should still be watched—US engineers can quickly repair both bridges, allowing Marine vehicles to pour across.

Maps: 32- and 64-Player

Adjacent Bases/ Control Points:

- Cement Factory
- Train Accident
- Warehouse

Gatehouse Assets

USMC Control	MEC Control	16-Player	32-Player	64-Player
HMMWV	GAZ 39371	—	2	1
M1A2	T-90	—	1	—
N/A	Artillery	—	2	—
N/A	UAV Trailer	—	1	—
N/A	Radar Station	—	1	—
AT Turret	AT Turret	—	1	1
Machine Gun	Machine Gun	—	1	1

Cement Factory

Just south of the Gatehouse is this sprawling industrial complex. The control point's flagpole is positioned in the yard, north of the factory building. This yard is surrounded by a fence with entry points to the west and east. MEC defenders should use the Cement Factory to cover the river ford to the west. Like the bridges near the Gatehouse, the river ford is another potential avenue of attack for Marines looking to gain a foothold on the eastern control points. Defenders can use the factory itself to attain a height advantage on the river ford. An upper level walkway on the western side of the factory is an ideal spot for snipers and anti-tank troops. This walkway can also be used to cover the southern approach in the event the Marines attack with APCs from the bay.

Engineers spawned at the Cement Factory should also place some mines in the river ford. Locking down the bridges and river ford are key to keeping the Marines isolated to the western side of the city.

Maps: 64-Player Only

Adjacent Bases/ Control Points:

- Gatehouse
- Train Accident
- Warehouse

Cement Factory Assets

USMC Control	MEC Control	16-Player	32-Player	64-Player
HMMWV	GAZ 39371	—	—	1
AT Turret	AT Turret	—	—	1
Machine Gun	Machine Gun	—	—	1

Warehouse

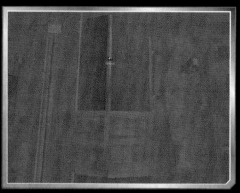

The Warehouse's interior flagpole presents unique challenges to attackers and defenders, often resulting in close-quarter firefights. Entry can be made through the large doors on the structure's northern and southern sides. Attackers should always enter from the south as the southern facing machine gun (near the flagpole) has a more limited firing arc than the one covering the northern entrance. To enhance defenses to the south, defenders should take up positions on the catwalk overlooking the southern door. MEC troops should only fall back to the Warehouse's interior if necessary. Their defensive efforts are more successful when focused around the building's perimeter and surrounding control points. Whichever side controls the Warehouse should avoid getting pinned inside. Otherwise the enemy can simply surround the building and blast anyone that tries to exit. If this is the case, stop spawning here and secede the control point to the enemy—it will probably save you tickets in the long run.

Maps:
64-Player Only

Adjacent Bases/ Control Points:
- Cement Factory
- Factory
- Gatehouse

Warehouse Assets

USMC Control	MEC Control	16-Player	32-Player	64-Player
HMMWV	GAZ 39371	—	—	1
Machine Gun	Machine Gun	—	—	2

Factory

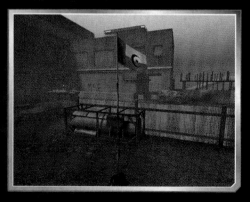

On the 64-player map, the Factory is the MEC's core control point, producing the bulk of their vehicles as well as housing their artillery and other Commander assets. As expected, this large facility is well fortified too, with a fence surrounding the perimeter and only a few narrow entry points. The northern and western entries are protected by guard posts, each equipped with a machine gun. The southern approach is more open and as such should be watched by MEC defenders. The Marines may attempt an amphibious assault from the bay using APCs. The flagpole is located in the center of the facility, partially surrounded by a small fence with entries from the east and west. Just north of the flagpole is a build with an accessible rooftop. Defenders should use this spot to deter attackers from converting the control point. Snipers can also be placed around the facility's perimeter, including on the huge smoke stacks to the far east and the large shipping container lift to the south.

Maps:
64-Player Only

Adjacent Bases/ Control Points:
- Warehouse

Factory Assets

USMC Control	MEC Control	16-Player	32-Player	64-Player
HMMWV	GAZ 39371	—	—	1
LAV-25	BTR-90	—	—	2
M1A2	T-90	—	—	1
N/A	Artillery	—	—	2
N/A	UAV Trailer	—	—	1
N/A	Radar Station	—	—	1
AT Turret	AT Turret	—	—	1
Machine Gun	Machine Gun	—	—	2

KARKAND TACTICS

Street Defense

Mines are the key to shutting down Karkand's streets to enemy vehicle traffic. Place mines next to the various obstacles and barricades in the street so no vehicles can pass. This helps reduce the number of mines needed to completely block a street.

Don't underestimate the effectiveness of the mounted machine guns scattered across the map. Not only do they have unlimited ammo, but they're also very accurate and can fire in long sustained bursts. This is just one of many reasons why infantry should stay out of the streets.

Smoke screens deployed by tanks and APCs are a great way to provide temporary cover for infantry. These vehicles should be used to rush a control point and pop smoke while infantry follow closely behind and help secure the site.

Amphibious Sneak Attack

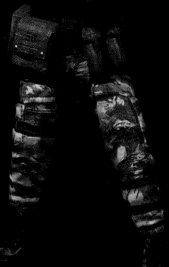

On the 64-player map, the Marine LAV-25s can be used to enter the bay and attack the Factory and Cement Factory control points from the south. All they need to do is enter the river ford (south of the Train Accident) and veer south, into open water.

Both the Factory and Cement Factory feature ramps like this along the southern docks. Once on dry land, the APCs can either rush the control points with guns blazing or unload troops for a more stealthy attack.

Karkand Sniping

Karkand is filled with various sniping opportunities. One of the best spots is the rooftop of the building next to the Square. From this roof, snipers can cover the Square, the Market, and the street near the Hotel. However, this spot is so popular, don't be surprised if the enemy Commander drops some artillery on this roof.

When taking up a sniping spot on a roof, look for rubble or any other objects that can be used for cover and concealment. Such objects can break up your visible profile against the sky, making you harder to spot by enemy troops on the ground.

Building interiors offer a bit more protection and much more concealment than rooftops. This apartment just south of the Square is an ideal defensive position in 16-player games. Simply pick off any hostiles that move next to the flagpole.

ZATAR WETLANDS

The Zatar Wetlands along the Red Sea coastline possess vital natural gas resources but create a difficult battlefield for US and MEC forces. Small tributaries break the landscape into isolated islands whose soggy marshes inhibit heavy vehicles. As American forces advance, MEC forces possess an initial advantage in the air, making control of an abandoned airfield crucial early in the battle, after which supply line protection will become an additional consideration.

16-PLAYER

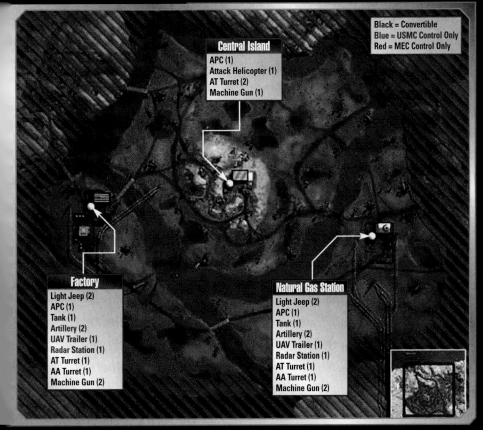

Black = Convertible
Blue = USMC Control Only
Red = MEC Control Only

Central Island
APC (1)
Attack Helicopter (1)
AT Turret (2)
Machine Gun (1)

Factory
Light Jeep (2)
APC (1)
Tank (1)
Artillery (2)
UAV Trailer (1)
Radar Station (1)
AT Turret (1)
AA Turret (1)
Machine Gun (2)

Natural Gas Station
Light Jeep (2)
APC (1)
Tank (1)
Artillery (2)
UAV Trailer (1)
Radar Station (1)
AT Turret (1)
AA Turret (1)
Machine Gun (2)

Game Type:
Conquest Double Assault
Total Control Points: 3
Convertible Control Points: 3

Take control of the Central Island quickly! Its high elevation and attack helicopter spawn point are the keys to victory.

US Strategy

Speed is the key to guaranteeing a quick victory on this small map. The first priority is to take the Central Island as soon as possible. From the Factory, send at least one DPV (with a couple of anti-tank troops and an engineer) to the Central Island control point. MEC troops are likely to do the same thing, so expect resistance on the top of the hill. Support the advance on the Central Island with the M1A2 and the LAV-25, using them to halt the approaching MEC units to the east. If your team manages to capture the Central Island, put the Super Cobra attack helicopter to work immediately, using it to blast enemy armor and APCs.

The hectic opening moments of a battle is the perfect time to hit the Natural Gas Station too, depriving the MEC units of their starting spawn point. While the bulk of the US forces move against the Central Island, use a squad of one or two special forces troops to advance on the Natural Gas Station using the second DPV. Avoid contact with other enemy units near the Central Islands by using the southern approach. Before moving in on the control point, eliminate the artillery guns with C4 charges. Failing to take out the artillery guns leaves your attackers open to counter-attack as they try to convert the control point. Once both artillery guns are smoldering, rush into the facility and take up defensive positions around the flagpole.

MEC Strategy

Since both sides are on an even footing at the outset of the battle, the MEC forces should closely mirror the US strategy. The Central Island is still the key focus, not just to attain the attack helicopter, but to prevent the US forces from spawning one. Use at least one FAV to rush the control point and take immediate steps to fortify it from APC and tank attacks approaching from the west. Another FAV should be sent to the Factory, in an attempt to capture it while the US forces are preoccupied with the Central Island. However, if the Factory can't be captured within the first few minutes of the game, swing all offensive efforts to taking the Central Island. Simply holding the Natural Gas Station and Central Island is sufficient to keep US forces pinned at the Factory. Use the Mi-28 and frequent artillery strikes to pound the Marines until they run out of tickets. While suppressing their advances, look for opportunities to rush in and capture the Factory to bring the battle to a quick end.

BATTLEFIELD

32-PLAYER

MEC Base
Light Jeep (2)
APC (1)
AA Vehicle (1)
Tank (1)
Transport Helicopter (1)
Fighter (1)
Artillery (2)
UAV Trailer (1)
Radar Station (1)
AT Turret (1)
AA Turret (1)
Machine Gun (2)

Central Island
Light Jeep (2)
Tank (1)
Attack Helicopter (1)
AT Turret (2)
AA Turret (1)
Machine Gun (1)

Village
Light Jeep (2)
APC (2)
RIB (2)
Machine Gun (2)

Airfield
Light Jeep (2)
APC (1)
AA Vehicle (1)
Tank (1)
Transport Helicopter (1)
Fighter (1)
Artillery (2)
UAV Trailer (1)
Radar Station (1)
AT Turret (1)
AA Turret (1)
Machine Gun (2)

Factory
Light Jeep (1)
APC (1)
AT Turret (1)
Machine Gun (2)

Natural Gas Station
Light Jeep (1)
APC (1)
AT Turret (1)
Machine Gun (2)

Farm
Light Jeep (2)
APC (2)
RIB (2)
Machine Gun (2)

Black = Convertible
Blue = USMC Control Only
Red = MEC Control Only

Game Type:
Conquest Head-On
Total Control Points: 7
Convertible Control Points: 5

Keep the attack helicopter near the Central Island and use it to defend the control point. Rockets and guided missiles are devastating against tanks and APCs.

US Strategy

While the Airfield is the staging area for the US attack, it can't be captured so don't worry about defending it from infiltration. Instead, focus your manpower on reaching the Central Island. The most effective way to do this is by loading up the Seahawk with troops and dropping them over the control point. An F-35B can get there quicker, assuming the pilot ejects and parachutes down to the flagpole. Equally important is taking control of the Factory and Village control points. DPVs and other land vehicles can reach these areas quickly. Holding these three control points causes a drain on the MEC tickets. Hold firm at the Central Island, and use anti-tank troops to pick off enemy vehicles approaching from the Natural Gas Station and Farm. The Central Island's Stinger turret is also useful for keeping Mig-29s and Mi-17s at bay.

MEC Strategy

Like the US Strategy, the Central Island is key to victory. The attack helicopter spawn point is less effective on this map since there are now fighters prowling the skies. But the actual location and elevation advantage of this control point makes it the ideal front-line position. Use the Mi-17 or Mig-29 to quickly gain control of the Central Island while ground units fall in from behind, capturing the Farm and Natural Gas Station. Holding these control points imposes a ticket drain on the US forces, giving the MEC an advantage the longer they can hold back attacks. Maintaining air superiority is also important. The Mig-29 should be used to attack the Marine F-35B and Seahawk at the Airfield—just be mindful of the Stinger turret and the M6 Bradley. Keeping these air units grounded greatly inhibits the Marine's expansion capability.

64-PLAYER

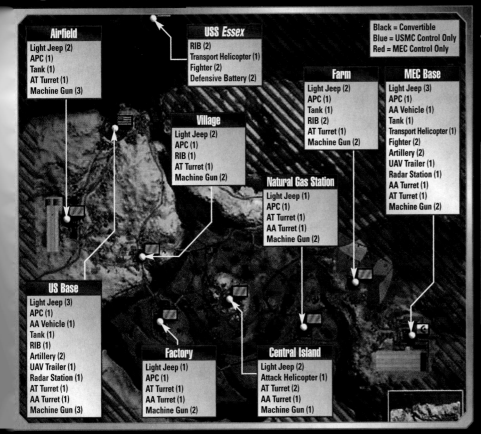

Airfield
Light Jeep (2)
APC (1)
Tank (1)
AT Turret (1)
Machine Gun (3)

USS Essex
RIB (2)
Transport Helicopter (1)
Fighter (2)
Defensive Battery (2)

Black = Convertible
Blue = USMC Control Only
Red = MEC Control Only

Farm
Light Jeep (2)
APC (1)
Tank (1)
RIB (2)
AT Turret (1)
Machine Gun (2)

MEC Base
Light Jeep (3)
APC (1)
AA Vehicle (1)
Tank (1)
Transport Helicopter (1)
Fighter (2)
Artillery (2)
UAV Trailer (1)
Radar Station (1)
AA Turret (1)
AT Turret (1)
Machine Gun (2)

Village
Light Jeep (2)
APC (1)
RIB (1)
AT Turret (1)
Machine Gun (2)

Natural Gas Station
Light Jeep (1)
APC (1)
AT Turret (1)
AA Turret (1)
Machine Gun (2)

US Base
Light Jeep (3)
APC (1)
AA Vehicle (1)
Tank (1)
RIB (1)
Artillery (2)
UAV Trailer (1)
Radar Station (1)
AT Turret (1)
AA Turret (1)
Machine Gun (3)

Factory
Light Jeep (1)
APC (1)
AT Turret (1)
AA Turret (1)
Machine Gun (2)

Central Island
Light Jeep (2)
Attack Helicopter (1)
AT Turret (2)
AA Turret (1)
Machine Gun (1)

Game Type:
Conquest Head-On
Total Control Points: 9
Convertible Control Points: 6

Ejecting from a fighter and parachuting down onto distant control points is the quickest way to capture them for your team. Don't worry about losing a fighter—more will spawn into place.

US Strategy

On this map, the Marines must capture and hold at least four control points to impose a ticket drain on the MEC forces. Using assets at the Beach and USS *Essex*, immediately branch out and begin capturing the neutral control points on the western side of the map. This includes the Airfield, Village, and Factory. Capturing and defending these three control points is the first priority as it prevents the MEC from bleeding your ticket count. But as proven on the smaller maps, capturing the Central Island is the key to making serious progress. Once the three western control points are under US control, stage an assault of the Central Island. Use artillery and air strikes to soften up any defenders, then move in with M1A2s and LAV-25s to wipe them out and assume control. Holding the four western control points not only drains tickets from the enemy, but setting up a defensive line at the Central Island makes it extremely difficult for them to breakout. But don't get greedy. Even with 32-players on your team, it takes just about everybody to hold the western control points. Prepare to repel frequent attacks at the Factory and Central Island, but watch out for sneak attacks on the Airfield and Village too.

MEC Strategy

Like the US, the MEC forces should focus on building a defensive line at the Factory and Central Island control points while using the Farm and Natural Gas Station to bleed tickets from the enemy. As soon as the game begins, push the fastest vehicles toward the Factory and Central Island. This may mean sacrificing the Mig-29s so the pilots can eject and parachute down to the control points. FAVs and the Mi-17 can also reach these control points quickly. The slower vehicles (like the T-90 and BTR-90) should split at the MEC Base and move toward the nearby Farm and Natural Gas control points. Once all control points are owned by the MEC forces, it's necessary to dig-in and hold them. Most resistance will be focused on the Central Island and Factory. Load up the Central Island with anti-tank troops and use the high elevation to fire down on Marine vehicles attempting to attack. Consider blowing up the western bridges too, using bombs dropped from the Mig-29s. The Mi-28 should never move far from the Central Island, using the helipad to repair and stock up on missiles. A disciplined defense of the four easternmost control points guarantees the MEC an eventual victory.

BASES AND CONTROL POINTS

US Base

In the 64-player map, this control point serves up the bulk of the Marine's land vehicles. Even though it can't be captured by MEC forces, these vehicle spawn points are well worth defending, especially against early air strikes. For this reason, defenders should consider keeping the Stinger turret (to the east) manned at all times. MEC air strikes aren't just likely, they're a certainty—especially as US forces attempt to spread out from this point to other areas of the map. If necessary, the M6 Bradley can provide extra anti-air deterrence from its spawn point to the west. Defenders should also be mindful of MEC troops infiltrating the Base to either steal or sabotage vehicles and artillery.

Maps:
64-Player Only

Adjacent Bases/ Control Points:
- USS *Essex*
- Airfield
- Village

US Base Assets

USMC Control	16-Player	32-Player	64-Player
DPV	—	—	3
LAV-25	—	—	1
M6 Bradley	—	—	1
M1A2	—	—	1
RIB	—	—	1
Artillery	—	—	2
UAV Trailer	—	—	1
Radar Station	—	—	1
AT Turret	—	—	1
AA Turret	—	—	1
Machine Gun	—	—	1

USS *Essex*

Like the Beach, the USS *Essex* is only available on the 64-player map. This large amphibious assault carrier features two separate spawn points. The western spawn point drops players onto the carrier's flight deck, giving them easy access to the aircraft or the two Phalanx and Sea Sparrow batteries. The eastern spawn point puts players inside the boat hangar at the ship's aft. This is where troops can board one of two RIBs and stage amphibious assaults.

As the primary source of US air power, the USS *Essex* is an attractive target for MEC pilots. The two F-35Bs and the Seahawk are all sitting ducks, vulnerable to bombs, rockets, and strafing runs. A well balanced and disciplined US team will keep at least one of the two ship's defensive batteries manned at all times—a lack of manpower shouldn't be a problem on a filled 64-player map. Just one Phalanx and Sea Sparrow battery is capable of turning back most air attacks. These batteries can also be used to help defend the Beach to the south.

Maps:
64-Player Only

Adjacent Bases/ Control Points:
- Beach

USS *Essex* Assets

USMC Control	16-Player	32-Player	64-Player
RIB	—	—	2
HH-60H	—	—	1
F-35B	—	—	2
Defensive Battery	—	—	2

MEC Base

Located on the eastern side of the map, this Base supplies MEC forces with the vehicles needed to quickly capture the nearby control points. FAVs or the Mi-17 can be used to take control of the Farm, Natural Gas Station, and even the Central Island in the early moments of 32- and 64-player games. This Base can't be captured but is still likely to experience some heavy attacks. Fortunately, most of the vehicle spawn points are protected by rooftops. Up to two Mig-29s are housed in the two aircraft hangars, protecting them from bomb attacks. But they can still be hit through the hangar doors by rockets or strafing runs. Since air power is so important on this map, defenders should position the Tunguska near the runway to better protect the Migs.

The hills on western edge of the Base are at a higher elevation than the nearby marshlands. Defenders should use the height advantage to fire down on any US units near the Farm or Natural Gas Station control points. Snipers and anti-tank troops are most effective at engaging enemies at this distance.

Maps: 32- and 64-Player

Adjacent Bases/ Control Points:
- Farm
- Natural Gas Station

MEC Base Assets

MEC Control	16-Player	32-Player	64-Player
FAV	—	2	3
BTR-90	—	1	1
Tunguska	—	1	1
T-90	—	1	1
Mi-17	—	1	1
Mig-29	—	1	2
Artillery	—	2	2
UAV Trailer	—	1	1
Radar Station	—	1	1
AT Turret	—	1	1
AA Turret	—	1	1
Machine Gun	—	2	2

Airfield

Holding the Airfield is important, since it provides a central location for friendly planes to rearm and repair without having to fly to the USS *Essex* or MEC Base. On the 32-player map, the Airfield serves as the US staging area and cannot be captured by the MEC forces. But this control point is up for grabs on the 64-player map. Whichever side controls the Airfield should take steps to defend it by covering the entry points.

Vehicle infiltration can be halted by placing mines at the main entrances to the east and north. The perimeter guard posts (with machine guns) are useful for holding back infantry assaults. Defending the control point from air assault is easy for the Americans in 32-player, as the control point spawns an M6 Bradley Linebacker as well as a Stinger turret near the helipad. But the situation is different on the 64-player map, producing no anti-air units. Since the Marines are most likely to hold this control point, they should consider moving the M6 Bradley from the Beach to this area.

Maps: 32- and 64-Player

Adjacent Bases/ Control Points:
- Beach
- Village

Airfield Assets

USMC Control	MEC Control	16-Player	32-Player*	64-Player
DPV	FAV	—	2	2
LAV-25	BTR-90	—	1	1
M6 Bradley	N/A	—	1	—
M1A2	T-90	—	1	1
HH-60H	N/A	—	1	—
F-35B	N/A	—	1	—
Artillery	N/A	—	2	—
UAV Trailer	N/A	—	1	—
Radar Station	N/A	—	1	—
AT Turret	AT Turret	—	1	1
AA Turret	AA Turret	—	1	—
Machine Gun	Machine Gun	—	2	3
			* = USMC Control Only	

Village

Its close proximity to several control points makes the Village a popular staging point for assaults. On both maps the Marines are likely to capture this control point early. They can then use it and its RIBs to launch amphibious assaults on other control points like the Factory or Natural Gas Station. Just as useful as the vehicle spawn points is the higher elevation offered by the large hills surrounding the control point. Defenders can use this height advantage to defend the control point or to support assaults on the Central Island or Factory. The open nature of the Village makes it susceptible to fast vehicle attacks rushing for the flagpole. To prevent these attacks from succeeding consider placing mines and claymores in the area surrounding the flag.

Maps: 32- and 64-Player

Adjacent Bases/ Control Points:
- Beach
- Airfield
- Central Island
- Factory

Village Assets

USMC Control	MEC Control	16-Player	32-Player*	64-Player
DPV	FAV	—	2	2
LAV-25	BTR-90	—	2	1
RIB	RIB	—	2	1
AT Turret	AT Turret	—	—	1
Machine Gun	Machine Gun	—	2	2

Factory

Of all the control points, the Factory is one of the most difficult to capture, requiring attackers to climb to the roof of the central industrial structure where the flagpole is positioned. However, the control point can also be converted by a hovering helicopter—making a juicy target for any nearby enemies. Whatever the method, defenders have several options to flush out attackers before they can claim the control point for their team. The easiest is to place claymores near the flag, preferably at the top of each staircase to the north and west. Snipers and other troops can also climb on top of the nearby storage tanks to cover the flagpole. The porous perimeter fence surrounding the facility makes it difficult to predict the direction of an assault, so go easy on mines in these areas. Instead, focus mines and other defensive features on the flagpole.

Maps: All

Adjacent Bases/ Control Points:
- Village
- Central Island

Factory Assets

USMC Control	MEC Control	16-Player	32-Player	64-Player
DPV	FAV	2	1	1
LAV-25	BTR-90	1	1	1
M1A2	T-90	1	—	—
Artillery	N/A	2	—	—
UAV Trailer	N/A	1	—	—
Radar Station	N/A	1	—	—
AT Turret	AT Turret	1	1	1
AA Turret	AA Turret	1	—	1
Machine Gun	Machine Gun	2	2	2

Central Island

The Central Island is often the most contentious piece of territory. Not only does it posses the only attack helicopter spawn point, but it's also the highest point in the center of the map. As a result, whichever team captures this control point first has a good chance of holding onto it—but only if it's defended properly. Defenders should first take note of which team controls the surrounding control points and shift defenses accordingly. Anti-tank troops are devastating from this location, capable of spotting and engaging any approaching vehicle at long range. Engineers and snipers can also come in handy, using mines and claymores to protect the area around the flag.

Maps: All

Adjacent Bases/ Control Points:

- Village
- Factory
- Farm
- Natural Gas Station

Central Island Assets

USMC Control	MEC Control	16-Player	32-Player	64-Player
DPV	FAV	—	2	2
LAV-25	BTR-90	1	—	—
M1A2	T-90	—	1	—
AH-1Z	Mi-28	1	1	1
AT Turret	AT Turret	2	2	2
AA Turret	AA Turret	—	1	1
Machine Gun	Machine Gun	1	1	1

Since the control point is easily defended, both sides should try to reach this spot first. If the enemy reaches this spot first, stage a quick attack before their defenses are setup. DPVs and FAVs are a good option, capable of rushing across the marshland and getting troops near the flag. Transport helicopters are effective too. Passengers should jump out over the control point and parachute down to convert it.

Natural Gas Station

This control point is laid out much like the Factory, with a perimeter fence and entry points to the north and south. However, the Natural Gas Station's flagpole is positioned in the middle of the facility, making it relatively easy to capture. Mines can be deployed at the entry points, but must be placed so friendly vehicles can maneuver around them. A safer option is to mine the area around the flagpole. For additional security, snipers and/or anti-tank troops should be positioned on the nearby refinery tower to the west. From this elevated position, defenders can fire down on any attackers, often catching them by surprise before they even enter the facility.

Maps: All

Adjacent Bases/ Control Points:

- Farm
- Central Island
- MEC Base

Natural Gas Station Assets

USMC Control	MEC Control	16-Player	32-Player	64-Player
DPV	FAV	2	1	1
LAV-25	BTR-90	1	1	1
M1A2	T-90	1	—	—
N/A	Artillery	2	—	—
N/A	UAV Trailer	1	—	—
N/A	Radar Station	1	—	—
AT Turret	AT Turret	1	1	1
AA Turret	AA Turret	1	—	1
Machine Gun	Machine Gun	2	2	2

Farm

The Farm sits on the eastern edge of the marshlands. Like the Village, the Farm's high elevation provides a good view of the surrounding control points. Defenders positioned on the hill just west of the control point can engage enemies approaching from all directions. More importantly, they can help cover the northern entrance of the Natural Gas Station, as well as its flagpole. The Farm also produces two RIBs (on the docks to the west), giving MEC troops an option for staging quick amphibious assaults on distant control points like the Factory or Village.

Maps: 32- and 64-Player

Adjacent Bases/ Control Points:

- Natural Gas Station
- Central Island
- MEC Base

Farm Assets

USMC Control	MEC Control	16-Player	32-Player	64-Player
DPV	FAV	—	2	2
LAV-25	BTR-90	—	2	1
M1A2	T-90	—	—	1
RIB	RIB	—	2	2
AT Turret	AT Turret	—	—	1
Machine Gun	Machine Gun	—	2	2

ZATAR WETLANDS TACTICS

Refinery Tower Tips

The heat signature of the flames rising from the natural gas refinery towers can fool heat-seeking missiles. In addition to using flares, fly low and amongst these towers to shake a missile lock.

 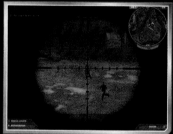

Some of the refinery towers can also be climbed, making them ideal (but predictable) sniper perches. Always fire from a prone position in an attempt to remain concealed. Consider placing claymores near the ladders to prevent enemy troops from sneaking up on you.

Central Island Defense

 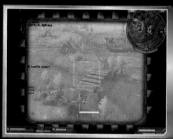

The Central Island control point spawns the only attack helicopter on the map. The guided missiles offered by both the AH-1Z and Mi-28 can quickly turn any armored advance into a smoking pile of rubble within seconds. The pilot should maintain a low hover near the Central Island and simply point the chopper at the incoming enemies, allowing the gunner to do the rest. Use the control points helipad to repair and stock up on ammo.

Two or three anti-tank troops can inflict some serious damage when positioned on the hills surrounding the control point. But they'll need to be stocked with plenty of replacement missiles. Request a supply drop from the Commander to place a crate where the defenders can easily restock.

Marshland Maneuvers

To avoid slowing to a crawl when crossing the marshy center of the map, steer clear of the dark brown areas. These muddy marshes slow your vehicle significantly, making them an easy target for ground-pounding pilots and anti-tank troops.

Remember, the APCs are amphibious and don't need to rely on the narrow wooden bridges to cross the various tributaries. Use this to your advantage by surprising enemies from an unexpected direction.

RIBs are available to both sides on the 32- and 64-player maps. These fast moving boats are an attractive alternative to move troops through the expansive marshland territory. Tanks and other vehicles will have difficulty depressing their guns to fire on these boats, since the tributaries are often at a significantly lower elevation. Consider using RIBs to conduct raids on enemy control points.

If you're satisfied with your team's holdings, destroy any bridges that may give the enemy an advantage. This forces the enemy to deploy engineer units to repair the bridge or simply route their vehicles over the shallow river fords. These delays simply give defending anti-tank troops more time to rack up more vehicle kills.

APPENDIX A: FIREARMS

Firearms Comparison Chart

Kits and Weapons	Damage	Cyclic Rate	Magazine Capacity	Minimum Deviation	Deviation When Standing/Crouching/Prone	Deviation Added per Shot	Deviation Mod when Zoomed	Recoil	Recoil when Zoomed Mod
Pistols									
92FS	20	—	15	0.5	—	0.125 (3.5)	0.5	0.5-0.8	0.25
MR-444	20	—	15	0.5	—	0.125 (3.5)	0.5	0.5-0.8	0.25
QSZ-92	20	—	15	0.5	—	0.125 (3.5)	0.5	0.5-0.8	0.25
Antitank									
MP5	19	900	30	0.8	1.4 / 1.3 / 1.2	0.3 (2)	0.8	0.4-0.6	0.7
PP-19	19	900	45	0.8	1.4 / 1.3 / 1.2	0.3 (2)	0.8	0.4-0.6	0.7
Type 85	19	900	30	0.8	1.4 / 1.3 / 1.2	0.3 (2)	0.8	0.4-0.6	0.7
DAO-12 (unlock)	12x8	—	12	1.5	—	0.2 (3.2)	0.9	3	0.7
Assault/Medic									
M16A2	30	900	30	0.3	1.5 / 1.3 / 1	0.2 (2)	0.8	0.1-0.6	0.8
AK-101	37	600	30	0.45	1.5 / 1.3 / 1	0.25 (2)	0.8	0.4-0.6	0.8
AK-47	38	600	30	0.45	1.5 / 1.3 / 1	0.25 (2.3)	0.8	0.4-0.6	0.8
G3 (Assault Unlock)	40	600	20	0.5	1.5 / 1.3 / 1	0.25 (2.5)	0.8	0.3-0.5	0.7
L85A1 (Medic Unlock)	32	600	30	0.3	1.5 / 1.3 / 1.2	0.3 (2.5)	0.8	0.3-0.5	0.6
Engineer									
M11-87	25x8	—	7	0.75	—	0.2 (3)	0.9	3	—
S12K	12x8	—	7	1.5	—	0.2 (3)	0.9	2	0.75
NOR982	25x8	—	7	0.75	—	0.2 (3)	0.9	3	—
MK3A1 (Unlock)	15x8	300	7	1.5	—	0.3 (3)	0.9	4	1
Special Forces									
M4	25	600	30	0.15	1.5 / 1.2 / 1	0.15 (1.7)	0.65	0.3-0.5	0.75
AK-74U	29	600	30	0.2	1.8 / 1.4 / 1	0.2 (2.5)	0.65	0.3-0.6	0.75
QBZ-97	25	600	30	0.15	1.5 / 1.2 / 0.7	0.15 (1.7)	0.6	0.25-0.45	0.75
G36C (Unlock)	25	600	30	0.12	1.5 / 1.2 / 1	0.15 (2)	0.65	0.2-0.4	0.5
Sniper									
M24	95	—	5	5	—	2 (3.5)	0.01	4-5.2	0.25
SVD	45	—	10	5	—	2 (3.5)	0.02	4.5-6	0.25
Type 88	45	—	10	5	—	2 (3.5)	0.02	4.5-6	0.25
M95 (Unlock)	95	—	5	5	—	2 (3.5)	0.02	4-5.2	0.25
Support									
M249	25	900	200	0.8	2 / 1.5 / 0.8	0.4 (1.2)	0.8	0.25-0.45	0.5
RPK-74	35	600	130	0.8	2 / 1.5 / 0.8	0.4 (0.8)	0.8	0.25-0.45	0.5
Type 95	25	900	100	0.8	2 / 1.5 / 0.8	0.4 (1.2)	0.8	0.25-0.45	0.5
PKM (Unlock)	45	450	100	0.8	2 / 1.5 / 0.8	0.4 (0.8)	0.8	0.25-0.45	0.5

APPENDIX B: AWARDS

Battlefield 2 awards are granted based on your performance, both over time and during a single game round. You are rated on several criteria, and the ratings are:

- **Satisfactory**
- **Good**
- **Skilled**
- **Outstanding**
- **Excellent**

Each award may require you to fulfill one or more of the following criteria. To achieve more advanced awards, you need to achieve a higher rating for each criterion. The criteria are:

Army Combat Effectiveness: Wins with a particular army.

Army Combat Rating: Score in a particular army.

Army Service: Time in a particular army.

Battlefield Commendation: Refers to the three end-of-round awards (gold, silver, bronze stars) that are awarded to the three highest scoring players.

Combat Proficiency: Time spent playing as a particular kit.

Combat Qualification: Time spent playing in a particular vehicle.

Combat Qualified: Qualified with all combat badges at a specified level.

Combat Rating: Kills with kit or vehicle.

Command Proficiency: Total commander score.

Command Qualification: Time as commander.

Command Rating: Single-round commander score.

Conduct Rating: Awarded for good conduct.

Driver Rating: Driver score.

Parachute Qualification: Time in a parachute.

Specialist Rating: Score with a specialist ability, such as the medic, engineer, or support kit.

Squad Leader Qualification: Time as squad leader.

Squad Member Qualification: Time as squad member.

Team Player Rating: Teamwork score.

Time in Service: Total time since you enlisted.

Time in Theater: Having played all of the maps from a specific theater.

Weapon Rating: Total kills with a weapon.

Weapon Proficiency: Kills with a weapon in a round.

Medals

Medal	Name	Description	Criteria
	Air Combat Medal	Awarded to any person who has distinguished themselves by superior achievement while participating in aerial combat.	Vehicle Qualification: Outstanding; Vehicle Combat Rating: Outstanding; Vehicle Proficiency: Excellent
	Armor Combat Medal	Awarded to any person who has distinguished themselves by superior achievement while participating in armored combat.	Vehicle Qualification: Outstanding; Vehicle Combat Rating: Outstanding; Vehicle Proficiency: Excellent
	Bronze Star	Awarded to those individuals who have distinguished themselves through proven skill and teamwork.	Combat Qualification: Good; Battlefield Commendation
	Combat Action Medal	Awarded to any person who has distinguished themselves by superior achievement while participating in infantry combat.	Time in Service: Outstanding; Combat Rating: Outstanding
	Combat Infantry Medal	Awarded to individuals who have distinguished themselves above and beyond that normally expected of infantry in a combat situation.	Time in Service: Good; Combat Qualified: Basic Infantry
	Distinguished Service Medal	Awarded to individuals who distinguish themselves through exceptionally meritorious service in a duty of great responsibility.	Command Qualification: Outstanding; Squad Leader Qualification: Outstanding; Squad Member Qualification: Outstanding; Team Player Rating: Excellent
	Gold Star	Awarded to those individuals who have distinguished themselves through excellent skill and teamwork.	Combat Qualification: Outstanding; Battlefield Commendation
	Golden Scimitar	Awarded to members of the Middle Eastern Coalition for extraordinary heroism in action while engaged in military operations involving conflict with an opposing foreign force.	Army Service: Outstanding; Army Combat Rating: Excellent; Army Combat Effectiveness: Excellent
	Good Conduct Medal	Awarded to those individuals who, through exemplary conduct while among their comrades, have shown themselves to be models of efficiency and fidelity.	Time in Service: Outstanding; Conduct Rating: Excellent; Combat Rating: Excellent

Medals (cont'd)

Medal	Name	Description	Criteria
	Helicopter Combat Medal	Awarded to persons who have distinguished themselves by superior achievement while participating in helicopter combat.	Vehicle Qualification: Outstanding; Vehicle Combat Rating: Outstanding; Vehicle Proficiency: Excellent
	Marksman Infantry Medal	Awarded to individuals who have distinguished themselves by sustained meritorious achievement during combat situations.	Time in Service: Good; Combat Qualified: Veteran Infantry
	Medal of Valor	Awarded to individuals who distinguish themselves through gallantry and intrepidity at the risk of their lives above and beyond the call of duty; the deed performed must have been one of personal bravery or self sacrifice so conspicuous as to clearly distinguish the individual above his/her comrades and must have involved the risk of life.	Time in Service: Excellent; Team Player Rating: Excellent
	Meritorious Service Medal	Awarded to an individual for exceptional conduct in the performance of outstanding services and achievements in support of their comrades.	Time in Service: Skilled; Medic Specialist Rating: Outstanding; Engineer Specialist Rating: Outstanding; Support Specialist Rating: Outstanding
	Navy Cross	Awarded to members of the United States Armed Forces for extraordinary heroism in action while engaged in military operations involving conflict with an opposing foreign force.	Army Service: Outstanding; Army Combat Rating: Excellent; Army Combat Effectiveness: Excellent
	People's Medallion	Awarded to members of the People's Liberation Army for extraordinary heroism in action while engaged in military operations involving conflict with an opposing foreign force.	Army Service: Outstanding; Army Combat Rating: Excellent; Army Combat Effectiveness: Excellent
	Purple Heart	Awarded to any member of the armed force who has been killed in any action with an opposing armed force of a foreign country.	Combat Rating: Outstanding; Battlefield Commendation
	Sharpshooter Infantry Medal	Awarded to individuals who have excelled in every action expected of the infantry in a combat situation.	Time in Service: Good; Combat Qualified: Expert Infantry
	Silver Star	Awarded to those individuals who have distinguished themselves through superior skill and teamwork.	Combat Qualification: Skilled; Battlefield Commendation

Ribbons

Ribbon	Name	Description	Criteria
	Aerial Service	Awarded to recognize individuals who performed their duty while engaged in active aerial combat.	Vehicle Qualification: Satisfactory; Vehicle Combat Rating: Satisfactory
	Airborne	Awarded to recognize individuals who have participated in sustained airborne operations during combat situations.	Parachute Qualification: Good
	Air Defense	Awarded to recognize the individual who performed their duty while engaged in active air defense combat.	Vehicle Qualification: Satisfactory; Vehicle Combat Rating: Satisfactory
	Armored Service	Awarded to recognize the individual who performed their duty while engaged in active armored combat.	Vehicle Qualification: Satisfactory; Vehicle Combat Rating: Satisfactory
	Combat Action	Awarded to recognize active participation in ground or air combat.	Combat Rating: Skilled; Combat Qualification: Good
	Crew Service	Awarded to recognize the individual who performed satisfactory duty while on flying status as a crewmember.	Driver Rating: Skilled; Combat Rating: Good

Ribbons (cont'd)

Ribbon	Name	Description	Criteria
	Distinguished Service	Awarded to recognize the superior achievement of an individual in all aspects of unit command.	Squad Member Qualification: Good; Squad Leader Qualification: Good; Command Qualification: Good; Team Player Rating: Good
	Far East Service	Awarded to recognize service in the Far East Theater.	Time in Theater, Time in Service: Good
	Good Conduct	Awarded to recognize exemplary behavior, efficiency, and fidelity in active service.	Time in Service: Satisfactory; Combat Rating: Satisfactory; Conduct Rating: Outstanding
	Ground Defense	Awarded to recognize individuals who participated in sustained ground combat.	Vehicle Qualification: Satisfactory; Vehicle Combat Rating: Satisfactory
	Helicopter Service	Awarded to recognize individuals who performed their duty while engaged in active helicopter combat.	Vehicle Qualification: Satisfactory; Vehicle Combat Rating: Satisfactory
	Infantry Officer	Awarded to recognize superior dedication of unit leaders during combat situations.	Team Player Rating: Good; Squad Leader Qualification: Satisfactory
	Legion of Merit	Awarded to recognize the individual who, through gallantry, determination and esprit de corps, succeeds in his/her mission while under difficult and hazardous conditions.	Time in Service: Good; Combat Rating: Skilled; Team Player Rating: Outstanding
	Meritorious Unit	Awarded to recognize an individual's contribution to their unit during sustained combat situations.	Squad Member Qualification: Satisfactory; Team Player Rating: Satisfactory
	Mid-East Service	Awarded to recognize service in the Middle East Theater.	Time in Theater, Time in Service: Good
	Staff Officer	Awarded to recognize superior achievement by unit commanders during sustained combat situations.	Command Qualification: Good; Command Rating: Satisfactory
	Valorous Unit	Awarded to recognize extraordinary heroism in action against an armed enemy.	Squad Member Qualification: Skilled; Squad Leader Qualification: Skilled; Team Player Rating: Outstanding
	War College	Awarded to recognize achievements which, through their dedication and gallantry, have set the individual apart and above other commanders.	Command Qualification: Skilled; Command Proficiency: Good; Command Rating: Outstanding

Infantry Badges

Badge	Name	Level	Description	Criteria
	Anti-Tank combat	Basic	Awarded to anti-tank personnel who have proven themselves during any period the unit was engaged in active combat.	Combat Rating: Satisfactory
	Anti-Tank combat	Veteran	Awarded to anti-tank personnel who distinguished themselves during any period the unit was engaged in active combat.	Combat Proficiency: Skilled; Combat Rating: Good
	Anti-Tank combat	Expert	Awarded to anti-tank personnel who served with excellence during any period the unit was engaged in active combat.	Combat Proficiency: Outstanding; Combat Rating: Skilled
	Assault combat	Basic	Awarded to assault personnel who have proven themselves during any period the unit was engaged in active combat.	Combat Rating: Satisfactory
	Assault combat	Veteran	Awarded to assault personnel who distinguished themselves during any period the unit was engaged in active combat.	Combat Proficiency: Skilled; Combat Rating: Good
	Assault combat	Expert	Awarded to assault personnel who served with excellence during any period the unit was engaged in active combat.	Combat Proficiency: Outstanding; Combat Rating: Skilled

Infantry Badges (cont'd)

Badge	Name	Level	Description	Criteria
	Command	Basic	Awarded on the basis of proven skill in the area of command.	Command Rating: Satisfactory
	Command	Veteran	Awarded on the basis of distinguished skill in the area of command.	Command Proficiency: Skilled; Command Qualification: Outstanding
	Command	Expert	Awarded on the basis of excellence in the area of command.	Command Proficiency: Outstanding; Command Qualification: Excellent
	Engineer	Basic	Awarded to engineering personnel on the basis of proven skill in the area of repair.	Specialist Rating: Satisfactory
	Engineer	Veteran	Awarded to engineering personnel on the basis of distinguished skill in the area of repair.	Specialist Qualification: Good; Specialist Rating: Skilled
	Engineer	Expert	Awarded to engineering personnel on the basis of excellence in the area of repair.	Specialist Proficiency: Outstanding; Specialist Qualification: Skilled; Specialist Rating: Excellent
	Engineer combat	Basic	Awarded to engineer personnel who have proven themselves during any period the unit was engaged in active combat.	Combat Rating: Satisfactory
	Engineer combat	Veteran	Awarded to engineer personnel who distinguished themselves during any period the unit was engaged in active combat.	Combat Proficiency: Skilled; Combat Rating: Good
	Engineer combat	Expert	Awarded to engineer personnel who served with excellence during any period the unit was engaged in active combat.	Combat Proficiency: Outstanding; Combat Rating: Skilled
	Explosive ordnance	Basic	Awarded to personnel who have proven themselves with explosive ordnance during any period the unit was engaged in active combat.	Weapon Rating: Satisfactory
	Explosive ordnance	Veteran	Awarded to personnel who distinguished themselves using explosive ordnance during any period the unit was engaged in active combat.	Weapon Proficiency: Skilled; Weapon Rating: Good
	Explosive ordnance	Expert	Awarded to personnel who excelled in the use of explosive ordnance during any period the unit was engaged in active combat.	Weapon Proficiency: Outstanding; Weapon Rating: Skilled
	First Aid	Basic	Awarded to medical personnel on the basis of proven skill in the area of field medicine.	Specialist Rating: Satisfactory
	First Aid	Veteran	Awarded to medical personnel on the basis of distinguished skill in the area of field medicine.	Specialist Qualification: Good; Specialist Rating: Skilled
	First Aid	Expert	Awarded to medical personnel on the basis of excellence in the area of field medicine.	Specialist Proficiency: Outstanding; Specialist Qualification: Skilled; Specialist Rating: Excellent
	Knife combat	Basic	Awarded to personnel who have proven themselves with a knife during any period the unit was engaged in active combat.	Weapon Rating: Satisfactory
	Knife combat	Veteran	Awarded to personnel who distinguished themselves using a knife during any period the unit was engaged in active combat.	Weapon Proficiency: Skilled; Weapon Rating: Good
	Knife combat	Expert	Awarded to personnel who excelled in the use of a knife during any period the unit was engaged in active combat.	Weapon Proficiency: Outstanding; Weapon Rating: Skilled

Infantry Badges (cont'd)

Badge	Name	Level	Description	Criteria
	Medic combat	Basic	Awarded to medical personnel who have proven themselves during any period the unit was engaged in active combat.	Combat Rating: Satisfactory
	Medic combat	Veteran	Awarded to medical personnel who distinguished themselves during any period the unit was engaged in active combat.	Combat Proficiency: Skilled; Combat Rating: Good
	Medic combat	Expert	Awarded to medical personnel who served with excellence during any period the unit was engaged in active combat.	Combat Proficiency: Outstanding; Combat Rating: Skilled
	Pistol combat	Basic	Awarded to personnel who have proven themselves with a handgun during any period the unit was engaged in active combat.	Weapon Rating: Satisfactory
	Pistol combat	Veteran	Awarded to personnel who distinguished themselves using a handgun during any period the unit was engaged in active combat.	Weapon Proficiency: Skilled; Weapon Rating: Good
	Pistol combat	Expert	Awarded to personnel who excelled in the use of a handgun during any period the unit was engaged in active combat.	Weapon Proficiency: Outstanding; Weapon Rating: Skilled
	Resupply	Basic	Awarded to support personnel on the basis of proven skill in the area of ammo resupply.	Specialist Rating: Satisfactory
	Resupply	Veteran	Awarded to support personnel on the basis of distinguished skill in the area of ammo resupply.	Specialist Qualification: Good; Specialist Rating: Skilled
	Resupply	Expert	Awarded to support personnel on the basis of excellence in the area of ammo resupply.	Specialist Proficiency: Outstanding; Specialist Qualification: Skilled; Specialist Rating: Excellent
	Sniper combat	Basic	Awarded to sniper personnel who have proven themselves during any period the unit was engaged in active combat.	Combat Rating: Satisfactory
	Sniper combat	Veteran	Awarded to sniper personnel who distinguished themselves during any period the unit was engaged in active combat.	Combat Proficiency: Skilled; Combat Rating: Good
	Sniper combat	Expert	Awarded to sniper personnel who served with excellence during any period the unit was engaged in active combat.	Combat Proficiency: Outstanding; Combat Rating: Skilled
	Spec Ops combat	Basic	Awarded to special forces personnel who have proven themselves during any period the unit was engaged in active combat.	Combat Rating: Satisfactory
	Spec Ops combat	Veteran	Awarded to special forces personnel who distinguished themselves during any period the unit was engaged in active combat.	Combat Proficiency: Skilled; Combat Rating: Good
	Spec Ops combat	Expert	Awarded to special forces personnel who served with excellence during any period the unit was engaged in active combat.	Combat Proficiency: Outstanding; Combat Rating: Skilled
	Support combat	Basic	Awarded to support personnel who have proven themselves during any period the unit was engaged in active combat.	Combat Rating: Satisfactory
	Support combat	Veteran	Awarded to support personnel who distinguished themselves during any period the unit was engaged in active combat.	Combat Proficiency: Skilled; Combat Rating: Good
	Support combat	Expert	Awarded to support personnel who served with excellence during any period the unit was engaged in active combat.	Combat Proficiency: Outstanding; Combat Rating: Skilled

Vehicle Badges

Badge	Name	Level	Description	Criteria
	Air Defense	Basic	Awarded to personnel who have been exposed to enemy fire while performing their duties in an air defense vehicle.	Combat Qualification: Satisfactory
	Air Defense	Veteran	Awarded to personnel who during combat situations have distinguished themselves while performing their duties in an air defense vehicle.	Combat Qualification: Good; Combat Rating: Skilled
	Air Defense	Expert	Awarded to personnel who during combat situations have excelled while performing their duties in an air defense vehicle.	Combat Qualification: Skilled; Combat Rating: Outstanding; Combat Proficiency: Excellent
	Armor	Basic	Awarded to personnel who have been exposed to enemy fire while performing their duties in an armored vehicle.	Combat Qualification: Satisfactory
	Armor	Veteran	Awarded to personnel who during combat situations have distinguished themselves while performing their duties in an armored vehicle.	Combat Qualification: Good; Combat Rating: Skilled
	Armor	Expert	Awarded to personnel who during combat situations have excelled while performing their duties in an armored vehicle.	Combat Qualification: Skilled; Combat Rating: Outstanding; Combat Proficiency: Excellent
	Aviator	Basic	Awarded to personnel who have been exposed to enemy fire while performing their duties in an airplane.	Combat Qualification: Satisfactory
	Aviator	Veteran	Awarded to personnel who during combat situations have distinguished themselves while performing their duties in an airplane.	Combat Qualification: Good; Combat Rating: Skilled
	Aviator	Expert	Awarded to personnel who during combat situations have excelled while performing their duties in an airplane.	Combat Qualification: Skilled; Combat Rating: Outstanding; Combat Proficiency: Excellent
	Ground Defense	Basic	Awarded to personnel who have been exposed to enemy fire while performing their duties in a ground defense vehicle.	Combat Qualification: Satisfactory
	Ground Defense	Veteran	Awarded to personnel who during combat situations have distinguished themselves while performing their duties in a ground defense vehicle.	Combat Qualification: Good; Combat Rating: Skilled
	Ground Defense	Expert	Awarded to personnel who during combat situations have excelled while performing their duties in a ground defense vehicle.	Combat Qualification: Skilled; Combat Rating: Outstanding; Combat Proficiency: Excellent
	Helicopter	Basic	Awarded to personnel who have been exposed to enemy fire while performing their duties in a helicopter.	Combat Qualification: Satisfactory
	Helicopter	Veteran	Awarded to personnel who during combat situations have distinguished themselves while performing their duties in a helicopter.	Combat Qualification: Good; Combat Rating: Skilled
	Helicopter	Expert	Awarded to personnel who during combat situations have excelled while performing their duties in a helicopter.	Combat Qualification: Skilled; Combat Rating: Outstanding; Combat Proficiency: Excellent
	Transport	Basic	Awarded to personnel who have been exposed to enemy fire while performing their duties in a transport vehicle.	Combat Qualification: Satisfactory
	Transport	Veteran	Awarded to personnel who during combat situations have distinguished themselves while performing their duties in a transport vehicle.	Combat Qualification: Good; Combat Rating: Skilled; Driver Rating: Outstanding
	Transport	Expert	Awarded to personnel who during combat situations have excelled while performing their duties in a transport vehicle.	Combat Qualification: Skilled; Combat Rating: Outstanding; Driver Rating: Excellent